SAP HANA for Project Managers

How to succeed in SAP HANA
Implementation Projects

■ ■ ■

Jayaraman Kalaimani

SAP HANA for Project Managers: How to succeed in SAP HANA Implementation Projects
Copyright © 2016 by Jayaraman Kalaimani

I would like to dedicate this book to my beloved Guru- Maharishi Vethathiri & my family

Contents

Foreword

Today, Information Technology (IT) is playing the role of an enabler, supporting business. In today's competitive market, faster you reach your customers through enhanced order fulfillment or sales and customer services, you win more business. Hence there is a compelling need for I.T to take the driver seat in enabling business rather than being part of back office operations by helping sales achieve targets, lean manufacturing, zero inventory to reduce product costs etc. The paradigm shift in business suite applications helps business achieve newer markets, avenues to conduct business in the unknown territory. Author focusses on the technology shift by demonstrating capabilities of SAP HANA as an enabler to conduct business faster, effectively by reaching customers more than ever with data available ant. Further, author has described the evolution of SAP HANA and demonstrates how it helps in driving the business.

Amrendra, Mishra
Sr.SAP Program Manager,
Alstom Transport,
Bangalore,
India.

Acknowledgements

I would like to thank Amazon for the opportunity to share my experiences with the world of SAP HANA consultants and project managers. It is a journey and SAP HANA is still evolving as a cutting-edge technology for the current and the future. It will remain as the pioneer with simple solutions to meet complex client requirements. SAP's BIG data is HANA. SAP has transitioned itself from shop-floor ERP to enterprise mobility by reinventing itself.

I would like to thank my Guru. Maharishi Vethathiri, family, friends, and colleagues. A book of this size would not have been possible without the support of them all. I would like to give sincere thanks to my team for the review and proofreading throughout the stages of this book. I would also like to thank Mr. Stefan Hetges, Founder & CEO SmartShift Technologies for contributing to the Methods & Tools for HANA Implementation chapter for their kind support.

    I would like to thank all of my colleagues for their enthusiasm and support for this project, and, finally to the Divine Space in me, thank you—for everything.

Introduction

This book is designed to help you understand SAP HANA technology and manage implementation projects successfully. It is a compilation of basic know-how to the implementation techniques that I have learned.

Often, the evolution SAP embarrasses me and how the massive structure of SAP has transitioned from shop-floor based ERP software to the enterprise mobility. SAP HANA is SAP's largest investment next to ECC to realize values to the customers by shifting itself to the next trending technologies in BIG data. Today, analytics drives business as you need to know the customer and predict his behavior. Hence, it is imperative to realize HANA as the game changer to justify it to the business. It is important to learn the concepts and the roadmap of the SAP HANA platform as a product suite and how to implement an SAP project. The objective of this book is to present quick artifacts of HANA product suite with road map to help you to succeed as a project manager or consultant to realize why HANA is a game changer.

This book is directed at project managers and consultants implementing SAP HANA, but is also a valuable tool for the IT/IS department to make decisions with deeper knowledge and understanding of the product.

As you read this book, you will learn evolution of SAP HANA the next generation database, application with architecture supporting your business requirements with S/4HANA suite for business. It will provide deep insights into HANA technology and as a platform supporting business requirements. Also, it helps in gaining deep understanding of the Technical and functional capabilities of the technology to leverage key business scenarios, Optimizing business process by leveraging simple logistics and simple Finance solution in HANA and above all leveraging the cloud infrastructure to ease operating key business processes.

SAP HANA for Project Managers will help you to understand SAP HANA from an end-to-end perspective, to help you manage HANA implementation projects. If you're a beginner, read this book completely and ensure that you run through the system to familiarize yourself with the concepts. Each topic discussed in this book will explain the background info regarding the concepts and processes. You can refer to the SAP HANA website (https://training.sap.com/us/en) for any additional information. This book is not a replacement for regular training, but it will help you to understand SAP HANA architecture and effective tips provided via the real-time case studies.

Chapter 1: Introduction to SAP HANA

The objective of this chapter is to help you understand the roadmap for SAP HANA, which stands for 'High Performance Analytical Appliance'. SAP has done two key innovations and the largest investment ever done to revamp its own product suite as illustrated below:

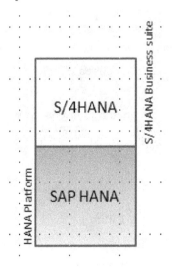

a. HANA as a platform comprising of HANA certified hardware, preinstalled HANA database with in-memory

b. S/4HANA Business suite for ERP which runs on HANA.

Now, let's understand the above two topics more closely. With SAP HANA massive amount of data can be analysed in quick turn-around. SAP HANA is a modern, in-memory database and platform that is deployable on premise or in the cloud. It's modern due to the in-memory capabilities with high data processing capabilities. The complete data is stored in-memory with the entire processing done in the RAM instead of hard disk. Thus, SAP HANA has significantly improved data processing capabilities with multiple CPU's, RAM. Therefore, SAP HANA is a platform which integrates HANA database, HANA studio and HANA client. SAP has partnered with HP, Fujitsu, IBM and Dell to sell SAP certified hardware for HANA. These partners offer HANA hardware on which HANA software can be licensed.

The evolution of HANA started from R/3 to ERP and finally to HANA. SAP was very successful in the ERP model; however every release took nearly 12-15 months. Thus, SAP landscape grew increasingly complex with disparate systems involving data warehouse applications. HANA answered simplification in the following points:

- Effort / Services / Admin – Less development, testing and maintenance with agile applications to deliver benefits to the users.

- Software – Reduced license costs

- Hardware – Reduced maintenance costs

Instead of spending time in maintenance, SAP's strategy is to spend time in innovation with more simplification and more profit. Thus, IT landscape is simplified in HANA with major TCO.

What is SAP HANA Platform?

The SAP HANA platform is a flexible data source agnostic in-memory database platform that allows customers to analyse large volumes of data in real-time. Now, you can perform business intelligence as real time as soon as transactions are punched without waiting for aggregates. It is also a development platform, which helps in application development. SAP HANA studio is a java based application development platform that runs on the eclipse platform. SAP HANA has leveraged integrated development environment (IDE) of eclipse platform. SAP HANA studio provides an environment for administration, authorization and data provisioning.

14

SAP's Big Data Platform

This is SAP's big data platform and S/4HANA is the next generation business suite which runs on HANA. Without this knowledge of roadmap of SAP HANA as platform with its unique S/4HANA business suite, SAP Project Manager's cannot comprehend the benefits of SAP HANA and the future vision of the product itself. Before we move on with SAP's big data strategy, let us understand the basics of analytic (OLAP), transaction data processing (OLTP), and concepts. The earlier approach to database design had been OLTP's, i.e. designing dB's for transaction processing aka 'OLTP's'. On the other hand the need for analytics aka 'OLAP' increased every year, with growing demand for analysing data to build intelligence, hence the need of DataMart(s), Data warehouse(s) spiked up. The real challenge had been synchronizing OTLP's and OLAP's (Data warehouse(s) with batch process. The bottom line story is that you'd never get up-to-date information from these Data warehouses due to the latency period between the OLTP's and OLAP's synchronization. As an end-result, enterprises suffered without being able to make quick decisions, despite costly Data warehouse(s) solution implemented. Today, SAP has challenged the way enterprise transacts and analyse data. SAP HANA has combined transactions and analytics processing into one powerhouse. Thus, it is fuelled to help enterprises to run simple, quick, enabling decision making abilities.

Innovation

Trend is that huge amount of data is generated by the enterprises; however without harnessing data for business decisions there is no use. Here is where technology strives to analyse data to come out with decisions. SAP HANA comes as a front-runner with in-memory technology to reduce lead time in transaction processing and analytical reporting.

Now, let us see HANA's innovation which analyses data at high speed. HANA is called as appliance because it is a combination of server and HANA dB with preconfigured HANA software. HANA hardware with in-memory configured in such a way it uses optimally. Thus, HANA box processes data in parallel at high speed. For example, if you give a task to HANA, it breaks into multiple tasks to process it at a high speed. This technique of storing data in-memory is known as in-memory database (IMDB) where data is stored in the RAM, instead of data storage in the hard disk.

SAP HANA database is an in-memory dB which stores everything as in-memory by using the HANA appliance. The unique column based data storage has many benefits such as partitioning for high speed query processing. It also supports row based data storage. For example, if you want to read a complete row at a time, it is better to use row based storage. On the contrary, if you want to read 2 columns, it is logical to use column based storage. Mostly, tables are used for fetching data from specific columns. There is no need to aggregate tables in HANA. For example, aggregate of sales data at month level. In fact the database writes are also faster. Thus, HANA server stores massive data and process data at real time. This is real time analysis. The transfer of data from hardware to RAM has always been a problem. Hence, it is possible to bring in complete data into RAM in HANA. At the same time, the top level CPU and cache memory gives you capabilities in multi-processing in parallel.

These are the major innovations in HANA.

HANA stores data; hence it can be used as a database for developing custom applications on HANA such as Java based application development. It uses calculation engine, which is used for retrieval of data. For example, Traditional dB will try to aggregate in Business Warehouse (BW) system to extract data. Hence, there is an item level parsing of data is required, however in HANA aggregate is done by HANA using calculation engine and returns output to the HANA server much faster. Thus, it helps in accessing data at high speed. There are other components in HANA such as Webserver engine that allows developers to build interfaces to the external applications. For example, html application can be consumed by mobile devices;

HANA is a platform with the ability to build applications on the HANA box, such as store data in the database, use calculation engine and build webserver engine for external applications. For example, HANA platform can be used by a bank to build the entire enterprise suite using the database, calculation engine and webserver engine. Hence, we call HANA as a platform as you can build your custom applications on the HANA box. As part of the HANA box, you'd get hardware with HANA database preinstalled and extract-transform and load (ETL) tool suite out of the box.

What is S/4HANA Business Suite?

S/4HANA Business suite is the next generation ERP that combines simple data model with an improved user experience with the result of improved capability to the business. It runs on HANA. For example, closing books as finance results in complex reconciliation process. Hence, financial closure is very complex in legacy. S/4HANA is unified in one data store with easy reconciliation with soft close. Another example is the simplest data model for inventory management. S/4HANA is the only ERP that leverages columnar data store and runs in-memory. No more constraints of aggregate and long run batch process as S/4HANA data model is simpler with columnar data access. For example, reports can be done on the fly with no indexes required. No more headers, status tables are required. S/4HANA is a huge innovation from SAP with simpler data model and helps in significant business benefits.

Deployment

SAP's big data platform is "HANA", which is not just a database, a whole new approach to data, which runs 350x times faster than its predecessor. It's a combination of enhanced hardware, database and preconfigured in-memory software for high performance using HANA appliance. Let us try to understand the basics of SAP's "Big data" strategy, and how do enterprises leverage it to benefit to maximize profit. The most awaited, and the most exciting enterprise software giant, has launched its innovative breakthrough technology after a decade of research and development by analysing data processing. If you have not heard it, here it is... The SAP S/4HANA is the future ERP suite with advanced in-memory capabilities... To be precise; HANA has evolved as a platform to provide a robust HW with preconfigured in-memory. On top of it customers can choose to run S/4HANA ERP suite. Thus, SAP has evolved with HANA as a platform and S/4HANA ERP suite for high performance. Existing customers can choose either of the two options to migrate to HANA as mentioned below:

a. Side-Car HANA – In Side-Car HANA, Customers running on legacy SAP systems can use SAP Landscape

Transformation (SLT) for real-time data access without replacing the legacy database as illustrated below:

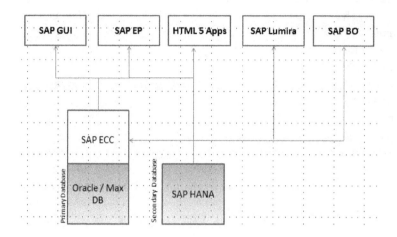

SAP Landscape Transformation (SLT)

b. Enterprise HANA – In enterprise HANA, you'd replace legacy database with HANA database. Since the database is changed and the entire application runs in-memory with significant performance benefits and real-time analytics as illustrated below:

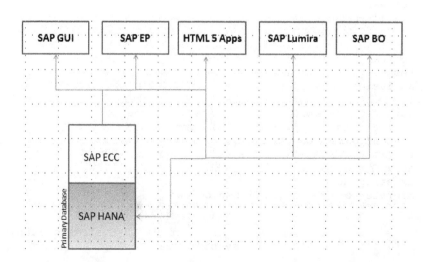

S/4HANA Business Suite

The SAP S/4HANA connect users, devices in real-time to support the development of business models. The SAP S/4HANA is exploding beyond frontiers, thus enabling customers to plan their enterprise for the future. As an SAP Consultant, SAP Project Manager, you should be able to guide the customers by explaining the roadmap for S/4HANA business suite and HANA as a platform. You should be able to explain the benefits of SAP's strategy. Let's us try to understand the roadmap for S/4HANA, which is the application suite and SAP strategy towards HANA as a platform in this chapter.

Today, the market is revolving around data, data and data. It's no longer useful, by just simply dumping data into DataMart(s) & data warehouse(s); it is how you're able to harness data for improving your business strategy. It is how you relate it to the customers, and change the focus of business. How do you accelerate the internet of things, connecting social media, retail customers? The answer is "Big Data". The SAP "S/4HANA" is SAP's business suite with native database and supports big data in analytics computing for real time access, anytime, anywhere. The SAP S/4HANA is a high performing business suite with simple logistics and simple finance, which is evolving at a high speed in-memory database, if you're wondering. What it is? Simply, understand this is something you can put a lot of data "in" and extract "out" in no-time and use it for valuable market, customer and sales volume analysis and insights. Gone are the days, where you'd run material resource planning ("MRP") and/or month-end financial account closure in the overnight batch run mode, with processes running in the background for hours.

Instead, you'd be able to access real-time data anywhere, anytime, thus, helping managers decide quickly. The SAP S/4HANA SPS 12 is a robust business suite that has simple finance and logistics processing with its unique capabilities of simple finance, and simple logistics which are steadily evolving to consolidate business applications. Further, S/4HANA business suite can be deployed on-cloud option to maximize performance. Especially with the interface applications such as SAP CRM and Success factors for HR services as part of the SAP cloud landscape.

It's time to fasten your seat belts to learn the new HANA technology breakthrough as a leader in the Industry with the benefits of S/4HANA, which is the breakthrough ERP application suite. With the advent of big data, enterprise can connect with customers and predict their needs based on analysing customer information. Thus, enterprises will be able to gain the necessary insights to provide personalized products and services. As an example, you will be happy to receive personalized offerings provided by your bank, isn't? Now, imagine a large scale enterprise, which is able to analyse customer, market and sales data in real-time. Now, with a smarter digital strategy, new age enterprises can retain customers, improve profitability by focussing on specific sales channels, and heighten the ability to respond to industry changes by collecting data from various channels such as mobile, internet, etc.

The SAP S/4HANA Business suite is the next generation ERP suite designed to run business applications run simple in the digital economy. SAP HANA is a revelation in true sense, with the computation capacity to read transaction and analytical data real time. This new suite developed with an in-memory platform with personalized user experience aka "SAP FIORI". The HANA suite can be deployed in the cloud or on premise, or even a hybrid approach is possible. The SAP S/4HANA is developed with simplicity in mind, to drive significant business value to the customers. Now, lets us understand a little bit about "predictive" analysis. A predictive analysis is how you'll be harnessing past data to predict the behaviour of the customer, sales & market trend with revenue forecasts etc.

Predictive Analysis

In legacy ERP systems redundant data model resulted in huge data stores which don't add value to the business. In HANA, with simplified data model, there are lot of benefits in terms of predictive analysis as highlighted below:

5 Key things that you gain out of predictive analysis:

1. Better understanding of the customer and the market trend

2. Improved customer satisfaction by focussed segments, sales channels with customized offers and services provided

3. Higher market penetration by understanding the market scenario with analysis of dynamically changing product pricing etc.

4. Improved supply chain processes

5. The predictive analytic solutions of the SAP HANA can help your business better with required insights!

Top 5 sources of data tapped for predictive analysis:

1. Sales

2. Marketing

3. Customer

4. Product &

5. Financial

If you observe, all of the above data, relate directly to revenue. It is staggering to realize more than 40% of companies are evaluating or planning to use social media data. Thus, predictive analysis will help enterprise gain competitive advantage with real-time predictive analysis. More and more enterprise is looking forward to the forward-looking view as illustrated below in Fig. 1-1 Predictive analysis. Now, let's examine the implications of predictive analysis in an enterprise.

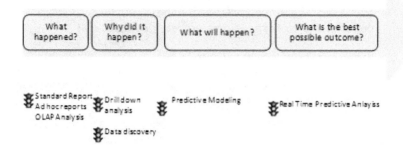

Figure 1-1 Predictive analysis

HANA Predictive Analysis helps you analyse the historical data assess the cause and forecast the future trend with the best possible outcome. In summary, it helps to predict trends in sales; customer and market trends gain competitive advantage. The above analogy helps you comprehend the power of harnessing data from various channels to increase your revenue with predictive analysis.

■ **Note** SAP S/4HANA aka SAP Business Suite for HANA

Why to choose SAP HANA as platform or S/4HANA Business suite?

Why do you think customer should switch to SAP HANA or S/4HANA business suite? There are critical factors such as increasing profit, TCO and analysing sales & market trend is critical for any business. One of the primary reasons is the ability to take quick decisions with the analysis and remain agile and innovative in the face of intense market pressure. No longer "IT" will remain as a back office, with the advent of SAP HANA as platform along with S/4HANA business suite, "IT" is simplified and it will transform as an innovation lab to help Organizations grow to the next level. The SAP Business Suite delivers simplicity, high agile applications that can run on cloud or on premise to help you take quick decisions and/or manage a business better without worrying about IT.

One of the common challenges in today's IT landscape is the heterogeneous platforms and the issues of integrating every single component in the landscape. The SAP HANA platform has the solution to integrate all components with one data source. SAP S/4HANA running on HANA is the next generation ERP business suite. The objective of HANA is to consolidate customer's "IT" landscape and system architecture, thus delivering functional improvements in ERP, and enhancing the user experience seamlessly as one unit. The new principles of User Experience are enhanced in SAP FIORI applications. The SAP S/4HANA is evolving with the following key aspects in mind:

a) Simplicity of business suite by integration all SAP Business suite under one roof of HANA

b) Enhance user experience (UX), which is the front-end

c) Ease of Integration in one platform as all products are under one-roof

d) Providing mobile, internet interfaces

e) Minimal changes to the system in terms of operating system, database changes etc.

f) Provide real time analysis by using in-memory techniques. Hence, SAP HANA runs 350x times faster access with increased RAM with the high performance analytic appliance

The above factors indicate how the business will run way forward. With these aspects in mind, if you visualize SAP S/4HANA, it can provide enhanced user experience, with simplicity and ease of using business suite. Also, it aids in the instant data analysis for managers to make quick decisions and helps organizations achieve operational excellence such as "quicker MRP runs", "quick month-end account closures" etc. SAP has delivered EHP 7.0 (Enhancement package 7) for SAP ERP 6.0 with lots of simplified financial transactions readily available for SAP HANA. It simplifies business transactions.

S/4HANA Roadmap

The roadmap for SAP S/4HANA business suite is to provide Simple Financials, SAP Simple Logistics, and Simple Operations to benefit from significant functional improvements that customer can leverage. The Simple financial application on HANA, enables "on-the fly" month-end closures using the high performance and agile HANA database. The simplification of the architecture indicates SAP products such as SCM, PLM, SRM, EP, and BI will run on SAP HANA as one source data, instead of multiple databases. Thus, integration of products is simpler as it sits on one database, "HANA" and data can be accessed real time, anytime, anywhere. This is the most exciting news of recent times as a breakthrough in technology, thus providing real functional and technical benefits to the customer.

Moreover, SAP IT systems will become lean with the advent of HANA as a platform, with the unified landscape with one source of data, HANA db. For example, instead of multiple database(s) in the legacy landscape, now it is possible to consolidate into HANA dB as a single source. All these SAP applications run on a single SAP HANA production appliance. There are three options to deploy SAP business suite on HANA, as MCOS, MCOD or co-technical deployment as illustrated below. I wondered, how these applications run on a single source and how are they deployed. The following Figure 1-2 explains the schema for each of these applications on the SAP HANA database. If you're aware of "schema" concept in a dB, you'll be able to appreciate these ideas. A simple example is how you'd organize your workplace, a big space or partitions for different purposes and/or all in one huge conference room. It is a choice for the manager to support his activities. In a similar way, SAP offers three options of deployment.

- In simple terms, 'MCOS' refers to the multiple components on one system as illustrated in Figure 1-2; each schema uniquely refers to the corresponding business application. In MCOS, there might be more than one HANA DB.

- Whereas, in MCOD DB which refers to the multiple components in one database as illustrated in Figure 1-2, all components are referred to the same HANA DB partitioned into one or more schemas.

- Finally, the co-technical deployment refers to the ADD-ON's on one unified schema of the single HANA DB.

As we keep talking about Big data, enterprise should be able to capture unstructured information such as marketing, sales data or prospect details in a text format from social media analytics. SAP provides integration with HADOOP as well as helping read unstructured data using SAP HANA Text analysis to derive meaningful information from the unstructured data.

The SAP HANA Platform provides the following services as highlighted in Table 1-1

Table 1-1. Services Provided by SAP HANA

Service Description	Interface	
1. Application Services	Webserver, Fiori UX	Java script, Graphic Modeler, ALM
2. Processing Services		Spatial, Graph, Predictive, Search, Function Libraries, Data Enrichment, Planning, Text Analytics Series Data
3. Database Services		OLAP+OLTP, Multi-core/parallelization, Advanced compression, Multi-tenancy, Multi-tier storage, Data model, open standards, high availability, disaster recovery

4. Integration Services	Data Virtualization, ELT & Replication, Streaming, Hadoop Integration, Remote Data Sync.

Let's see the SAP Business suite on HANA as illustrated below in Figure 1-2.

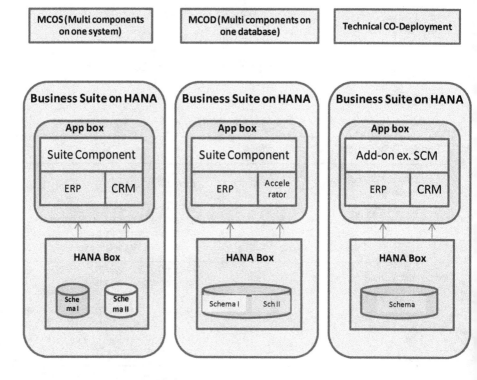

Figure 1-2 Illustrates SAP Business suite deployment on HANA

Overall, using SAP HANA platform you'll be able to reduce TCO, maintenance and overall OS/DB upgrade costs by effectively reducing the number of instances. Also, the required IT labour will be very minimal to support one database, instead of multiple database(s). The following Fig. 1-3 illustrates the legacy SAP IT landscape with no. of systems in the landscape. Now, if it is consolidated into one source of data, into SAP HANA with one or more schemas. Your productive landscape will be leaner instead of multiple instances. Let's see the legacy SAP landscape in Figure 1-3 illustrated below.

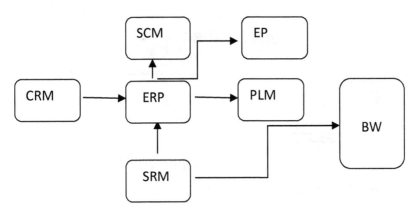

Figure 1-3 Illustrates a Legacy SAP Landscape with number of productive systems.

In summary, there are significant benefits of migrating or implementing SAP S/4HANA ERP suite by leveraging both technical and functional benefits discussed in this section. On the technical side, there are a huge system landscape consolidation and integration benefits by using HANA as a platform. On the functional side, there are benefits in terms of simple applications that are faster, real time by using the S/4HANA business suite. Thus, it makes it easy for existing and new customers adopt HANA to benefit from the current changes. The migration path provides a faster adoption of HANA from native legacy systems. Over a period of time your redundant master data across applications increases drastically. These multiple sources are now integrated into seamlessly one platform, relying on one source, which is 'SAP HANA'. Now, observe the lean SAP HANA IT landscape, thus simplifying your complex IT landscape from multiple productive systems (SIDs) into ONE single source of information.

You'd have observed the simplicity of integrating all components under one roof of the SAP Business suite running on S/4HANA. In addition, there are options to add-on non-SAP systems into HANA. The only additional investments would be hardware requirements with additional RAM space, on the required HANA appliances and SAP recommended HW for enabling in-memory capabilities. With the server costs going down every year, this is no big deal, when compared to the simplicity and the power of data computing that you'd gain. These HW recommended by SAP comes as ready to go as illustrated below in Figure 1-4.

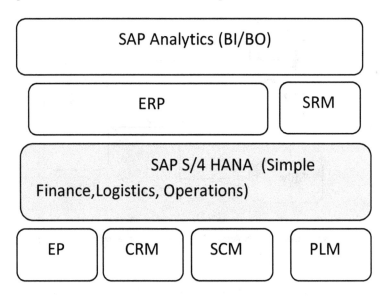

Figure 1-4 illustrates an SAP S/4HANA Landscape with one single source

SAP S/4HANA Landscape

Now, let's see how SAP's vision came true. The following Fig. 1-5 illustrates SAP S/4HANA landscape. If you had observed SAP Landscape with core ERP, Supply Chain (SCM), Supplier Relationship (SRM), Project Lifecycle (PLM), you'll be staggered with the amount of integration efforts required using Process Integration is known as "PI".

Now, the disparate SAP ecosystem has converged into one source of database in SAP S/4HANA. This is the most exciting news ever heard. Imagine a SAP system landscape, primarily a 4 system-landscape comprising of Sandbox, Development, Quality and Production. You would have 4 systems-landscapes for ERP, another 4 for SCM, 4 for SRM etc. In totally an SAP landscape will include near about ~ 20-25 systems to maintain, upgrade including hardware, operating system costs in addition to the number of database licenses. Now, wouldn't it be surprising if 25 systems in your landscape become just 4 systems with just one productive instance. It is true with SAP HANA platform, which becomes one source of data for all your SAP systems, thus the systems integration task is simplified and access is faster within one source of database, HANA.

For example...Now, let's see how a complex SAP legacy landscape is consolidated into SAP HANA, one source data as illustrated in Figure 1-5 illustrated below.

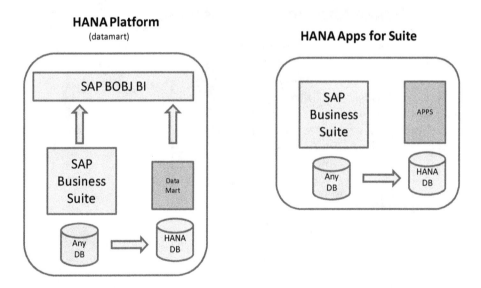

Figure 1-5 Illustrate SAP S/4HANA Architecture.

Hence, HANA is powerful with the integration of components with ease. Imagine in the landscape maintenance activities are over simplified with one "HANA" dB instead of 5X5 = 25 systems in the landscape to maintain. Imagine the operational costs involved, one side there is a significant IT cost reduction, and the other side Business users will enjoy access to data anytime, anywhere, thus increasing the efficiencies of the business. Moreover, the predictive analysis will help in improving revenue, by analysing the behaviour of customers, sales data, market data and products, etc. The HANA platform indicates the HW/HANA DB, whereas business suite for the business applications. The HANA on enterprise cloud provide details of the hosting business suite on a cloud platform, with an option of on premise business suite or on SAP enterprise cloud offerings.

Figure 1-6 Illustrates SAP S/4HANA for the business suite on one data source "HANA". All SAP software products rely on one source of data; hence there is no duplication of master data and/or integration between SAP systems. It can talk seamlessly as one unit.

HANA Apps for Business Suite

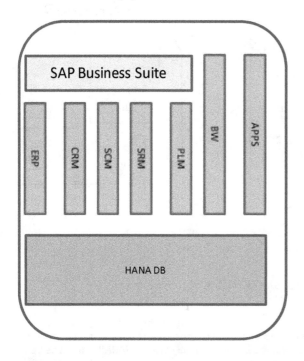

Figure 1-6 Illustrate SAP S/4HANA business suite

Real-time data processing

Now, let's try to understand the fundamentals of data processing. With the advent of high speed blade servers resulting in increased RAM-based storage solutions, with data stored in memory for quick access. It significantly reduces the turnaround time for data access using RAM. In addition, SAP HANA provides column wise compression techniques, which compresses data by column and partition data. This technique reduces data volume. A simple analogy is like file compression in windows. For example, it helps you compress data volumes from 2.75 TB to 600GB. With In-memory technology, it is possible to **process data at a speed of 100GB per second** by storing information in main memory (RAM), accessed directly on the motherboard, and instead of slow retrieved from the hard disk. The end-result for an end-user is the speed at which he is able to run transactions and access data.

The SAP HANA is a **preconfigured in-memory software, already optimized** that users can implement in combination with an SAP recommended HANA hardware, which comes with pre-loaded with SAP HANA and SUSE Linux, ready to go.

What's ahead for SAP HANA

It's apparent to realize SAP's vision on HANA. It's really going big! The entire business suite is moving to SAP HANA, products such as SAP Business One, SAP Customer Relationship Management, and SAP ERP. The ability to analyse data in real time and process large amounts of information is significantly greater than a normal db. The ability to do aggregate of data is faster. In addition, you can also analyse information from non-SAP systems as well.

Business Warehouse utilizes the power of the SAP HANA database. An enterprise can operate their BW systems on HANA without any changes to the application itself. The migration to SAP BW on SAP HANA is simply a database migration under the application. Further acquisition of Lumira business intelligence tools, Ariba & Success factors strengthen SAP in mobility and cloud based services. SAP has integrated the predictive analytics software Supplier Info Net with the Ariba Network to insight into the performance of its suppliers. The HANA-based software makes predictions by querying a combination of supplier information and relevant data about those suppliers drawn from a wide range of third-party sources, such as news

31

wires. SAP Lumira is a self-service solution that allows analysts and decision makers to access, transform, and visualize data. Now, let's understand the SAP Lumira cloud product, The SAP Lumira is a data visualization tool, primarily runs on cloud platforms. The user can analyse data from various sources in mobile, cloud with a simple browser for quick decision making. These products leverage power of HANA to be robust on the cloud, on premise and mobility.

One of the common pitfalls is that the project managers are unable to explain the roadmap of the SAP product suite, thus leading to poor planning. This will result in skill GAP over a period of time and the ageing infrastructure. Eventually, these projects fail to yield expected ROI. Hence, as a Project Manager, you must share the roadmap of SAP with HANA strategy to benefit the customer landscape, as often projects fail due to common pitfall such as lack of planning and lack of skills during the product evolution cycle.

Evolution of SAP HANA

Let's analyse High Performance Analytic Appliance with main components illustrated below in Figure 1-7

SAP High performance Analytic Appliance

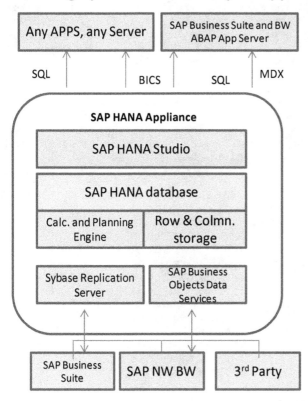

Figure 1-7 Illustrate SAP HANA High Performance Analytic Appliance

Now, let us understand the robust HANA architecture will help business run faster with in-memory, also you've realized the benefits of normalized transactions such as G/L in simple finance. S/4HANA provides Simple Finance with additional benefits due to optimized data model. For example, a G/L report program in ECC optimized utilization of tables than its predecessor in Simple Finance of S/4HANA. Thus, SAP has normalized its data model bottom up, to eliminate redundant tables. Secondly, we talked about the landscape itself is simplified as you'd remember all of its products sits on one source of database, HANA. Isn't that smart? If you ask your production plan engineer for time taken for "MRP" runs and/or accounting team for the month end close, these are endless tasks with the batch process running in the background. Hence, SAP thought through consolidating an analytical engine for faster access, where is a predominant read only. This had evolved in BW Analytics, over a period of time; the staggering amount of data in and out of OLTP's had a demand to retrieve faster, as well as written into the db. If you've designed dB in the past, you'd appreciate the fact of the combined power of OLTP/Data warehouse(s) which is for transaction processing and analytical processing both in the consolidated DB as HANA. It's like using the same DB for both purposes of analytics and transaction based processing. It helps you gain real time access, and consolidate data in one storehouse.

The main objective of SAP HANA platform is to provide real-time analytics by replicating data into in-memory, thus available for real-time analysis as OLAP. With the above points in mind, SAP NW architecture evolved into HANA architecture. The roadmap of the SAP suite of enterprise application is to run all SAP's applications on SAP HANA. As a result of this transformation, the entire SAP business suite will run seamlessly as one unit in SAP S/4HANA business suite, with high speed guaranteed. SAP has also provided additional Eclipse environment for custom development, to ensure optimized development of ABAP and/or Java. I believe there is a major challenge for enterprise migrating from legacy ECC environment to HANA as it will involve dB changes and functional enhancements migrating to simple finance, logistics and/or operations. Thus, it has eliminated all redundant data structure. This will be the next significant opportunity for most of the consulting organizations. The SAP business objects (BO) Strategic Workforce Planning is one of the foremost HANA-based applications. There are few pure HANA-based applications introduced by SAP, and the list is increasing as we speak, to name a few:

a) **Business Warehouse,**

b) **Analytics,**

c) **SAP Dynamic Cash Management &**

d) **SAP Controlling Profitability Analysis (COPA) Accelerator**

In addition, **SAP** provides the following in-memory solutions from **HANA**:

a) The Business Warehouse Accelerator (BWA) for accelerating queries by optimizing dynamic calculations and aggregates.

b) SAP Business Objects Explorer is a helpful tool for analysing large volumes of data.

c) Enterprise Search is very useful for structured as well as unstructured data analysis

d) SAP CRM Customer Segmentation is used for marketing campaigns, analysing millions of records in seconds.

e) SAP Advanced Planner and Optimizer with live Cache &

f) SAP Business By Design analytics

SAP Delivers Next Release of SAP HANA

SAP HANA delivers "better, faster, cheaper" alternative. The latest release is service pack SPS 12 for the SAP HANA platform, helping customers successfully extending core functionalities to deliver growing business requirements. For example, SAP delivered, Internet of Things (IoT) at enterprise scale, manage Big Data more effectively, further extend high availability of data across the enterprise and develop new applications. The SAP HANA provides a robust platform for SAP and non-SAP applications for transactional and analytical processing. Further, it extends to synchronizing data to any remote systems, high availability and disaster recovery of enterprise data to support advanced analytics.

Let's see the Figure 1-8 below illustrates the evolution of SAP application stack in HANA. It is self-explanatory, with ERP applications running on HANA. There are many virtual data marts enabled for real time data access and its integration with non-SAP.

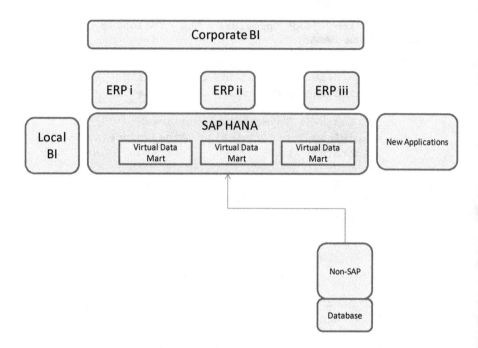

Figure 1-8 Illustrates SAP Application stack evolving in HANA

Evolution of Internet of Things (IoT)

What is IoT? Its how you connect your enterprise is connecting with physical objects, embedded with electronics, software, sensors and connectivity to achieve greater value. In simple terms, it is how your devices communicate seamlessly as one unit. With more and more demanding marketing situations with data coming in from mobile, internet and social media platforms. How do you synchronize data between mobile applications to the enterprise application? SAP HANA supports connecting from the remote applications; hence it is imperative to synchronize data between the enterprise and remote locations. Developers can now build "IoT" and data-intensive mobile apps that leverage SAP HANA remote data synchronization between the enterprise and remote locations. The "SAP SQL Anywhere suite" helps in synchronization. For example, stores can integrate to the main ERP real-time for availability check. Thus, Customers have the ability to analyse "IoT" data from remote locations, either online and/or offline.

Evolution of Big Data

More and more enterprise is challenged to make sensible analysis out of unstructured sales, marketing data from social media analytics such as Facebook, LinkedIn and many other social media. SAP HANA provides integration with Hadoop distributions to read such unstructured data.

There are rules that can be defined for data stored in-memory. For example, Insurance and/or financial corporate will need large data in-memory. Depending on the rules defined, in-memory data storage can be increased. The UI aka single user interface and Hadoop cluster increase the speed of data access. These rules provide multiple storage tiers based on the requirements of the business. Also, data can be cleansed, including duplicate analysis like any ETL operations, using HANA workbench.

Enabling High Availability across the Enterprise

One of the key challenges in today's enterprise is to manage disaster recovery and high availability to ensure data centre's ability to support operations 24X7. SAP HANA features 1-to-n asynchronous replication, auto-host failover for dynamic tier and incremental backups to reduce system downtime. In addition, enterprise information can use NUMA non-uniform memory access) to support large scale systems > 12TB of memory to improve system performance. The importance of ensuring reliability and certainty that IT operations will continue in the event of a failure cannot be understated. SAP HANA has been designed to provide a solid foundation that facilitates business continuity across the enterprise and reduces the risk of security breaches.

Quick decision using Analytics

The latest support pack is SAP HANA SPS 12, with the expanded data processing capabilities, primarily features of application development with advanced analytics. The new features provided in SPS 12 such as text mining, spatial processing enhancements help in extending to the next generation database with spatial expressions in SAP HANA models or SQLScript. These advanced visualization techniques can help in enterprise build robust data models to present data in real time analytics.

Which model is right for a customer?

There are various options provided by SAP. One of the fundamental questions is to go for pure cloud or hybrid on premise solution. Well, I wouldn't advocate entirely cloud or on premise and/or hybrid as it entirely depends on the customer situation.

For example, an enterprise with subsidiaries can go for the SAP Cloud finance edition for shared service centres, the cloud-enterprise edition for group subsidiaries. The on premise edition for core processes such as ERP. The enterprises can choose from the best suited operating models. Now, let's see HANA on cloud illustrated in Figure 1-9 for reference. Let's explore each of the cloud editions in the next section.

HANA on Cloud

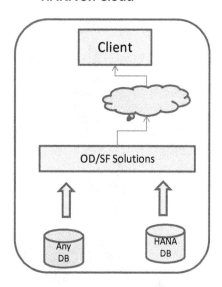

Figure 1-9 Illustrate SAP S/4HANA on-cloud

There are few options to run SAP S/4HANA:

1. SAP S/4HANA public cloud marketing edition

2. SAP S/4HANA public cloud edition

3. SAP S/4HANA cloud project services edition

4. SAP S/4HANA cloud enterprise edition

5. SAP S/4HANA Hybrid Cloud & On premise

SAP S/4HANA, public cloud marketing edition

The sales and marketing strategy has evolved over a period of time. The market segmentation has changed, with focussed customers and product segmentation. A simple marketing campaign for consumer products will need several marketing insights to analyse customer's behaviour using advanced predictive analysis. It means, harnessing past historical data to predict customers and product innovation. Therefore, the strategy of enterprises is to manage marketing campaigns as specialized task outside the core activities of the enterprise. The objective of such campaign is to assess customers through various channels, segment and analyse them, prior to launching the campaign. A simple example is a publishing company, publishing a new title with the focussed audience of a particular age group for selling fiction! This is a classic example. Now, it is easy to put your marketing data into cloud and operate without worrying about the complexities in the IT landscape. Thus, you'd be able to focus more and maintain cloud based services, which is easy to use!

SAP S/4HANA public cloud edition

Now, let's take an example of a group of companies with headquarters in Germany. It is obvious that headquarter will need an on premise solution for various reasons. Now, enterprises can leverage SAP Simple Finance delivers IFRS-compliant financial statements. There is an option for subsidiaries to leverage SAP HANA for cloud for simple financial solutions offered. SAP S/4HANA public cloud solutions cover all the core financial scenarios such as billing, invoice processing, payment, month-end closing, group closing, and IFRS-compliant financial statements. The core objective is to help enterprise save costs by driving significant infrastructure costs.

SAP S/4HANA cloud project services edition

Now, let's explore cloud project services edition. We discussed about the simple finance solution offered in SAP HANA S/4 Cloud. It will help enterprise explore financial statements with public cloud solutions. SAP S/4HANA is characterized by a carefully tailored functional scope and highly standardized processes that are ideally aligned to the project business. The basic framework would help services enterprise financial applications. The functions of simple finance map to the industry standard business process, thus meeting customer's demand.

SAP S/4HANA cloud-enterprise edition

Group subsidiaries: full range of ERP functions from the cloud. If it is not financially viable for a company to operate its own data centre "just" for HR, financial, and marketing processes, it may make sense to follow an approach in which the on premise systems at the headquarters are fully integrated with cloud-based systems at the subsidiaries. Employees won't have any idea that they are toggling between an on premise and a cloud system as they switch from working on financial transactions to placing an order or accessing the integrated HR systems.

Large enterprises: complete switch over from on premise to the cloud until recently, this scenario seemed little more than a vision for the far-distant future; the reason being that a manufacturing company's logistics processes are so tightly interwoven with its financial processes that both sets of processes needed to be supported by SAP S/4HANA to enable an entirely cloud-based deployment. However, the cloud-enterprise edition of S/4HANA now makes this scenario possible because it covers all the ERP functions — financials, logistics, manufacturing, supply chain, quality assurance and HR. It is the ideal edition for customers who want to move right over to working with standardized business processes in the cloud.

Large enterprises with legacy IT landscapes: IT landscapes that have grown organically over many decades and are still based on older versions of SAP R/3 are sometimes so complex that they are impossible to modernize. In this case, the only option is to start with a clean slate. This means either reinstalling the entire system or moving it to S/4HANA, cloud enterprise edition. Either way, an IT transformation roadmap is required. One of the benefits of opting for the cloud approach is that it gives companies standardized core processes that cover all their business operations, including those that are specific to their industry. Moreover, unlike the situation with on premise systems, companies don't have to worry about the total cost of ownership (TCO), because they no longer operate the software themselves. SAP takes care of everything, updates, testing, and corrections. Fees are paid per user, based on the application scenario.

Hybrid approach: cloud and on premise

The Hybrid approach gives an option to plan the critical data requirements, high availability as an on premise solution, whilst rest of HCM, Simple Finance can go with cloud option. It depends on customer's factors that are critical to the business operations. If you're a marketing organization, it makes sense to run the marketing application entirely on cloud, which is lean in terms of IT infrastructure requirements and cost effective cloud based solution. It depends on factors such as your core business operations, which you'd want to run on premise, customize as situations demand. On the other side, marketing and sales can be entirely running on Cloud without much hassle. For example, an automotive company's core business is manufacturing, hence you'd prefer entire supply chain on premise, whilst HR can be moved to cloud, as a hybrid approach. SAP provides an option with the inclusion of cloud based offerings such as success factors for HR offerings entirely on cloud and Ariba web shop, which helps you place an order.

Key Highlights:

SAP HANA is set to Transform Business Processes and Data Analysis for Banking and Insurance Customers. The SAP finance solution such as SAP Cost and Revenue Allocation will help you analyse past data to predict financial forecast with the ability to benchmark. It helps in real time analysis at the granular level of financial products. Above all, it helps Insurance and banking companies to integrate operations into one integrated IT platform, which SAP HANA fits in, by helping them seamlessly work as one data source to make valuable analysis. SAP Cost and Revenue Allocation for Financial Products is expected to improve business processes. There are specific allocation rules that will help large corporate to analyse data more effectively. SAP Cost and Revenue Allocation for Financial Products is designed to work seamlessly with the SAP Simple Finance solution, banking services from SAP and SAP Insurance Analyser analytic applications.

What is in store with SAP S/4HANA

The SAP S/4HANA business suite provides an end-to-end solution to business requirements. You'll be able to run the entire business on a global scale, with market-leading applications and technology combined with a fully integrated business suite. It will help you to stay on the cutting edge with continuous enhancements and innovations, all delivered without disruption. Above all, customers have the options to go on premise, cloud or even hybrid as discussed in this section. The simple user experience (UX) of HANA provides flexible and easy to access software from mobile, cloud platform with ease. In the end, you'd run a simple software from anywhere with absolute ease, powered by SAP HANA with innovations that will help you drive your business.

The adoption trend for software-as-a-service (SaaS) is significant for SAP's business. They have more than $1 billion in subscription now and they want to grow it over the next five years at a much faster rate.

SAP HANA SPS 12 Online Help and Release notes: http://help.sap.com/hana_platform/

Summary

SAP HANA as a platform with its unique S/4HANA is the next generation business suite, which combines the power of OLAP and OLTP into one db. SAP S/4HANA business suite running on HANA platform is helping customers achieve business goals without comprising anything. SAP HANA as a platform can help customers to build custom applications using JAVA/JSP or any other language. SAP provides various deployment options to run applications as on-premises or on-cloud. Customers can choose the best deployment option based on the enterprise strategy and requirements. Either they can go for HANA as a platform alone or perhaps combine the power of S/4HANA business suite as required. The entire SAP landscape can be designed lean by considering the deployment options.

As discussed there are significant benefits to the business by leveraging a simpler data model with columnar data access in S/4HANA business suite. The overall IT landscape is simplified with HANA as a platform with the native HW certified for HANA, preinstalled with HANA database and in-memory configuration. All of that helps customers to run business simpler with less maintenance costs. Further innovations into enterprise mobility and analytical solutions, helps business run faster, effective with analytical capabilities. Let's explore how these tools help you achieve a robust framework for a successful implementation in the upcoming chapters.

■ ■ ■

Chapter 2: SAP HANA DB System Architecture and Roadmap

The objective of this chapter is to help you understand the HANA DB system architecture and roadmap for HANA, which is SAP's investment and future strategy to evolve from ERP based software to end to end software that combines the power of transaction process with the analytical process. Also, we will discuss backup and recovery strategy with tools such as HANA cockpit used for backup and recovery

SAP HANA DB System Architecture

As you know the enterprise requirements have become complex with high volume data requirements. The SAP HANA database is a game changer in the technology, which runs on SUSE Linux Enterprise Server. It's a breakthrough in query processing using in-memory technology to support large enterprise applications. The main components of SAP HANA database consist of Index Server, Name Server, Statistics Server, Pre-processor Server and XS Engine as illustrated in Figure 2-1 below.

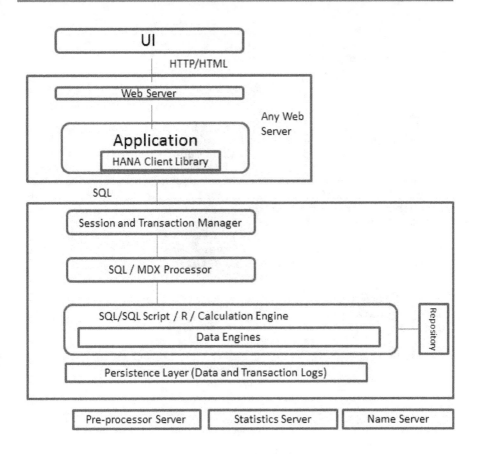

Figure 2-1. SAP HANA DB System Architecture

Let's explore each of the above core components of SAP HANA System. The above SAP HANA system with core components will ease data processing, as many database administrators concur, when compared to legacy databases. SAP HANA instance can connect to disparate client applications; also connect via XS Engine via http. The key components of SAP HANA architecture are:

1. Index Server,

2. Persistence Layer,

3. Pre-processer Server,

4. Named Server,

5. Statistical server,

6. Transaction & Session Manager and

7. XS Engine

Index Server - This is like the central nervous system of SAP HANA DB component, which takes care of all services. In any relational database management system (RDBMS), the key to data processing is how effectively you manage requests to the database using dB engines, which indicates servers with high computational capacity for multi-processing CPU's. This is like the steam engine that cranks enormous power, it helps in data process with high power of computing in terms of volume, speed etc. Hence, SAP HANA technology leverages index server, which consists of the actual data stores and the engine for data processing.

For example, When SQL is triggered; index server takes care of data processes. There are few operations that it does such as authenticating sessions and transactions besides data processing. Also, it helps in processing these commands by effectively coordinating with other servers. Thus, it helps in defying longer query process time with high computation capacity than the legacy databases.

Persistence Layer for data recovery - Next is the persistence layer, which helps in restoring database from the most recent commit points. If you're a DBA, you'd comprehend the benefits of restore as it is an elaborate exercise in legacy databases. As discussed, the requirement is enormous data processing such as analysing huge volume of text data with the advent integrated sales data from various interfaces like apps-Facebook, LinkedIn etc. SAP HANA uses pre-processor server for analysing text data with enhanced search capabilities used for analytics.

The Name Server - Primarily intended for identifying topology of SAP HANA system. Let's say in a distributed landscape, the name server helps in identifying key components that are running and which data is located on which server. The name server knows how data is spread across different servers.

The statistics server is used for collecting statistical data such as performance of the HANA system. It takes a lot of time to study the performance issues in legacy databases, where HANA uses statistics server to derive meaningful information about the status, performance and resource consumption of the servers in the SAP HANA landscape using system monitor.

Transaction Manager - Often times I.T managers are struggling to identify key transactions used in the SAP legacy system. Hence, there is a need for identifying key transactions used frequently used, which are active. Hence, it is essential to keep track of any rollback or commit that happens via transactions to update storage engines about occurred events. SAP HANA Transaction manager helps in analysing key transactions in the system. Finally, XS engine helps in accessing data from the backend SAP HANA database via http. It helps in static content search services to identify static data in the content repository.

Now, let's briefly look at the SAP HANA database Index server with its core components that does the magic with incredible computational power as illustrated in Figure. 2-2 below:

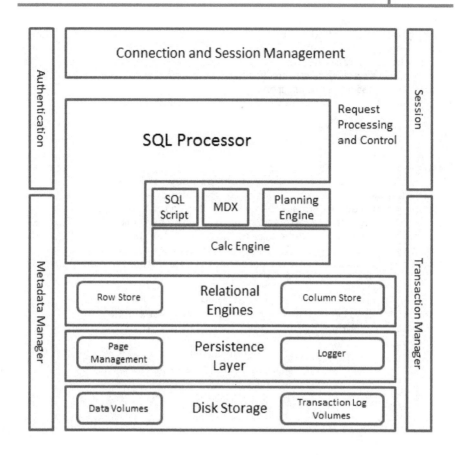

Figure 2-2: SAP HANA Database Index Server

The main components of SAP HANA DB Index Server consist of:

a. Connection and Session Management

b. Authorization Manager

c. Request Processing and Execution Control

d. SQL Processor & SQL Script

e. Multidimensional Expressions (MDX)

f. Calculation & Planning Engine

SAP HANA for Project Managers

g. Transaction & Metadata Manager

h. Row & Column Store

The connection and session management is used for creating and managing sessions and connections for the database clients. For example, as soon as the session is established, clients can communicate with the SAP HANA dB using SQL statements.

The Authorization Manager is primarily used for managing user authorization and access controls. We have detailed chapter 10 discussing authorization concepts in SAP HANA. This component checks user roles and privileges, authorizations mechanism and access rights for specific action performed. It will suffice if you understand the authorization manager helps you in controlling user access to information in the HANA system.

The request processing and execution control helps in handing client requests. For example, each of the incoming requests are analysed and executed by the set of components. The execution layer engages different engines for processing and routes intermediate results to the next execution step.

The SQL processor handles updates to the backend database using transactions. For example, data manipulation statements are executed by the SQL processor. Other requests such as transaction control statements are managed by the transaction manager, planning commands are routed to planning engine and procedure calls via stored procedure processor.

SQL Script is like any other RDBMS SQL's, however this is exclusive and a native SQL language designed for SAP HANA database with high optimizations and parallelization technique. SQLScript is a collection of extensions to SQL. It breaks down SQL query into sets for parallel processing. If you've executed queries that take lot of time to run, you'd understand the value of SAP HANA SQLScript, which helps quick turn-around time in fetching database from the database by offloading data-intensive application logic.

Multidimensional Expressions (MDX) is primarily a language used for query and manipulation the multidimensional data stored in OLAP cubes. The incoming mdx requests are processed by the MDX engine. The Planning Engine is primarily used for huge volume data analysis such as analysis of past 5 years of historical data for sales operation plan. Thus, planning Engine helps you in analysing financial planning applications to execute basic planning operations in the database layer. One such basic operation is to create a new version of a data set as a copy of an existing one while applying filters and transformations.

Now, let's look at the calculation engine, which is used for computation using SQLScript and planning operations. Now, let's say an end-user running a key transaction for analysing sales data. In this case, calculation engine will break it into logical execution plan. Thus, it uses pockets of SQLScript, MDX and Planning Model into operations that can be processed in parallel mode effectively. In similar terms, transaction manager is responsible for managing codes and it tracks if effectively. For example, when a code is committed or rolled back, the code manager informs the respective engines about the event to execute necessary actions.

SAP HANA stores metadata in a database catalogue for all stores. The dB catalogue is stored in tables in row store. Remember, HANA provides in-memory relational data engines, which helps in row-based or column-based data processing. A store is in-memory storage.

SAP HANA stores metadata of all these types is stored in one common database catalogue for all stores. The database catalogue is stored in tables in the Row Store. The features of the SAP HANA database such as transaction support and multi-version concurrency control are also used for metadata management. In the centre of the figure you see the different data Stores of the SAP HANA database. A store is a sub-system of the SAP HANA database which includes in-memory storage, as well as the components that manages that storage.

SAP HANA Platform strategy

Why do you think customer should switch to SAP HANA as a platform? There are critical factors. It's more than a DB as SAP HANA is the platform which supports applications as it just more than a DB with a consolidated suite of business functions to support real-time business critical operations as illustrated below in Figure 2-3 below.

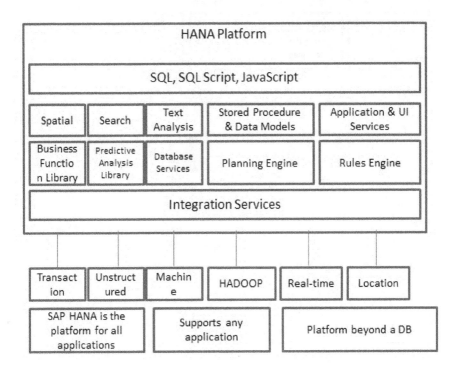

Figure 2-3 SAP HANA Platform.

As illustrated above, SAP HANA combines the power of transactional database and analytical processing with in-memory techniques to transform transactions, analytics, text analysis, predictive and spatial processing to support business operating in real-time. Let's recap platform capability as illustrated below in Figure 2-4.

Figure 2-4. SAP HANA Platform Capability.

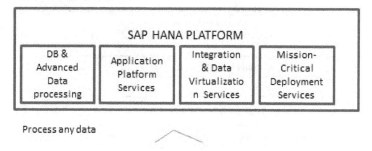

Figure 2-4

Let us take a look at the innovations as illustrated below in

Table 2-1. Innovations

Category	Innovations
Managing Workload	Multi tenancy & workload management support
Reporting Capabilities	Intelligent data tiering
Big Data Capabilities	Graph services and AFL SDK
Enterprise reality deployment capabilities	Additional Cloud deployment opportunities

Cloud Deployment

Enhanced Hadoop Integration

Enhanced openness and application support

Enhanced developer, administration, operations and modelling capabilities

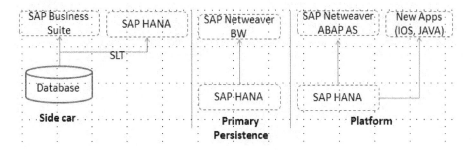

Figure 2-5 SAP HANA Implementation Scenarios

As highlighted above Figure. 2-5 SAP HANA Implementation scenarios to provide an integrated environment combining various applications built on SAP HANA application services. Each of these scenarios can help maximizing investments by leveraging the existing infrastructure using side car option along with the existing systems or use SAP HANA BW for reporting with HANA db. With HANA as platform it will help you build non-SAP applications running on HANA platform as illustrated above.

Let us explore the row vs. column store as you know column store is one of the highlights of the SAP HANA DB. In the next section, let's discuss about the row store and the column store which are unique in SAP HANA.

Row store vs. column store

Typically, relational database use row store, however column store is more suitable for many business applications. SAP HANA supports both store options. The column store is highly optimized. Now, let's look at an example:

Table 2-1 Row based storage:

Table - 'EMP'

EMP	Name	Country	Amount
AB	Abraham	USA	$ 1000
SA	Saleem	UAE	$ 2000
JA	Jayaram	India	$ 3000
AB	Abishek	Singapore	$ 4000
AB	Abirut	Malaysia	$ 5000

As illustrated above in the above Table 2-1 data is stored in a sequence of rows. In the above example, row # 1 refers to record details of Abraham with details of country with amount. As you know records are fetched from tables using structure query language (SQL) in a simple query that matches a specific criteria as highlighted below.

```
SELECT EMP,
       NAME,
       COUNTRY,
       AMOUNT
FROM EMP
WHERE EMP = AB;
```

Result:
Table 2-2 Result of the above SQL:

EMP	Name	Country	Amount
AB	Abraham	USA	$ 1000
AB	Abishek	Singapore	$ 4000
AB	Abirut	Malaysia	$ 5000

Every time you execute a SQL query as highlighted above, table is scanned for the search criteria EMP = 'AB'. If data is on disk, your request will read all columns. Hence, there is an intensive data scanning to meet the search criteria specified. Now, imagine million rows of data. For example, you can create index on Column Emp to keep search faster based on frequently used column. However, there is an intensive amount of data read from the disk. Time for data retrieval depends on the amount of data read from the disk. It is interesting to see how data read operation is done as illustrated below in Figure 2-51:

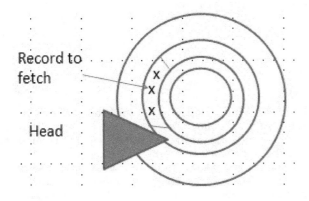

Figure 2-51 Record to fetch from disk

Data resides on cylinder of a disk. How long does it take data to access from the disk? As highlighted above in Figure 2-51, when data pass through the 'head' it is read. Imagine the disk underneath the head is spinning and it is read once it passes through head like a gramophone record player. Here in the above example, 'x' refers to data, it is read once it passes under the head. If the record is random over multiple columns, your reads from the disk will be multiple times as every pass will pick up respective data under the head. If you want nth song, it has to come to that point in the disk to read it. Even though we need only EMP and amount details, data is on disk, hence your query will read all columns sequentially to fetch records meeting your criteria. Let's say you have 1 billion rows of data with each row is 100 bytes long in a table with access speed at @100GB/sec. Therefore, total time to evaluate the above query with 1 billion records would be appx ~ 1000 seconds. In the legacy databases, there is an option to create index. For example, you can create index on Column Emp to keep search faster, based on the on frequently used column. However, there is an intensive amount of data read from the disk. Time for data retrieval depends on the amount of data read from the disk.

Columnar Store (C-Store):

Let us evaluate the above query to fetch employee = 'AB' to analyse the amount (salary) details.

```
SELECT EMP,
       AMOUNT
FROM EMP
WHERE EMP = AB;
```

Whereas, in a columnar storage, required scan time for access is significantly reduced by storing each column in a separate file. Thus, column representation will reduce scan time as illustrated below in Table 2-3 by specifically matching the search criteria instead of scanning the entire table. Furthermore, the column EMP is compressed for better performance during read operation. For example, it compresses column EMP with data stored as "AB X 3" for faster access to reduce the disk read operation discussed in the above example. Thus, in a table with Column EMP with over a billion records, you'd effectively compress EMP column in to few thousand rows EMP column data stored as 'AB X 3' etc. Column stores (C-Stores) can further be optimized with the additional tricks such as the following:

a. To Parallelize across many machines

b. To support efficient loading of new data

c. To optimize read-only queries in the presence of updates

EMP	Amount
AB	$ 1000
AB	$ 4000
AB	$ 5000

Table 2-3 accessing column stores

Now, let's analyse how memory is managed in the column store - The column store is the key highlights of SAP HANA database. It is optimized for read and writes operations.

This is achieved through two data structures as illustrated below in Figure 2-6.

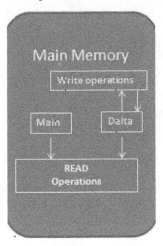

Figure 2-6 HANA Main Memory

Main storage and Delta storage - Each of these storages is useful to optimizing query read/write operations. Now, let us explore merge operations on tables. The key aspect is to understand how data is processed during read/write operations in tables. These merge operations are unique for HANA that helps in optimizing overall query performance. If you have written SQL queries, you'd comprehend the values of the enhanced merge operations available in the HANA system. Now, let's analyse how data is transferred from main memory to the main storage. This operation is called delta merge operation as discussed in the next section.

DELTA MERGE OPERATION

The delta merge operation helps in transfer of data from the memory location to the main storage as illustrated below in Figure. 2-7. there are various techniques involved in moving data from the temporary memory location to the main storage such as a. auto merge operations, b. smart merge & c. critical merge.

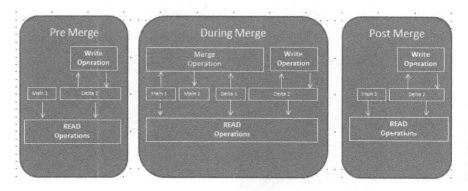

Figure 2-7 Delta Merge Operation

The request to merge the delta storage of a table into its main storage can be triggered in several ways using merge operation listed below:

a. Auto Merge is the standard method for initiating a merge in SAP HANA. It helps in checking the column store tables that are loaded to determine whether merge is required based on configuration. For example, Size of delta storage, available memory, time since last merge, and others.

The smart merge is a function that helps in automatic determination of the delta merge required based on the system checks. Now, let's explore hard and forced merges. These are delta merge operations for a table can be manually triggered using an SQL statement programmatically. This is called a hard merge and results in the database executing the delta merge immediately once sufficient system resources are available.

A critical merge helps in keeping the system functions stable. In case of any eventuality where auto merge is not working and/or smart merge hints does not function property, then the critical merge starts working based on a certain threshold to avoid system failure, thus it avoids eventual system crashes by maintaining stability of the system. Now, let's analyse benefits of the columnar storage in the next section.

Benefits of Column-based storage:

In addition to a classical row-based data store, SAP HANA is able to store tables in its column-based data store. It is important to understand the differences between these two methods, and why column-based storage can highly increase certain types of data processing.

Historically, column-based storage was mainly used in the datawarehouses, where aggregate functions play an important role. On the other hand, using column stores in Online Transaction Processing (OLTP) applications requires a balanced approach to insertion and indexing of column data, in order to minimize cache misses.

The SAP HANA database allows the developer to specify whether a table is to be stored column-wise or row-wise. It is also possible to alter an existing column-based table to row-based, and vice versa. Thus it helps in managing memory for faster query processing time. As you know database table is a two-dimensional data structure with cells organized in rows and columns. The computer memory functions as a linear structure. There are two options in order to start table in linear memory as follows:

6. As in a typical record in a row-based approach stores a table as a sequence of records, each of which contain the fields of one row.

7. In a column-based table, the entries of a column are stored in contiguous memory locations.

Key Pointers in row based storage vs. Column based storage

Now, it is important to analyse which option can be utilized for faster access. Perhaps row store makes sense in case of reporting all columns of a table because reconstructing the complete row is one of the most expensive operations for a column-based table. Whereas column store is better if you're accessing huge volume of data that are required to be aggregated and analysed; now, let us analyse commenting patterns used in SQL, identifiers and operators.

In the next section, let us analyze the unique features of SAP HANA backup and recovery procedures.

Backup and Recovery

SAP HANA delivers "better, faster, cheaper" alternative. The latest release is service pack SPS 12 for the SAP HANA platform, helping customers successfully extending core functionalities to deliver growing business requirements. For example, SAP delivered, Internet of Things (IoT) at enterprise scale, manage Big Data more effectively, further extend high availability of data across the enterprise and develop new applications.

The SAP HANA provides a robust platform for SAP and non-SAP applications for transactional and analytical processing. Further, it extends to synchronizing data to any remote systems, high availability and disaster recovery of enterprise data to support advanced analytics. In-memory computing is safe: SAP HANA holds the bulk of its data in memory for maximum performance, but still uses persistent storage to provide a fall back in case of failure. During normal operation, data is automatically saved from memory to disk at regular save points. Additionally, all data changes are captured in redo log entries.

New features of Backup & Recovery in SPS 12 include the following:

a. Scheduling Backups

b. Resume Uninterrupted recover

c. SAP HANA cockpit enhancements and

d. Recovery enhancements

You can create schedule in HANA is done using 'xs' job scheduler. The interesting point is that you can recover from a specified fall-back point. Here is a quick comparison of backup and recovery options between SPS 10 and SPS 12 as illustrated below in Figure 2-71.

61

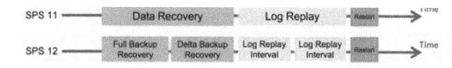

Figure 2-71 Backup & Recovery SPS 12

As illustrated in Figure 2-71, you can separate the delta backup recovery point. You can recover database using SAP HANA cockpit or SQL console.

A redo log entry is written to disk after each committed database transaction. After a power failure, SAP HANA can be restarted like any disk-based database and returns to its last consistent state by replaying the redo log entries since the last save point as illustrated below in Figure 2-8 below:

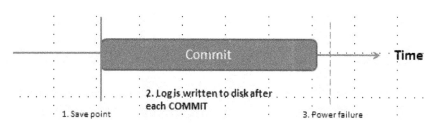

Figure 2-8 Commit

Why Backups?

There are different techniques available to schedule backups. Backup doesn't just refer to the data back in the disk. Indeed, SAP HANA stores enormous data as in-memory. Hence, there is a compelling need to write to the disk without losing data in terms of 'commit' operations to the database. Either you can use HANA studio tool or backing process to do the backup. Each of these techniques can be applied depending on the scenario. For example, you may want to backup to an external disk or internal etc. Typically save points and redo log helps in protecting your data against potential failures, however this does not help when the persistent storage itself is damaged. Backups complement other availability strategies such as system replication or storage replication as illustrated below in Figure 2-9.

SAP HANA DB

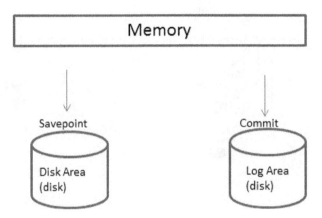

Figure 2-9

Memory-Disk-Backup

A full data backup saves all current data that is contained in the data area (payload only). Delta backups save subsequently changed data. A snapshot saves the content of the whole data area. Snapshots are an alternative to full data backups. Data backups and snapshots are executed manually (scheduling possible) Log backups. Log backups save the redo log entries that are contained in the log area and Log backups are carried out automatically (asynchronously) as illustrated below in Figure. 2-12

SAP HANA DB

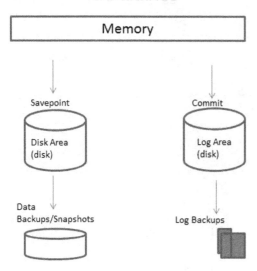

Figure 2-12 Backup from memory

Backup and Recovery Options

Now, let us understand the simple concepts of how to backup and recovery data quickly in SAP HANA with options provided.

Data Backups (Full vs. Delta)

A full data backup contains all current data. Old data that is no longer valid but might still be physically present in the data volumes is not part of the data backup. Delta backups contain data that was changed since an earlier data backup Two types: incremental and differential. In contrast, log backups contain redo log entries (=sequence of changes). Therefore, delta backups cannot be used together with a snapshot for recovery.

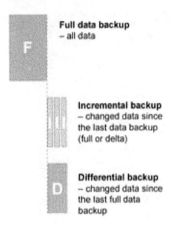

Full data backup
– all data

Incremental backup
– changed data since
the last data backup
(full or delta)

Differential backup
– changed data since
the last full data
backup

Figure 2-13

Incremental backups:

a. The smallest data backups as unchanged
   data will not be backed up in multiple
   backups for the faster backup

b. Restored one after the other during a
   recovery. Longer recovery times
   Differential backups.

c. Increase the amount of data saved with
   each backup with longer backup times

d. Reduce the number of data backups during
   recovery with faster recovery

Note: You can also mix incremental and differential
backups in your backup strategy

What happens during a data backup?

While backups are running, users can continue to work
normally. All services that persist data are backed up. It

Synchronizes across all hosts and services ⎩ No user interaction for synchronization required! Data marked in the global backup save point is read from the data volumes and written to the backups

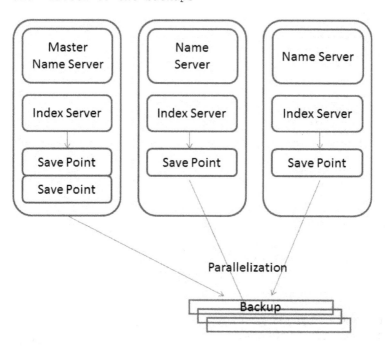

Figure 2-14. Synchronized backup savepoint

There are different options for carrying out backups for SAP HANA as highlighted below:

a. Backups to the file system,

b. Backups via the "Backint for SAP HANA" API to 3rd party tools and

c. Data snapshots using storage tools

Note: You can mix different backup options, e.g. write the data backups to the file system and the log backups to Backint. Now, let's see data backup using tools.

Data Backup Options:

You can back up data and logs to the file system Data backups can be triggered using the following tools:

a. SAP HANA Cockpit

b. SAP HANA Studio

c. SQL commands &

d. DBA Cockpit (scheduling) Log backups are written automatically More information:

Please note file systems that are not supported: SAP Note 1820529. The backup scheduling using SAP HANA studio data backup into file system is illustrated below in in Figure 2-15:

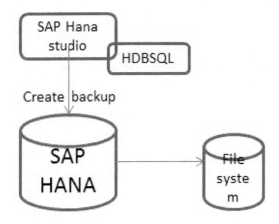

Figure 2-15 SAP HANA Backup

You can back up data and logs using 3rd party backup tools SAP HANA provides an API ("Backint for SAP HANA") via which 3rd party backup tools can be connected. These third party backup agent runs on the SAP HANA server as backups are transferred via pipe direct integration with SAP HANA. Backint can be triggered using SAP HANA Cockpit, SAP HANA Studio, SQL commands, or DBA Cockpit (scheduling). These Log backups are automatically written to Backint (if configured) as illustrated below in Figure 2-16

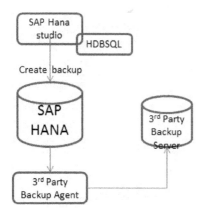

Figure 2-16 Backup using 3rd Party servers

For improved performance Backint can now use multiple parallel streams for data backups if parallel streams have been configured, the individual service backups are distributed across all available streams. Backups will only be distributed if they are bigger than 128 GB. In order to configure the number of parallel streams, use the parallel_data_backup_backint_channels ini file parameter (default: 1, max: 32) as illustrated below in Figure 2-17.

■ Note: It is recommended to adapt the configuration of the 3rd party backup tool accordingly.

| Overview | Landscape | Alerts | Performance | Volumes | Configuration | System Information |

Filter: parallel_data_backup ✖

Name	Default	System
◢ 🗎 global.ini		◆
◢ [ ] backup		◆
parallel data backup backint channels 1		● **3**

Figure 2-17 Configuration setting for backup

As illustrated below in Figure 2-18, 3 parallel streams have been configured. The index server backup is distributed across 3 streams. If both name server and XS engine backups are smaller than 128 GB, they are not distributed across. Using 3rd party backup as illustrated below.

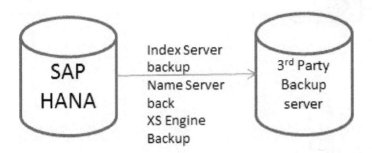

Figure 2-18 Backup configuration of index, name server

As an alternative to data backups to the file system or to Backint, you can use snapshots (data only) in the following steps:

a.   First, you trigger the creation of an internal data snapshot in SAP HANA using SAP HANA Studio or SQL commands ("prepare database")

b.   Using a storage tool or similar, you create a snapshot of the whole data area and

c.   Confirm the snapshot as successful, using SAP HANA Studio or SQL commands. This is necessary to include the snapshot in SAP HANA's backup catalogue. Note: No other data backup is possible until the snapshot has either been confirmed or cancelled as illustrated below in Figure 2-19.

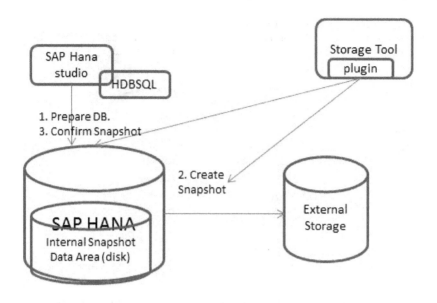

Figure 2-19 External storage for backup

Options for backup: Comparison

Table 2-5 Backup Options

Sol	File System	Backint	Snapshot
Advantages	Consistency checks on block level	Consistency checks on block level Additional features, e.g. encryption or de-duplication Data center integration Backups available for recovery	Restored fast Negligible network load
Disadvantages	Additional storage File system level need to be monitored	Network load	No consistency check on block level

Tools for Backup - The following tools are available for backup from SAP:

1. SAP HANA Cockpit (web-based administration tool)

2. SAP HANA Studio (Eclipse-based administration tool and IDE)

3. DBA Cockpit (ABAP-based tool for high-level database administration tasks)

Recovery

You can use SAP HANA Studio or SQL commands to execute a recovery. For a recovery, SAP HANA will be shut down In the Systems view in SAP HANA Studio, choose Backup and Recovery - Recover System... from the context menu of the database and enter credentials of the SAP HANA operating system user 'adm' Note: Recovery is not yet available in SAP HANA Cockpit as illustrated below in Figure. 2-28 below:

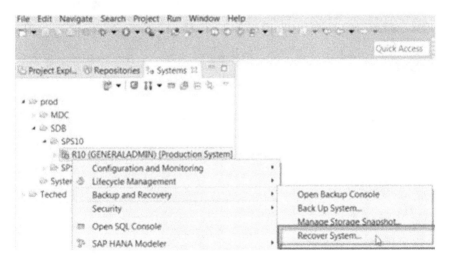

Figure 2-28 recovery settings

Recovery to the most recent state (option A)

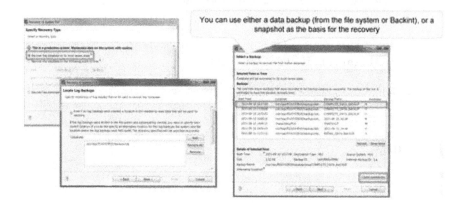

Figure 2-29 backup snapshot

The option (B) involves recovery to a past time.

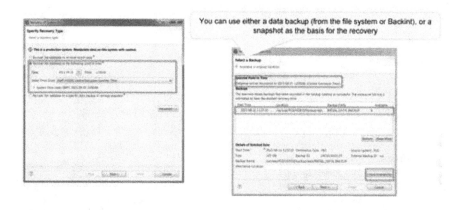

Figure 2-30 backup snapshot for recovery

Now, let's explore recovery using a specified data backup or snapshot option C

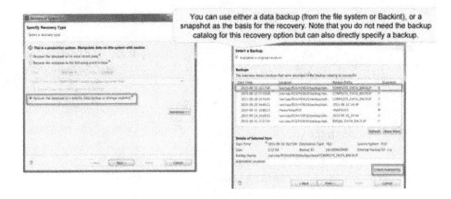

Figure 2-31 snapshot options

Further recovery settings, e.g. use of delta backups during recovery, which includes delta backups automatically SAP HANA automatically determines the best recovery strategy based on all available backups, including delta backups. If you do not want SAP HANA to use delta backups for the recovery, de-select Use Delta Backups when specifying your recovery settings

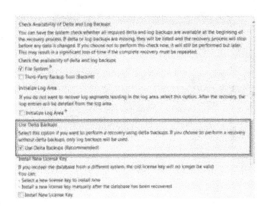

Figure 2-32 delta backup setting

Recovery Phases:

After the initial collection of system information required for the recovery, there is the following recovery phases described below:

a) Data recovery step involve backups using data backups or snapshot plus delta backups procedure available

b) Log recovery step involve redo log entries are replayed from the log backups and/or - from the log area (if still available/required) &

c) Restart SAP HANA.

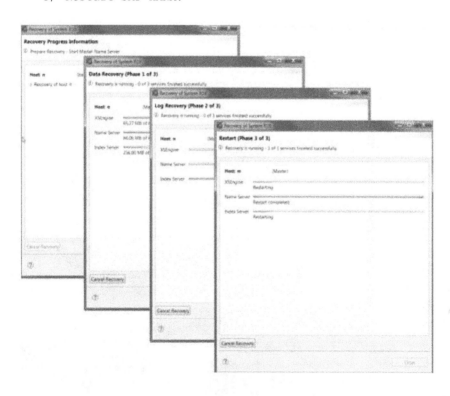

Figure 2-34 recovery

Preparation of a recovery using a snapshot as an alternative to a full data backup to the file system/Backint as illustrated below in Figure 2-35 using SAP HANA recovery from external storage.

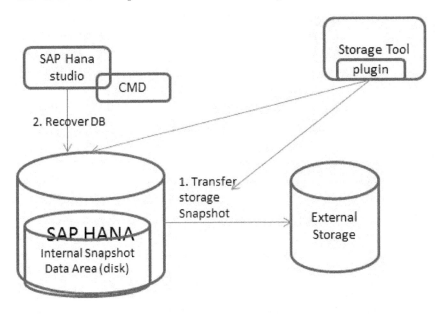

Figure 2-35 recovery from external storage

Multitenant database containers allow you to run multiple applications on one SAP HANA system. The system database and multiple tenant databases are shared installation of the database system software as illustrated below in Figure 2-26. The system database contains information about the system as a whole and is used for central system administration.

■ Note: SAP Note 2096000

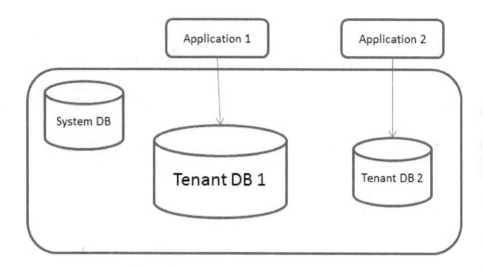

Figure 2-36 Multi Tenant DB on HANA

The MDC system follows the same backup/recovery principles as single-container systems. The system database plays a central role for MDC backup and recovery; however, it can support backups of the system database and the individual tenant's databases. A tenant database can also carry out its own backups unless this feature has been disabled for this tenant database.

Key Highlights

You can use SAP HANA Cockpit, which is simple tool for backup and recovery to create data backups of the system database or backup of individual tenant databases. Let's explore an option to use SAP HANA cockpit for backup.

Log on to the relevant database and click on the Data Backup tile. Then, create data backups and view backup information in the same way as for single-container databases as illustrated below.

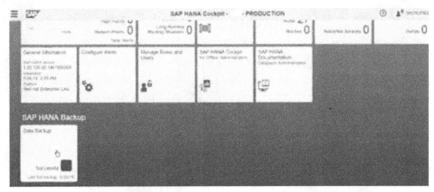

Figure 2-37 SAP HANA Cockpit

Step 1 - In the above SAP HANA cockpit in Figure 2-37, select the   [SAP HANA Backup] to open the catalogue.

Step 2 - Backup catalogue as illustrated below in Figure 2-38:

Figure 2-38 Backup Catalogue

Step 3 - Select the option from the list [Prefix]

Figure 2-39 Search

Step 4 -

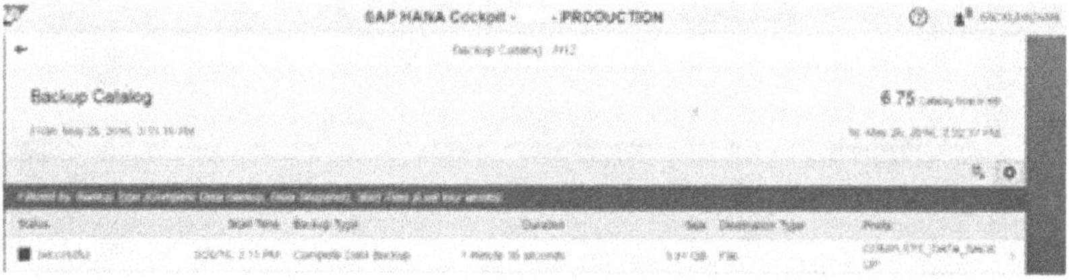

Figure 2-40

Step 5 - You can specify backup file destination with prefix for complete or incremental backup options as illustrated below in Figure 2-41:

Figure 2-41
Step 6 -

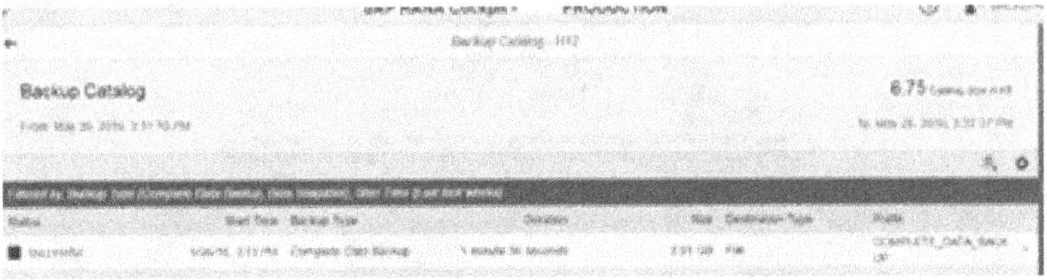

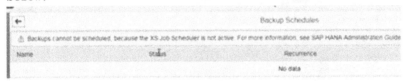

Figure 2-42

Step 7: Schedule using XS Job Scheduler as illustrated below:

Figure 2-43

Step 8: Activate XS Job scheduler as mentioned below in the XS admin tool:

Figure 2-44 XS Job Scheduler

Step 9 - Select job schedule details in XS dashboard as illustrated below:

Figure 2-45 XS Job Dashboard

Figure 2-46

Step 10 - Assign User and [Save Job] as illustrated below:

Figure 2-47

Step 11: If you return back to the cockpit, you can create the schedule with backup prefix and destination as illustrated below:

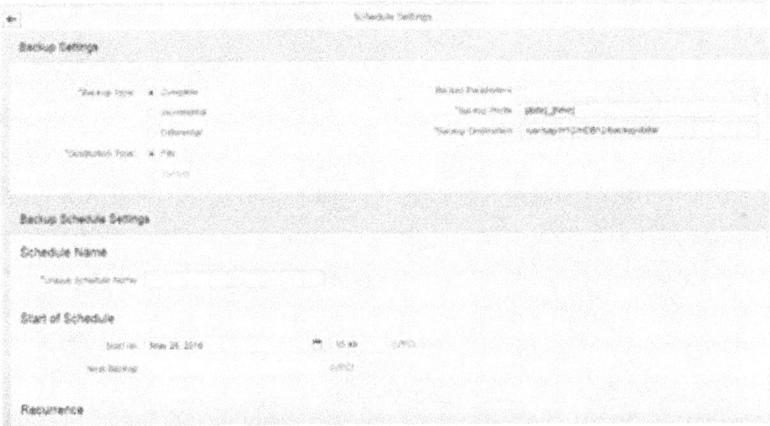

Figure 2-48

Step 12 – You can mention recurrence of the schedule weekly, monthly and save the schedule as illustrated below:

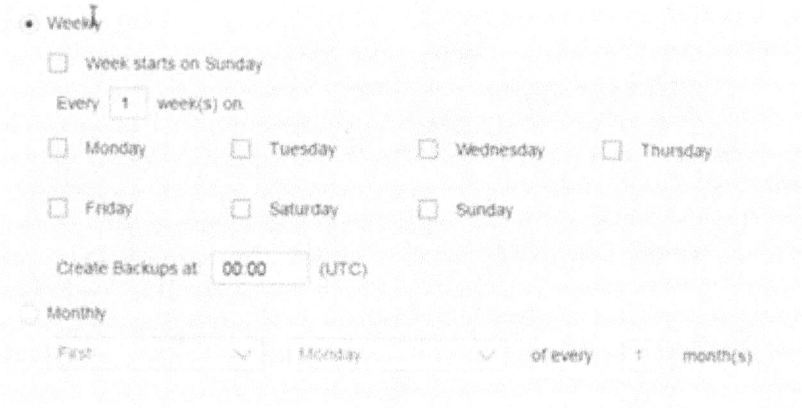

- Weekly

  ☐ Week starts on Sunday

  Every 1   week(s) on

  ☐ Monday   ☐ Tuesday   ☐ Wednesday   ☐ Thursday

  ☐ Friday   ☐ Saturday   ☐ Sunday

  Create Backups at   00:00   (UTC)

  Monthly

  First   ∨   Monday   ∨   of every   1   month(s)

Figure 2-49 Schedule recurrence

Step 13 – Log Recovery with resume point specified as illustrated below in Figure 2-50:

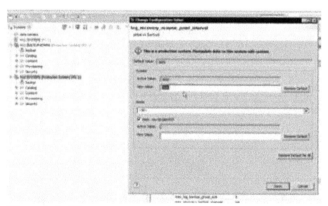

Figure 2-50 Log recovery

Summary

In this chapter, you've studied the SAP HANA architecture, roadmap with database backup and restore methods Also, we discussed about the concept of column compression techniques widely used in SAP HANA Db with backup and recovery options using HANA cockpit. In essence, HANA has simplified the way you perform various dB administrative activities, also leads me to believe the next generation technology to support clients worldwide to harness the power of computing. Each of the above database administrative activities in SAP legacy or any other systems takes several years of practice with manual tasks involved, which are prone to errors. However, it's easy in SAP HANA to train new administrators faster and effective without any loss of productivity.

■   ■   ■

Chapter 3: SAP HANA for Analytics

There are two primary objectives to ensure SAP's investment in HANA Analytics is justified. One is to provide real-time access to data at anytime, anywhere and secondly provide detailed view of data such as sales volume analysis for predictive analysis. Thus, data is available for developing insights about the customer behaviour, demographics and product analysis to improve market insights. Gone are the days where you'd implement complex data warehouses, data marts etc. to harness data available in the OLTP systems. As a Project Manager, you'd have struggled with number of backend jobs running to update OLAP analytical systems updated from real-time data in the OLTP systems in the I.T landscape. It's complex to manage multiple instances with increased costs of maintenance and subsequent developments. End of the day, if sales profitability analysis is required based on your corporate performance for last 5 years; you'd be running around I.T department with additional queries developed to fetch details from several database instances.

If you would like to assess scope of corporate performance based on historical evidences of sales volume, procurement and internal production capacity analysis is very complex. Each of it will need significant efforts to develop ETL (extract, transform and load) tools to extract data in relevant formats, and then transform and loading it in respective data marts is a project by itself. By the time data warehouse project is done, business would have closed the books for the accounting year without much interest with any further analysis. There are critical tasks such as sales operation planning, which needs detailed historical analysis of sales volume for the past years. In summary, harnessing data for analysing corporate performance in one go has never been easier. Moreover, year-end closure takes a lot of time to complete due to

85

extensive data computations in the backend with several jobs running in the background. This would impact other processes too. Hence, there was a need for running queries faster, gaining analytical insights and improving sales channels by leveraging data from disparate platforms such as mobile computing; social media network to develop market insights by interacting directly with the customers.

The SAP HANA Analytics suite provides enhanced reporting capabilities with the products such as Business Intelligence, Business Objects, Crystal Reports and SAP Lumira with plethora of designer tools to get out-of-box reporting solutions. This solution enables customers to select from the cloud based or on-premises installation deployment options. SAP HANA is the complete solution of data warehouse solutions with user-friendly tools to access enterprise information quickly. Most of the customers using legacy database have issues in the following areas:

1. A lot of time is spent on how to build data warehouse(s), instead of spending quality time in strategy. Often, it turns out to be a project by itself in building data warehouses without realizing ROI

2. Often, executives are dabbling with excel files to aggregate data in required format during analysis, thus losing focus

3. Extract, Transform and Load (ETL) process is always time consuming and expensive

4. Business benefits are not realized after a long hauling I.T projects

5. Enterprise wide reporting and/or at the transaction level has always been an issue

6. Lack of quick turnaround time in responding to queries raised by the end-users such as a reporting request. Even accounting departments struggle with the month-end closure, which usually takes longer.

Today, market has changed. It has primarily become customer friendly and demanding, and market is revolving around BIG data in every part of business. This paradigm change in the industry to consumer base has necessitated need of data available in handheld devices or enterprise mobility that is scalable with the advent of smart phones. You might have shopped online or mobile using your smart phone isn't? It's interesting to see companies such as a major online retailer can fulfil order in quick turn-around time. I am amazed with the point to point order to deliver process that can be tracked every moment. As a customer, I feel delighted to see the planning and execution of the on-time delivery by the retailer.

This is just a simple example of analytics supporting enterprises, moreover there were few options provided to customers based on the product search. Thus, a prospective buyer purchases product in quick turn-around and the order is fulfilled. This is a good example of real time analytics data helping enterprise increase sales.

This is an example of predictive analysis, where enterprises can analyse customer behaviour. I would rather call predictive analysis as the third-eye of the enterprises that can help companies to forecast precisely. Further, integration in to external applications that has a huge customer base such as LinkedIn, Facebook can help organizations grow by providing more value to the customers. It's time to market; fulfilling customer requirements in less time and delighting customers by providing detailed analytics. It is easy to maintain -- order history, expenses and manage orders and delivery. The return process is also simple without any hassles of waiting in the queue.

In this chapter, you would see how to benefit by using SAP's HANA analytics solution with details of complete suite of solution, hands-on building attribute views, and modeller and reporting capabilities.

■ **Note:** SAP HANA analytics solution supports harnessing data for the enterprise with advanced in-memory capabilities. Thus, it has transformed data marts into data engines for quick access to enterprise wide data.

SAP Analytics Solution

The SAP analytics solution is primarily used for the following, to provide intuitive analytical capabilities as illustrated below:

The SAP HANA Platform provides the following services as highlighted in Table 3-1 below:

Analytic Solution	Description
BI Solutions	Used for enterprise reporting, dashboards, mobile, data exploration and analysis
Crystal Solutions	Used for interactive report from any data source
Business Objects	Used for complex queries with high performance
Sybase PowerDesigner	Used as metadata solution for data modelling
Enterprise Information Management	Used for consolidating data for compliance

Table 3-1 Services provided by HANA

One of the retail giant based out of USA runs on SAP HANA. It highlights the need of retaining customers; build more value with the partners by engaging. This can be possible with tools such as Business Intelligence (BI) to increase the value proposition to the business. The above suite of analytics solution from SAP covers predictive analysis, data modelling with wide range of the products suite for small, medium or large enterprises. Thus, there is a definite need for transforming data into outcomes. Few quick wins as listed below:

1. Convert prospect to sale in quick turn-around

2. Customer behaviour analysis and provide viable product offerings

3. Quick order fulfilment process

4. Time to deliver in quick turn-around and

5. Predictive customer behaviour analysis

In the above scenario, based on online retailers ability to provide the right product suite resulted in increased sales. For example, a customer has an option to research mobile phones in a major online portal. Thus, intelligence is gathered to the extent of stating what type of smart phone with design, brand, colour, quality, operating system, software and hardware that a customer will like the most based on the search criteria. A customer can analyse the best option to choose from the catalogue. This is primarily customer driven, isn't? It's more exiting without additional resources to market and sell products which might be priced higher. This is a simple market intelligence based on customer's behaviour on the portal using search criteria.

Today, it's simple. A buyer can research about a product inside and out. Then, he or she would go online to buy a product based on his own findings. Hence, there is a definite need to gather details of buyer preferences before giving out options. Thus, companies can provide the best options with tools capable of enhanced predictive abilities to win order along with the customer confidence. Thus, tools have helped in consolidating data, building insights with a positive impact to the customers as illustrated below in Figure 3-2.

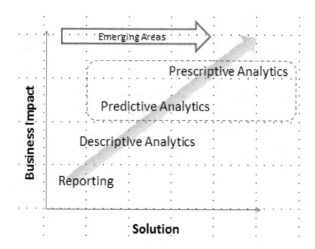

Figure 3-2 Maturity of Analytics solution

Let's look at HANA architecture with predictive analysis capabilities using HANA analytical process as illustrated below with HANA studio to build Queries using SQL or MDX. As shown below, data sources can be external 3rd party services as illustrated below in Figure 3-3.

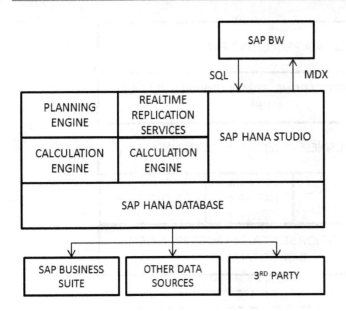

Figure 3-3 SAP BW powered by HANA

Let's take a quick look at SAP's BIG DATA. The moment you think BIG data, it refers to accessing data from various platforms including database, flat files or unstructured data from social media network. It should have capabilities to extend presentation in various platforms including mobile platform as illustrated below in Figure 3-4.

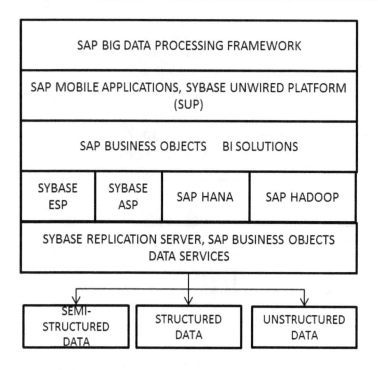

Figure 3-4. SAP analytics solution powered by HANA

Now, let's try and build attribute view. In simpler terms, a view represents logical group of data for your assessment. A schema refers to the database model with collection of tables, views to hold data required for quick analysis. It has facts and dimension tables as part of the schema. As you know star schema is the most prevalent ones in the data warehouse model. There are various types of views which are logical grouping of data such as attribute view, calculation view with specific purposes highlighted below. In the next section, let's take a quick look at building your first attribute views.

Build your first attribute view

Now, let's take a simple case study to build attribute view. Let's understand the basics of attribute view. It is typically created for maintain master data in SAP HANA system or also known as dimension in star schema. Point here is that data is not stored physically, it is fetched from source at run-time, whenever you execute at run-time. Now, you've asked this question about start schema. Let's step back to understand the basic data mart star schema model, which consists of fact and dimension tables as illustrated below in Figure 3-5.

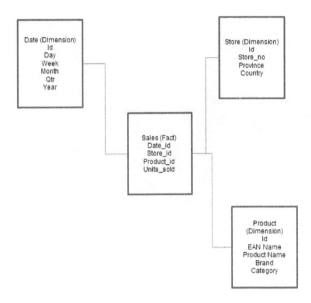

Figure 3-5 Star Schema

The above star schema refers to one fact table (SALES) with multi dimension tables referencing product, store and date tables as highlighted.

In the above example, you have developed a simple star schema for analysing sales volume of an enterprise. Hence, you have built a simple model to sales volume. In this scenario, table holds fact table holds information about the sold quantity, data, and store with product details. We will need additional supplementary details about each of the ID's stored in the fact. As you see in the above scenario, you'd like to know more about the product details such as EAN name, brand and category. This is true with date specifics and store details with its precise details. Hence, you'd need dimension tables for all such supplementary details as 'Dimension' tables, whereas 'FACT' remains the focal point as illustrated above. You may have one or more 'FACT' core table depending on the complexities of the data model. Once you've identified the tables required for analysis, now the next step is to build attribute view for each individual dimension and you can join them to fact table in analytic view. The following flow demonstrates step-by-step process in creating attribute views in Figure 3-6 below:

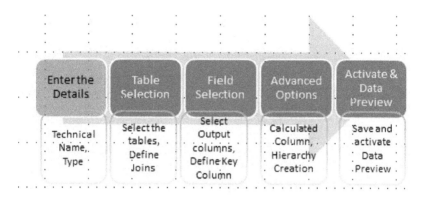

Figure 3-6 Attribute View Creation Flow

There are few pre-requisites before you start creating the attribute view. You can ensure user has select; execute privileges on the specific schema where tables are residing. Tables must be from HANA source. Now, let's analyse steps for creating a package for attribute views as detailed below in steps.

Step1. Create package with package technical details entered as illustrated below in Figure 3-7.

Figure 3-7 Create Package

Enter technical details as part of step 1 as illustrated below in Figure 3-8 below:

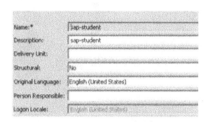

Figure 3-8 Enter Package Details

Now, let's move on to the next step 2. Now, right click on the package and follow NET – ATTRIBUTE-VIEW to start the attribute view creation process as illustrated below in Figure 3-9 below to enter details of the attribute view as soon as created.

Figure 3-9   Create Attribute View

Next step is to create as you can choose to create standard, time or derived attribute view as illustrated below in Figure 3-10:

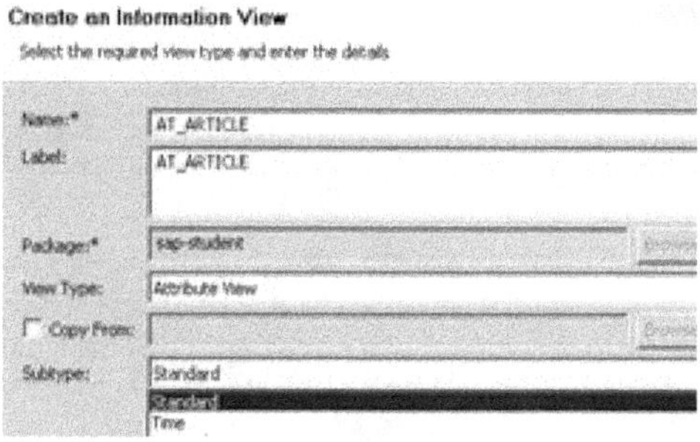

Figure 3-10 Select View Type

As a final step, you can click [Finish] to go to attribute view building screen as illustrated below, which has screens for semantics and data foundation for information about source tables and joins required which represents specific criteria that are used to join two tables for required output in Figure 3-11 below:

Figure 3-11 Output

You can add tables to data founding by using simple drag and drop options from the systems view. Once the tables are added, then you can select columns for output as illustrated below in Figure 3-12.

Figure 3-12 Add to Output

Thus, you will be able to create a simple attribute view based on the star schema designed in the HANA system. Once you activate the above model in the HANA system, it is available for reporting. In the above scenario, you'll be able to easily join tables to derive output. Once you drag and drop to join tables, there are options provided as illustrated below to specifically mention type of join as illustrated below in Figure 3-13.

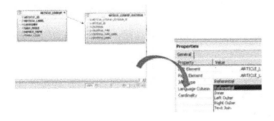

Figure 3-13 Join properties

Reporting Capabilities

Now, let's explore report capabilities using SAP BI in HANA, which primarily a data warehousing and reporting tool. BI provides user friendly tools to design and deploy. It supports many databases, you will be able migrate from source data to SAP HANA. In this section, let's review SAP BI architecture and how it works.

SAP BI runs on three tier architecture which comprises of DB server, Application and presentation server. The SAP Bex Query Designer can access SAP HANA view and display data in Bex as illustrated below in Figure 3-14:

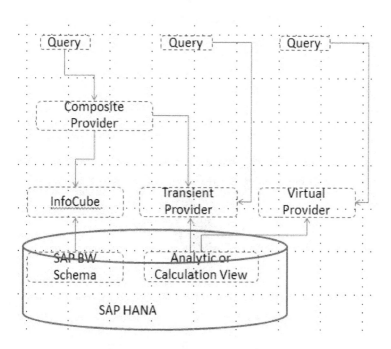

Figure 3-14 SAP BI Architecture

SAP Business Objects Web Intelligence (SAP BO WebI) is part of SAP Business Objects Platform (SBOP). It allows JDBC/ODBC driver to connect to source system. It is used for adhoc and detailed reporting. Users can create and modify queries. Hence, they don't need to wait for sending request to the I.T. It's like do it yourself. You need to install JDBC/ODBC drivers post SAP HANA client installations to enable usage. These drivers' help in connecting to the SAP HANA DB as illustrated below in Figure 3-15.

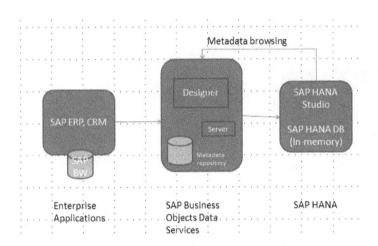

Figure 3-15 SAP BusinessObjects Data Services

Creating Business Objects Universe:

Business objects universe refers to semantic layer between database and the end-user. It is a business representation of data warehouse or transaction layer. For example, a business objects universe may contain a schema of tables and joins or SQL structures in the database.

Now, let's explore creating universe using a designer tool.

Create Universe using information design tool.

Step-1: Create universe using information design tool (IDT). As discussed earlier, HANA can be accessed via ODBC/JDBC drivers, and its tables can be defined and queried with SQL. Tables are managed with a tool called HANA studio.

Launch IDT by navigating to [Start Menu] - [SAP Business Intelligence] - [SAP Business Objects BI Platform Client Tools] - [Information Design Tool] as illustrated below in Figure 3-16 to create business layer, on which reports can be developed:

Figure 3-16 Information Design Tool

2. Navigate to project option as below:

   8. Click on file

   9. Click new option & c. Select project with details of the project entered as illustrated below:

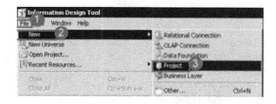

Figure 3-17 Create Project

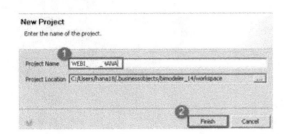

Figure 3-18 Enter new project

Project name will appear under local projects table as shown above. A project is a local workspace where you store the resources to build universes. Now, let's see type of connections available to connect to the universe:

Relational - To access data from table

OLAP - To access data from the applications

Let's create a relational connect. Go to [Project] - [New] - [Relational] as illustrated below. Enter resource name and description.

Figure 3-19 Enter Resource name

A pop-up for dB middleware driver selection will appear to select [JDBC] driver option as illustrated below.

Figure 3-20 Select JDBC Driver

Now, enter authenticate mode, user name and password as highlighted below

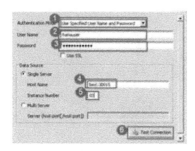

Figure 3-21 User Authentication

You have an option to [Test Connection] as highlighted above. Once you're done sample test connections. Next step is to publish connection for consumption of the universe by webi, dashboards or crystal report for enterprise as illustrated below.

Figure 3-22 Publish connection to repository

A pop-up is displayed indicate a successful connection as illustrated below:

Figure 3-23 Publish connection

Lastly, you'll be able to create universe by using SAP HANA Business layer for users. As discussed earlier, universe represents business information or transaction database. It allows users to interact with data without knowledge of complexities of the Database. Now, let's see how crystal reports help in building analytics for enterprises. Let's see a sample report developed using crystal reports as illustrated below.

Figure 3-24 SAP HANA Business Layer

You'll be able to drag and drop required objects in the business layer to build your own analytical reports as illustrated below in Figure 3-25:

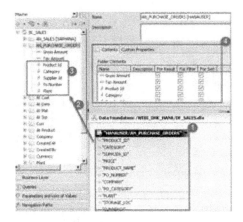

Figure 3-25 Building analytical reports

Now, let's analyse reporting using Crystal Reports which is a user friendly tool for building complex visualization as illustrated below:

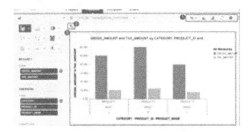

Figure 3-26 Visualize reoport

The above report is developed using [Crystal Reports] – [Data Explorer] console by using this designer tool that connects to the SAP HANA view in the backend as illustrated below. User can select required fields to build the report based on the data sources that are available in the view as illustrated below in Figure 3-27 Crystal Report.

Figure 3-27 Crystal report

Reporting using SAP Lumira

SAP Lumira helps in analysing and visualizing data. Using Lumira, you'll be able to visualize data, create interactive map, charts etc. It can also import data from excel and other sources. It can access HANA views. Let review the steps to setup lumira for data visualization as illustrated below with high quality analytics as illustrated below in Figure 3-28:

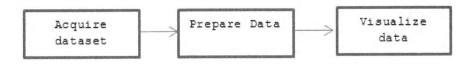

Figure 3-28 Building report in Lumira.

Reporting using Excel

It's easy to connect to HANA using excel. Select [From Data connection wizard] – [SAP HANA MDX Provider] – [Provide Link details with user name and password] – [Select Analytic view] and finally to build excel report as illustrated below in Figure 3-29

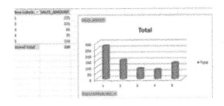

Figure 3-29 MDX Report

SAP HANA Modeller

Typically, model is the way you want to interpret data in the system by slicing and dicing the way you want to analyse. Our first step is to model a business case using content data. The content data can be classified in to attribute (for example. City, Country and customer ID) and measure (for example, Quantity sold). Now, let's talk about HANA modeller. It is a simple tool that allows create and edit data models (content) and stored procedures. You can also create analytic privileges that govern the access to the models, and business rules to implement. You'll be able to create a. Attribute b. Analytic and c. Calculation views.

Now, let's see modelling process overview as illustrated below in Figure 3-30:

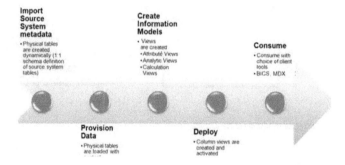

Figure 3-30

It's easy to connect to HANA Modeller using HANA studio which is the app to connect to SAP HANA database. As soon as you connect, you're in the modeller perspective, which is a modeller view as illustrated below, where you'd create model.

SAP HANA Modeller

106

Figure 3-31 Modeler Quick Launch

You can create attribute views, analytic privileges, calculation view which are required to support in creating logical views and authorizations etc. In data option, you can create time specific data. Data provisioning option is used to pull data from the respective schema, tables in the SAP HANA source system. You can select which tables you may want to replicate using simple graphic interface by defining the source and replication parameters as per requirements. For example, you may want to analyse sales data. You would select table [VBAK] with respective columns that you want to analyse. There are views that are readily available for your requirements. You can select [Attribute] view or [Analytic] view or [Logical] view. Transaction data is stored in the typical star schema as fact and dimensions. Calculation views are basically aggregate data available for your reporting requirements as illustrated below.

Figure 3-32

The below table lists the tasks you can perform in the SAP HANA Modeller perspective. Let's review list of tasks that can be performed in the Modeller as described below.

Table 3-2 List of tasks in SAP HANA Modeler

SAP HANA for Project Managers

2016

Task	Description
Import metadata Load data	Metadata refers to the table definitions imported from source system
	Load data refers to table definitions loaded in the target by leveraging load controller, SAP Sybase replication server or SAP SLT tool suite.
Create packages	Create package refers to grouping objects in structured way such as tables, views in a package.
Create Information views	Create information views represents slice and dice options of data available in HANA for reporting
Create procedures Create analytic privileges	Create procedures refers to implementing specific logic for business requirements
	Create analytic privileges refers to the authorizations controls for accessing data

SAP Analytic Privileges

Now, let's understand the concept of analytic privileges. Analytic privileges are used to provide read access to data which are primarily evaluated at run-time during query processing. This privilege is evaluated during query processing. These analytic privileges grant different user access on different part of data in the same information view based on user roles. Hence, it is used in SAP HANA database to provide row level data control for individual users to view data in the same view. Now, let us understand the process of creating SQL Analytic privilege and adding dependent objects in SAP HANA as illustrated below:

Step 1: To create a new analytic privilege, we need to go content, right click on package – New – Analytic privilege as illustrated below in Figure 3-33:

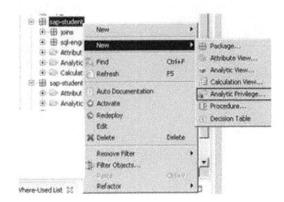

Step 2 – Enter details such as technical name, description and then select the type of analytic privilege that we would like to create as illustrated below in Figure 3-34:

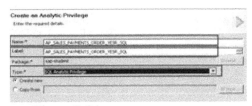

Figure 3-34

Step 3 – Select information models on which you'd like to apply the analytic privileges analytic privilege that we would like to create as illustrated below in Figure 3-35. There are three types of views to which you can apply SQL Analytic privileges:

    a. Attribute view,

b. Analytic view,

c. Calculation view &

d. Views

Now, let's apply analytic privileges on final calculation view CA_SALES_PAYMENTS for attribute ORDER_YEAR. Select the calculation view CA_SALES_PAYMENTS, add the right side and click [Finish] as highlighted below in Figure 3-36:

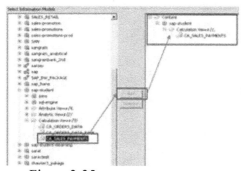

Figure 3-35

Step 4- This is the analytic privilege design area where we will define all the settings relevant to analytic privilege as illustrated below in Figure 3-36.

Figure 3-36

This screen is same as the one we see while creating classical analytic privilege as illustrated below in Figure 3-37.

Figure 3-37

By default when we create modelling objects in SAP HANA, these are secured by classical analytic privileges. We can check this option in 'semantics' of the modelling object as illustrated below in Figure 3-38.

Figure 3-38

Before we create SQL Analytic privileges on modelling objects, we have to change the apply privileges option to 'SQL Analytic Privileges' and activate it. This can be done depending on the modelling objects. Let's say you'll need to perform this for calculation view CA_SALES_PAYMENTS and analytic views AN_ORDERS_SALES, AN_PAYMENTS.

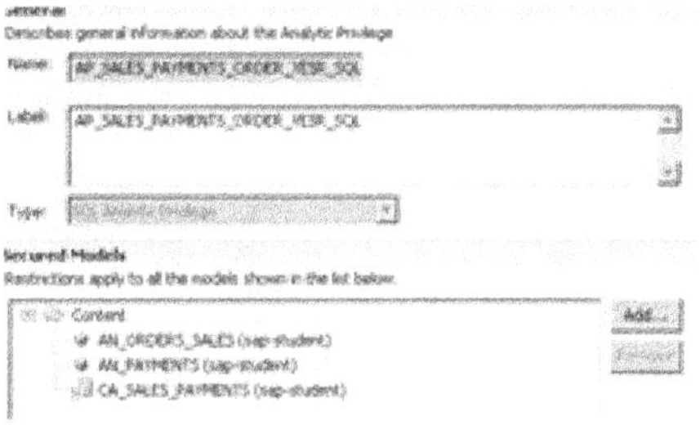

Figure 3-39

Analytic privileges are used to control access to row-level data in SAP HANA. It can be XML based or SQL based analytic privileges or classic privileges.

111

STEP 5- The key difference between SQL based analytic privilege and classic privileges. Attributes is used for simple data filtering, whereas SQL Editor gives you the flexibility to write a filter condition in SQL. You can write complex filter condition, which includes sub-queries as well using this option. For example, let's consider restricting data for user for ordered year 2003 can be done using filter condition in SQL.

■ Note: Procedures created under Database schemas are called catalogue procedures and the procedures created under packages are called repository procedures.

Step 6-We can use one of the three options available in SQL analytic privilege for data restriction. We used dynamic option and assigned procedure 'RUNTIME_FILTER_FOR_AP' to the SQL Analytic privilege. Now, the next step is to activate the SQL Analytic privilege and ensure it is successfully executed as illustrated below in Figure 3-40.

Step 7 - Once the SQL Analytic privilege is active, assign it to user 'KEY_USER' and check data preview to view data is restricted to year 2003 as illustrated below in Figure 3-41.

■ Note: SQL Analytic Privileges are only working on objects that are created directly on physical tables but not on the objects that include other modelling objects as source.

HANA Data Provisioning

Often you would have noticed several challenges in data loads from the legacy environments. Now, let us understand a high level overview of the SAP HANA Data provisioning, which refers to the data-replication techniques in HANA. It helps you to define the extract from SAP or non-SAP systems. It can be from any source, say for example. A flat file format, the following data mart refers to the operational data mart. This data model reflects the level of data detail in the application. You can do a real-time replication of data for reporting on operational data as illustrated below in Figure 3-42.

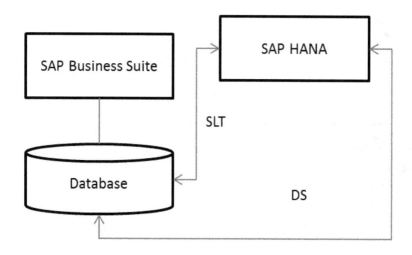

Figure 3-42 *Operational data marts*

There are few steps to implement an operational data mart:

1. First step is to load tables in to HANA using data provision methods.

2. As the next step, you can create data model

3. Create analytic views to combine master data with the fact table data

Summary

SAP HANA provides advanced analytical solutions for harnessing data into meaning report for enterprise data analysis. It's simple to build views and data stores with analytic privileges for end-user computing. The real time case studies yield several benefits of SAP HANA Analytics solution. We discussed about the importance of predictive analysis and the value it creates to the enterprises.

Moreover, the intimacy between customer and the enterprise is increased with the level of transactional data that analytics solutions provide. The entire suite of SAP HANA Analytics package comprising of reporting tools, designer tools can help you in building views with capability to designing data marts in quick turn-around. Moreover, there are deployment options to install as cloud based Enterprise analytics or on premise solution. In summary, it provides enhanced user experience with ease of data availability in the required format.

■   ■   ■

Chapter 4: SAP HANA for Enterprise Mobility

Gone are the days of heavy desktop computing. Today, employees prefer mobility to support customer requirements as time is the essence to win orders. It's all consumers driven industry with customers want orders fulfilled in no time. The advent of robust mobile operating system such as Android has revolutionized the way we do things from analytics to transactional computing such as raising orders in zero time. I can use 'OLA' app to book a cab or book a table at a restaurant in one click, without having to pick up my mobile responding to the calls from the agent or waiting in the long queue. Moreover, in countries like India, It is a maze to give someone real road directions. Imagine waiting in the queue for an hour at a bank for a simple transaction. I can do all of that using my m-banking services in any bank that offers mobile banking services. Each of them is competing in terms of providing the best mobile banking services. On top of it, one of the reputed banks has enabled an easy access option where you can key in 4 char numeric to quickly access to the account details without any hassles of even remembering passwords. Therefore, enterprise mobility has gained space in every industry from banking, manufacturing to retail. For example, e-commerce sites such as Amazon, flip kart are all turning into m-commerce for quick access to information and transactional processing done in zero time. In due course, e-retail will become m-retail, so on and so forth. This is spiking innovation in the mobile HW manufacturers innovating rigorously in server configuration in mobile phones with over 120 GB space and RAM > 5 GB is increasing.

The above trend of innovative HW products with enhanced OS will continue, thus packaging several mobile apps coming to the market. Moreover, the apps development platform, which is the complete suite of mobile apps design, development and implementation, is all gearing up in full swing with every enterprise application provider such as Microsoft, Oracle, and SAP are providing a robust platform for faster deployment. However, SAP is a pioneer as it is constantly re-inventing itself to provide mobile application platform in SAP Mobile application platform aka "SMP" to help you quickly design, develop and implement mobile applications on-cloud, or on-premises to enable enterprise mobility with rapid packages available as services to consume, which means there is least time spent on development as you'll get pre-configured scenarios as apps to activate and consume as services. Isn't exciting?

Imagine you can put sales order or manufacturing production orders tracking using simple apps! Or even CRM sales lead generation list using simple mobile. Most of your work is done using the mobile app itself. Therefore, in a decade or so, mostly you can work anywhere, anytime with all tasks managed using mobility apps.

Thanks to the technology, with google map app, it's easy for a cab driver to identify where you're or track your employee vehicle in GPS to increase safety. You can book a cab based on the next availability on the route, which is most economical or perhaps you can book a dedicated cab which might be a little expensive. The same is spiralling to carpooling, where you can get a ride cheaper than riding in an 'auto rickshaw' (3 wheeler hybrid of motor bikes) anywhere in India. The deadly combination of apps on HANA cloud platform can precisely measure the depths of the ocean or perhaps scale up the heights of the Everest and much more into identifying trajectory of rockets venturing into the vast space. It's all possible. The SAP HANA technology with FIORI apps can help you to venture into new age of enterprise mobility to delight customers. There are many examples of enterprise computing, one classic example is the way consumers use apps such as education app for personalized tuitions, or even a mobile app that can support end-to-end operations of m-school. In near future the concept of schooling can be entirely mobile based due to the increased constraints of space in major metropolitan cities, especially places like Mumbai, Pune,

Chennai, Kolkata, New York, Los Angeles, Bangalore are all crowded with cars hogging at every signal. You may have used amazon for buying anything, anywhere at any time, which seems to be the concept of generation x. SAP HANA can help beyond technology from reducing costs of supply chain by enhancing enterprise mobility to reaching out to the poor by reducing the cost of overheads by predictive analysis. It has demonstrated its use in the major healthcare sector to the clinical trials etc.

Now, it's easy to analyse a product in amazon and checkout to book your orders and get it delivered in short time, instead of driving to a store to do it. Who knows, in a decade or so, most of you would be logging in to the enterprise mobile office to perform your daily tasks and schedule events with your global clientele. With the Govt. of India initiatives in mobile computing to interact closely with farmers to facilitate supply chain, enterprise mobile computing has become a necessity, as part of day-to-day life of several millions of users. This initiative has been planned by the Prime Minister of India; Mr. Modi to ensure every farmer gets his fair price in the market without suffering during with low prices due to irregularities. Similarly, rapid digitization and m-commerce is catching up-to-speed in many developing countries. Hence, there is a lot of traction to improve speed of the OS platform in Android, Google or Microsoft to enable quick access to data in mobile platform, and help users to connect worldwide across the countries beyond barriers. Now, SAP HANA initiatives in bridging the GAP between disparate systems using SAP HANA enabled by the robust mobile application platform can help enterprises quickly re-design its landscape in least investments to plug in the mobile platform enabled on SAP HANA layer

The entire World has shrunk as one Global village in the space of enterprise mobility. Furthermore, the shrinking costs of Operating systems with high inter-operability and enhanced RAM supporting in-memory can run monthly book closure using mobile app. In my view, FIORI supports as the front-end with backend HANA running in a cloud based network, however it may be possible in a decade to run entire HANA suite with enhanced in-memory in mobile platform. In summary, your mobile appliance can work as a higher end server. The HANA appliances with network cables would have gone into history with mobile platform servers supporting customer requirements in enterprise mobility space. It may be possible to run dB apps in mobile with the mobile platform itself turning in to mini-servers. The concept of large cloud may shrink to mini-pocket cloud as m-cloud computing, wherein each of your enhanced mobile platforms can be turned to a mini-mobile server. Each of these mobile pocket servers can communicate at rapid speed with increased mobile hardware with scalable OS such as android, google etc. The entire business operations from accounting, sales, Supply chain & marketing apps can be done end-to-end in mobile platform. It will be entirely on mobile with the need of expensive servers and network cables gone into history. The net benefit is the computing speed, ease of portability and mobility itself. Your virtual reality can be true with higher end apps simulating customer behaviour, patterns to increase customer satisfaction. Now, let's come back to the presence. Let's explore the architecture of the SAP HANA front-end made for mobility, which is FIORI. It consists of packaged set of pre-configured mobile applications. These assets can be used for specific solutions depending on client requirements. The SAP HANA enterprise mobility runs on a robust HANA platform with security risks mitigated with its unique architecture as illustrated below in Figure 4-x to extract data from disparate systems in the landscape without much of investments.

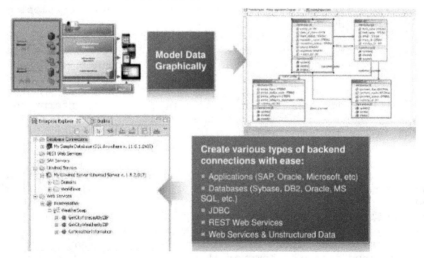

Figure 4-1 Mobile data access from disparate systems

With SAP Fiori UX the new face changed SAP's image of complex ERP software to simple mobile solution. It gives users a delightful experience, unlike the yester years of complex SAP screens in R/3. The combination of SAP HANA platform with enterprise mobility layer supported by cloud is the break-through in terms of design, development and usage of applications based on consumption based model. Thus, the leader-SAP has transition itself to the next age enterprise giant to sustain its growth by re-inventing itself. Finally, SAP's investment on SAP HANA for enterprise mobility is the answer to all impending questions from the customers to move on to the next generation of building mobile apps to delight customers with its unique SAP Mobile Platform (SMP). Let's understand SMP architecture with its benefits and implementation.

Note: SAP Fiori provides a high quality visuals across platforms for all users, be it mobile or Laptop or any handheld devices. It is easy to navigate with its unique design principles. It helps simple finance users to quickly access information without much time spent on searching for information.

Enterprise Apps Implementation Approach

There are two broader approaches in implementing enterprise apps.

a. Thin clients without using any middleware such as point solutions where the business application is rendered over the mobile browser. For example. You'll connect via browser to the chat services etc.

b. Thick clients using middleware such as standalone applications are installed on the device for better user experience. For example. Game apps installed in your mobile device.

An example of the thin client architecture using Webdyn pro is illustrated below in Figure 4-1:

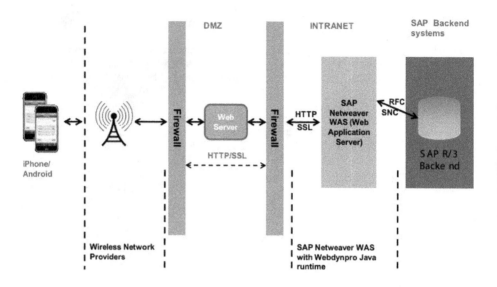

A detailed comparison is illustrated below in Table 4-1- Comparison of approach

Table 4-1. Comparison of Enterprsie mobility solution approach

Success Factors	Thin Client (browser based)	Thick Client (point solutions)
App development environment	Costly incremental changes	Higher costs due to limited portability
Centralized management	Based on backend	Security strategies are embedded within app
App Management	Not needed	Less Control
Device Management	Not needed	Required

SAP Mobile Platform (SMP)

SAP's mobile platform for mobile solution is known as SAP AFARIA that combines mobile device management and mobile application management technology. It is also available as an offering in the cloud via Amazon (AWS) as services, or alternately as on-premises deployment. It helps organizations to maximize investments using SMP platform with ease of managing end-to-end mobility applications. Most of the organizations have launched BYOD (Bring your own device) which means you can use your personal mobile for accessing enterprise information. Hence, it is important to ensure security measures are taken care to provide access to the BYOD configuration for enterprise data. Using AFARIA platform you can control access via role based option to ensure enterprise data is secure.

SMP helps you in quick deployment of mobility solution by using your existing landscape. The SMP platform helps you to rapidly deploy apps for customer-facing mobile applications across a range of device platforms. As stated, SMP is available with on-premises version or cloud. It offers enterprises access community of resources and connections to speed application development. Let's see architecture of SMP as illustrated below in Figure 4-2:

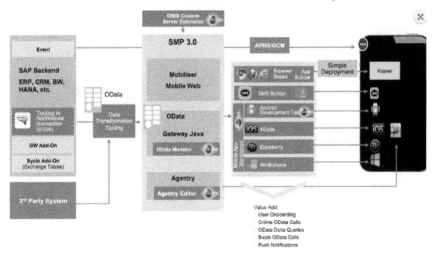

Figure 4-2 SMP Architecture.

The SAP Mobile Platform (SMP) comprises a development environment known as Sybase Unwired Platform (SUP). As mentioned earlier, Afaria mobile devise management tool is used for device specifics. The entire suite of SMP is an off-the-shelf mobile application development environment for rapid deployment of enterprise mobile applications to integrate easily into existing landscape with following benefits:

a. Easy and rapid mobile application implementation

b. Integration with the external applications

c. Ability to access in online and/or offline modes. d. Employees can remotely receive and process from corporate information systems and

d. Easy to integrate with any mobile device to finalize documents and business tasks, as well as receive reports as scheduled

Now, let's take a look at the framework of SAP HANA Mobile platform in the Cloud Architecture.

The key features of mobile platform in SAP HANA Cloud:

- Enhanced authentication services with secure on boarding

- Ease of administration, monitoring and registration

- Simplified push notification &

- Usage analysis report on mobile apps

Mobile platform on SAP HANA cloud supports a framework of services that can be consumed as illustrated below in Figure 4-2 Mobile platform in SAP HANA Cloud architecture. It also supports apps developed in third party SKDs. The Mobile application framework is one of the key features in SAP HANA with reusable components to accelerated mobile apps development illustrated in Figure 4-3.

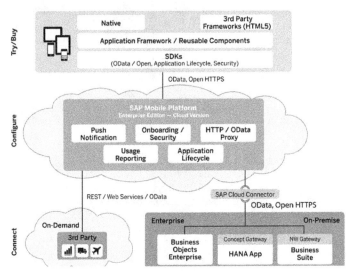

Figure 4-3 SMP Enterprise Edition

As discussed, it is easy and quick to deploy SMP platform. It helps organizations to deploy mobility rather quickly as a shrink wrap product. Moreover, it provides users with the options to customize and manage the lifecycle of the enterprise mobility solution for developers by providing accelerators for implementation. Thus, Organization can manage enterprise mobility platform as illustrated below in Figure 4-4:

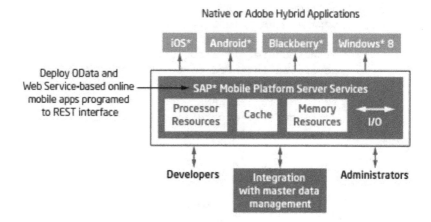

Figure 4-4 SMP Service Services

It is logical to plan for rapid inclusion of consumers of enterprise mobility application as you can observe a large increment to the users to use the mobile app. Hence, there is a need for concurrent users and testing can be done by simulating high number of concurrent users. One part is concurrent users, and the second part is with the type of network say for example, Wi-Fi. These scenarios can be tested using simulation options provided in the SMP platform used for optimizations. Thus, SAP Mobile Platform provides high and scalable performance with resources to support extensibility of the app scalability and stability for supporting large and complex environments. Let's see an example of SMP platform supporting multi-users using Wi-Fi connectivity with test constraints as illustrated below in Figure 4-5:

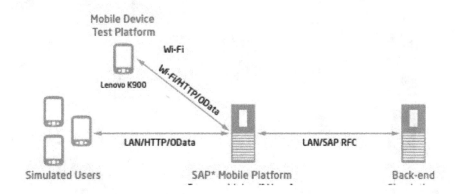

Figure 4-5 Mobile Device Platform

The mobile device passed requests to the SAP Mobile Platform over the corporate Wi-Fi* network. Load servers passed simulated user requests to the SAP Mobile Platform for processing. The SAP Mobile Platform server processed the requests, accessing the back-end data server to retrieve and write records. Back-end data responses were consistently delayed an additional 100 Ms. to simulate real-world response conditions in business transactions.

Let's take a quick look at the thick clients using Sybase Unwired Platform (SUP) platform for implementing mobile applications. The SUP platform allows users to package mobile applications and deploy in quick time. In this architecture, the run-time server takes care of communication between the backend data source with the mobile device, scheduling, transaction processing and security. The Sybase Control Centre (SCC) is a web-console used for configuration and managing unwired servers and its components. The Sybase Unwired Workspace (SUW) is the mobile application development environment used for design, development and testing of the mobile applications. Here is an example of thick client applications using Sybase Unwired Platform (SUP) as illustrated below in Figure 4-6:

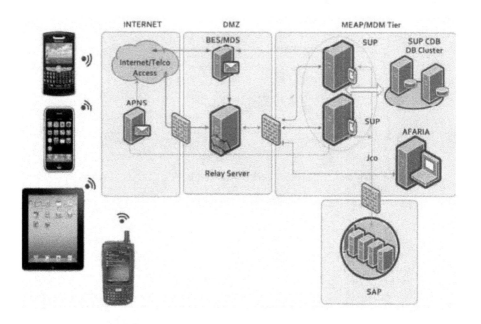

Figure 4-6 Thick client applications using Sybase Unwired Platform (SUP)

SAP FIORI

So far, World has perceived SAP as a complex software for large enterprises. However, this image of complex software has completely redefined by the concept of FIORI design principles introduced in HANA. It's easy to use, easy to navigate and find information. Thus, FIORI is SAP's innovation in a new user experience (UX) that applies modern design principles. The new design principles include:

a. Role-based authorizations for the end-users

b. Consistent look and feel, whether you're raising sales order or checking production order status

c. Device free, meaning regardless of any mobile device, it looks great

For example, as illustrated in Figure 4-7 in sales lead details. It will help them manage and follow up on sales prospects effectively as illustrated below in Figure 4-7.

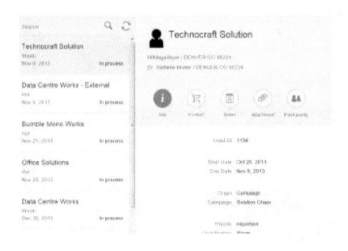

Figure 4-7 Sales view in FIORI

Overall, FIORI helps in boosting end-user productivity, greater adoption of business process and it's easy to implement. Moreover, it has been observed with FIORI the training costs of using the app is very low with reduced errors identified during usage. It's easy to deploy mobile applications in hours without investing much on the development using graphic builder as illustrated below in Figure 4-x, which works across devices. Basically, these services generated are consumed by the mobile devices using the Sybase unwired platform (SUP). As discussed, now the second key question post deployment is how to manage device settings and applications, here is where SAP AFARIA helps you achieve by using the AFARIA central web console as illustrated in Figure 4-8.

Figure 4-8

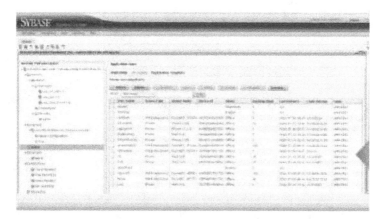

Figure 4-9 SAP AFARAI Centralized web console

SAP AFARIA provides extensive support in managing and securing the device life cycle, such as re-provision, and disable lost/stolen device.

FIORI Landscape

Let's look at the deployment architecture of the SAP FIORI Landscape as illustrated below in Figure 4-7.

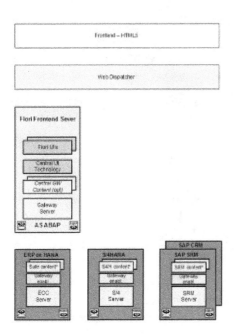

Figure 4-7 FIORI Landscape

SAP FIORI Front-End Server is based on the following main technical components:

SAP Web Dispatcher which serves as reverse proxy

SAP Fiori front-end server which is based on the SAP NW AS ABAP which contains:

UI's with FIORI Launchpad content

SAP Gateway server components with optional central gateway

SAP application back-end systems which contain core Fiori apps with backend OData integration, deployed either via Add-Ons or support packages

SAP Gateway backend components

Fiori Architecture

The FIORI architecture is shown in Figure 4-1. As you can see, mobile devices access SAP applications via SAP Net Weaver Gateway.

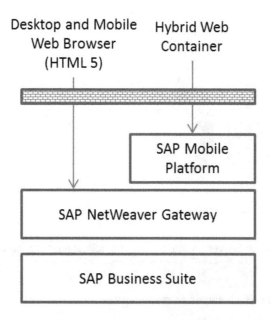

Figure 4-1. High-level architecture

Figure 4-2 shows key areas of the Fiori implementation, with back-end SAP implemented for FI/MM, HCM, and procurement solutions.

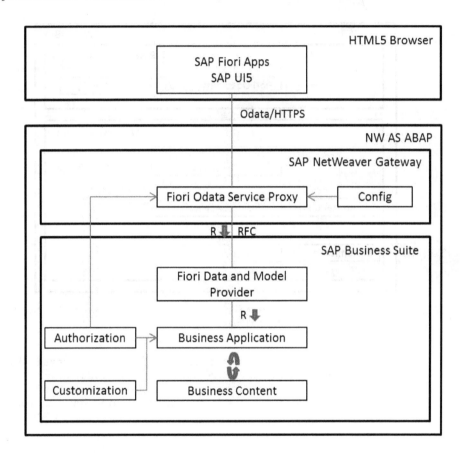

Figure 4-2. Fiori implementation

The SAP Net Weaver Gateway

Design Considerations

Let's look how Fiori is deployed: Figure 4-3 shows the architecture.

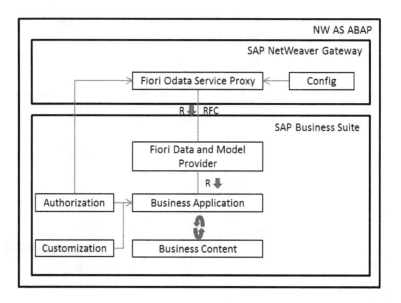

Figure 4-3. SAP NW Gateway architecture

SAP UI5 is an extension of the HTML libraries available in the SAP service marketplace. OData is standard; you can change or create new scenarios as you need them for customers. There are two ways to deploy Fiori applications, as shown in Figure 4-4.

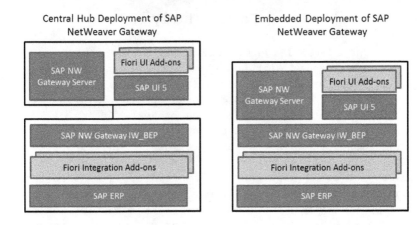

Figure 4-4. SAP Fiori app deployment options

You can have multiple ERP systems with one hub to represent data from the back-end or CRM system. The back end uses add-ons to communicate with Fiori apps. Using the SAP NW Gateway infrastructure, instead of deploying an additional NW ABAP stack for Fiori, you can use the existing ECC infrastructure, thus reducing your upfront investment. The following Table 4-2 describes the key factors to consider during mobile deployment with deployment options such as on-cloud or on premise. Let's take a look at on premise rapid deployment (RDS) options with scenarios mentioned below:

Note: See the following link for more information: Help.sap.com/fiori.

Case Study

One of the large Organizations in the Airline industry struggled with huge number of transactions and the ability to provide quick access to core apps via mobile. The apps were designed and deployed related in a few weeks, instead of a long duration of the project. It basically involved allowing quick check-out options via mobile, track flight schedule using the app provided. It saved a lot of time for the passengers to book, reschedule flights with ability to do a quick check-in instead of waiting in the long queue for check-in. Indeed, this app provided ability to support customer's flight schedule information, delays to re plan etc. It improved customer satisfaction based on customer satisfaction survey. Therefore, this app provided cycle time reduction up to 50% to ensure customers are able to access main information about their schedule with preferences such as aisle seat and meal preferences with upgrades to the business class all in one place.

This app was one of the key differentiator that helped agents to provide higher levels of services as strategic initiates.

Moreover, agent app helped in areas such as departure control, flight information, and passenger information. From a security standpoint, it helped in addressing concerns around access to unauthorized information etc. These inputs were highly critical for the airline industry. One aspect of key concerns addressed by this app is the security part, where airline found a way to manage and control the risk around the devices and apps containing this sensitive information using SMP platform, it was secured.

The entire app was deployed in quick turn-around based on cloud as SaaS based offering to deploy with custom based solution specific to the airline requirements. The SMP platform helps in managing the apps with periodic updates with device management capabilities. For example, it helps in managing apps on the iPad and devices. Some of the key benefits include, quick turn-around in enterprise mobile deployment, which was less than a month. Hence, the developed was used as a key differentiator by the business users.

This fast time to market was a key benefit the airline was looking for as it wanted to start rolling out the new apps to its employees as quickly as possible. The deployment of mobile enterprise management software delivered all the positive outcomes achieved by the mobility project, as it was critical to manage the potential risk if the device was lost or stolen or landed in the wrong hands. This organization believes that it's mobile application enablement project — powered by mobile management and security software — has provided better customer service and satisfaction, higher rates of customer retention, and increased revenue.

Summary

SAP provides ground breaking technology to resolve the myth of complex enterprise mobility into easy to implement apps using Fiori. Thus, enterprise can leverage mobility adoption in quick time by maximizing the existing investments in SAP platform transitioned to SAP HANA based enterprise mobile applications. Moreover, HANA has redefined enterprise mobility with the advent of robust enterprise mobility platform discussed for rapid deployment, customization and managing app in the app life cycle and maintenance. Above all, the simplicity it provides in Fiori user interface is very exciting with easy to use app for all complex applications in the backed. This will help them scale up in the enterprise mobility to meet customer requirements. SAP HANA provides mobility apps as pre-configured app scenarios ready for deployment for each of the package. As best practices, you must identify the pre-configured scenarios that you can implement to avoid time consuming.

■ ■ ■

Chapter 5: SAP HANA Cloud Platform

Let us explore the benefits of SAP HANA Cloud Platform. Most often, implementation projects fail due to cost, schedule issues, or complexity of the business process. Many enterprises fail in the bottom line expenses due to increased IT, Infrastructure and resource costs year-on-year. This is impacting the investors, customers and employee confidence. Whilst on one side enterprises are promising high customer satisfactions by lowering product price with value added services due to competition. It's not just the e-commerce or m-commerce; it is the way to build relationships with clientele by effectively leveraging the IT landscape. This is an interesting concept, with less interaction with the customers, you read those details using analytics and the buying behavior, and patterns of search yield tons of data available for analytics. It's ready to use data with useful analytics such as predictive behavior analysis using 'BIG' data. You'll need scalable platform to host such a robust landscape with proper hardware, software, operating system, database and overall IT architecture tuned for high performance.

In the maze of a complex landscape where the interface complexity is very high, it's even a bigger deal to manage environments. End result, IT managers and the product owners are really stressed to provide just-in-time services to adapt to the changing business requirements. Today, business will need information right now and there is no time to await extensive batch process running queries etc. Today, we need data anytime, anywhere in any device and imagine the type of landscape that is required! SAP

HANA Cloud platform offers ready to consume services to address these issues discussed above.

Be it a laptop, mobile or any other handheld devices. Overall your IT landscape is in a state of conundrum due to several interfaces evolved in the landscape as add-ons, thus increasing operational expenses. Hence, there is a compelling need to move away from the traditional deployment options, which is expensive to move to the future, which is the scalable model and is expandable at no additional costs to the business. There is absolutely no need to worry about implementation cost, schedule and budget. All of that is taken care by using deployment options provided in the SAP HANA Cloud Platform (HCP) with major deployment risks mitigated. The SAP HANA Cloud platform is an open platform-as-a-service (PaaS) model with its unique in-memory database with suite of application services. You can leverage HCP benefits by transitioning or extending your landscape to HCP without having to build a complex landscape on your own. In a changing IT landscape, it makes little sense to invest as capex on them. It may take few weeks of planning to leverage the benefits using SAP HANA Cloud platform and it's ready to use. Large enterprises such as Amazon, OLA have changed the entire business model with its unique m-commerce capabilities. Indeed, it started with e-commerce portal with millions of users registered and then started the brick-and-mortar company. Thus, to scale up to the new model, technology is rapidly changing to cater to the needs of the demanding customer. One aspect is speed to delivery, ease of using the app and customer satisfaction by reducing operational expenses.

This model of enterprise mobility using cloud platform is expanding from groceries to manufacturing in a distributed model with ease of managing apps. Gone are the days of expensive ERP software deployed as on-premises that helped you manage the sales, marketing to production. Hence, the new age architecture is mapped to one huge server which hosts the entire architecture involving your hardware, operating system, database, application, development platform and front-end mobile servers which is flexible to change with the business requirements. All of that in one place known as SAP HANA Cloud platform (HCP). If you're running business for a long time with heavy investments in IT landscape, then you can plan for a transition over the stages to leverage benefits in HCP, however it is rather easier for the startups to directly start with the HCP cloud infrastructure.

Wouldn't that be nice for any enterprise, if you're able to raise sales orders, analyze sales or close a contract without even worried about the backend database or middleware of HW and/or DB or server upgrade or migration? If I were to play the devil's advocate for a moment, any enterprise would love to hear the ease of conducting business without IT expenditure or outage that is managed without any impact to the business. From a business perspective, business community would love to stay focused on strategizing in terms of improving sales, product line and services to the customer. For a startup enterprise or an existing enterprise to maximize investments, it is easy to enable rapid digitization by connecting apps, systems and business process in one platform. There is no upfront capital expenditure (capex) in services based model. For example, you can leverage a simple app for order to cash process with simple finance to start with in the cloud model and then you can maximize investments by enabling process that is required for core business operations. It is imperative to evolve in a constantly changing business landscape; hence, your IT landscape evolves involving enterprise app store, ease of adding solutions will evolve over time to meet customer requirements. SAP HANA Cloud platform provides it all.

In a nutshell, the SAP HANA cloud platform provides the following benefits for organizations:

- Simplicity and Flexibility in terms of readiness of app usage
- Ability to easily add new features to cloud solutions
- Enhanced Disaster Recovery services
- Freedom from capital expenditures

- Quick software updates and enhancements (For example. OS, DB and software upgrades, enhancement packages or even HW platform switch)

Let us understand the cloud service model as illustrated below in Figure 5-1

Traditional IT Services	IaaS (Infra as a Service)	PaaS (Platform as a Service)	DaaS (Database as a Service)	SaaS (Software as a Service)
Applications	Applications	Applications	Applications	Applications
Database Administration	Database Administration	Database Administration	Database Administration	Database Administration
Software / Tools	Software / Tools	Software / Tools	Software / Tools	Software / Tools
OS Administration	OS Administration	OS Administration	OS Administration	OS Administration
Network Management	Network Management	Network Management	Network Management	Network Management
Storage	Storage	Storage	Storage	Storage
Hardware	Hardware	Hardware	Hardware	Hardware

Legends
Customer Managed
Managed as Service

Figure 5-1 Cloud Service model

You can choose the appropriate model depending on your organization strategy as illustrated above. The above Figure illustrates managed services by the service provider, whereas customer managed is in-house.

In a traditional IT services, everything is managed by the enterprise as on-house with huge upfront investments to setup infrastructure and resource costs. In the IaaS service model, your infrastructure such as OS/network, storage and HW are managed by the service provider example, HP as illustrated above. If you look as PaaS the entire set of SW/Tools, DB and OS including network and storage are managed by the service provider, example. SAP HCP. On the contrary DaaS is managed by the service provider or SaaS is end-to-end from app managed services to HW, storage, NW and OS including SW/Tools example, SAP HCP.

There are many service providers those who are providing these services, however SAP has provided the thought leadership in PaaS with the advent of providing a robust HANA platform that is scalable for increasing customer requirements. It has re-engineered the entire IT landscape to ensure a high performance is provided to the apps managed as services by SAP. Thus, the traditional ERP on-premises solution with several interfaces has changed into a simple HCP running on SAP HANA platform with IoT connecting external devices and applications seamlessly as one operational unit. This is an incredible story and key

142

accomplishments of SAP, who had re-structured its operating model from licenses to subscription based model to stay ahead of the curve. Also, had pioneered in enterprise mobility by enhancing its development environment such as Eclipse to cloud factory to support open source environments; Indeed, this revolution is the evolution of a new platform known as HANA Cloud Platform, surpassing a million miles ahead of any other competitors in the market. This is the only platform that addresses all key concerns of the business requirements with the new era of technological advancements by leveraging high performance with the backend of robust technology using in-memory capabilities. In my view, hybrid cloud is best for the customers who have already invested in the on-premises solution which allows some flexibility in customization and releases as per business requirements, however if you're striving for standardization, perhaps apps on HCP in private cloud as managed services may be a better option in terms of costs and standardization etc.

There are three types of cloud:

a. Public cloud - So, the point is in the public cloud infra is hosted by the service provider in their own premises. Therefore, customer's data is stored in the service provider's data centre with responsibilities of manage data. However the only concern is regarding infrastructure shared between multiple customers. Many public cloud services runs in a shared environment

b. Private Cloud-Cloud is managed as exclusive for the customer without any infrastructure sharing as described in the above type and

c. Hybrid Cloud is a combined approach of the public and private cloud as illustrated below in Figure 5-2

Figure 5-2 shows a classic case study of a hybrid cloud model.

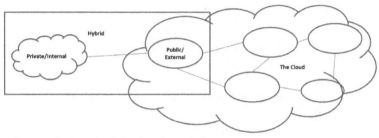

Figure 5-2 Hybrid cloud model

Scenarios of HCP

Let's explore various cloud scenarios on SAP HANA Cloud platform as illustrated below in Figure 5-1:

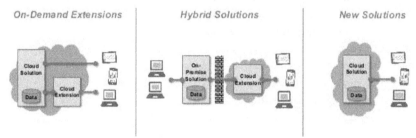

Figure 5-1 typical scenarios on SAP HANA Cloud Platform

- On-Demand Extensions: You can extend the cloud solution with custom extension, which is also running in cloud (Example. Success Factor).

- On-premise Solutions: As illustrated above extending on premise solution to the cloud extension. You'll be able to leverage existing investment with addition custom app developed in the cloud extension (Example. SAP Business suite)

- New Solutions: You can build new custom solutions on-Cloud

The next section discusses the cloud platform architecture.

SAP HANA Cloud Platform

The objectives of providing HANA services into robust cloud platform, is to provide a full feature in-memory platform as a service. In other words it helps you rapid deployment of apps by leveraging SAP Database in the backend. In addition, cloud platform provides runtime environment for cloud applications. These dB and App services can be consumed quickly with ease of deployment in weeks instead of months and years. SAP Hana Cloud platform architecture is illustrated below in Figure 5-2.

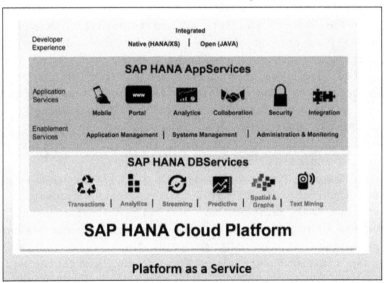

Figure 5-2 SAP HANA Cloud platform architecture

Now, let's look at the critical components of the SAP Hana cloud platform. The SAP HANA DB services is the backend database of the SAP HCP platform with it's unique in-memory dB with application platform with runtime environment. It provides unique column store capabilities for increased performance along with in-memory techniques. In addition, HCP provides libraries for query and data manipulations such as predictive analysis. It also provides enhanced query processing such as fuzzy search, text mining, GEO-Spatial and graphic functionalities as a bundled services. The extensions such as 'XS' APPS can help in custom development for specific customer requirements with ease of deployment. For example, developers can develop 'XS' apps and deploy quickly.

Now, let's look at the enhanced HANA APP Services. These app services are primarily referred to as enablement in HCP. For example, you'll find a wide range of enablement services such as connectivity, identify and document management etc. These app services are complimented by profile and monitor tools such as enhanced log-on capabilities with remote debug options available on-cloud. Thus, it helps customers to innovate, deploy solutions by subscribing to these apps.

The SAP HCP platform offers best practices and rapid deployment. For example, Apps services enable quick authorization control, profiling and app monitoring that is required for the app life cycle from an end-to-end perspective in rapid design, deployment and maintenance cycle of the app using app services like downing monitor etc. Hence, customers will have the ability to focus on innovation, solution deployment in quick turnaround, thus enabling increased value for IT spending.

One more interesting factor with the above HCP is the IoT (Internet of Things), which means connecting SAP customers and partners to develop applications that can leverage IoT services, cloud integration and in-memory capabilities of SAP HANA and HCP. There is a portfolio of IoT applications such as SAP connected manufacturing, SAP connected assets solution, and SAP connected logistics and predictive maintenance and services solution. *Following table 5-1 highlights the revenue forecast in the cloud based services, which is a clear indication of way forward in the IT industry*

Table 5-1 Cloud Services Revenue Forecast

Cloud Type	Year 2011 $ B	Year 2020 $ B
Public Cloud	25.5	159.3

	7	66.4
Private Cloud		
Virtual Private Cloud	7.8	15.9

According to a Forrester report, cloud computing consists of IT-based services that are offered by service providers using Internet protocols and that scale automatically to demand. Figure 5-3 shows the key attributes of the cloud computing model.

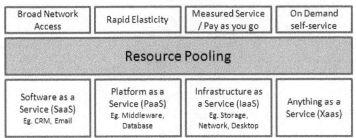

Figure 5-3 Cloud computing attributes

SAP HANA Cloud platform has set standards in the PaaS category with end to end solution for business. SAP's investments in cloud foundry, which further helps clientele in transitioning to cloud rapidly with the innovations of cloud based open platform for developers known as 'Docker'. As a result, IT can ship faster and run the app much faster in any device or cloud. Now, let's checkout few cloud deployment options as illustrated below in Table 5-3.

Table 5-2 Cloud Deployment Options

Key Attributes	Public	Private	Hybrid
Infrastructure and services	Mega scale	Finite	Combination of two or more clouds
Publically available	Yes	Enterprise owned	Mixed usage of private and public
Multitenant applications and services	Yes	Charged back to LOBs	Yes

Access virtually unlimited applications	Yes	Cloud computing in company's data center	Yes
Mixed usage of public and private access	No	Only private access	Yes

Figure 5-4 shows a classic case study of a hybrid cloud model.

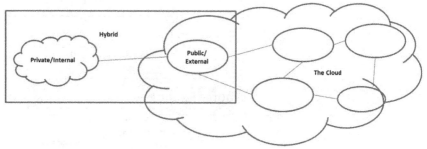

Figure 5-4 Hybrid cloud model

Now, let's look at the benefits of Cloud foundry:

1. Portability of app

2. Rapid development by providing open source environment for developer

3. Centralized Logging with centralized administration

4. Role Based Access

5. Infrastructure Security

6. Application Health Management

Deployment

As discussed, there are various options to deploy your applications on cloud. Since, SAP HCP is focused on the services based model; it would be easier to venture in to SAP HCP. Typically n a public cloud setup, service provider manages the entire scope of software services such as modifications, enhancements including software patches and upgrades etc. These changes are pushed automatically by cloud service providers. For example, Hybris, C4C, Success Factor, etc.

On the contrary, if you're planning to go with the private cloud setup, where software is managed entirely by the service provider, however any update is done after agreement with the customer. Perhaps, this is a more viable option in my view with the flexibility that you may want in your apps to customize as per your specific requirements. However, customer can still remain with the traditional model of SAP implementation as on-premises and standalone with huge capex and opex. The key constraints that are needed to discussed while designing a landscape on Cloud as follows:

a. Existing infrastructure renewal with licenses costs
b. Frequency of custom development and cost of changes
c. Interference of the non-SAP product, which has high bandwidth and security requirements
d. Business acceptance to adapt to the standard SAP package and best packages
e. Frequency of adhoc requirements such as analytics

Based on the above analysis in the respective landscape, customers can plan to go for either public, private or hybrid options.

Today, enterprises need a robust cloud platform to host applications securely and with high efficiency. SAP HANA is the answer: it provides a secure platform as illustrated below in Figure 5-5 Cloud hosted services

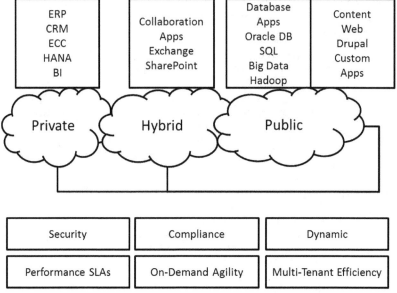

Figure 5-5. Cloud-hosted services

Deploy, Operate and Monitor the Experience

Now, let us see how to deploy, operate and monitor apps in SAP HCP as illustrated below in Figure. 5-6

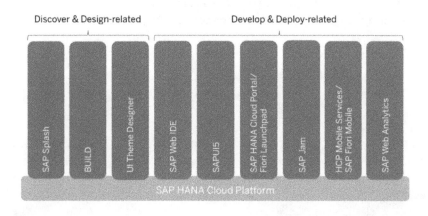

Figure 5-6. SAP HCP Deploy & Monitor apps

You can deploy new and extended applications with modern user experience or modernize the user experience (UX) of on-premises apps with SAP FIORI. For example, you can deploy apps using SAP FIORI securely to a user centric corporate app store. It provides extensive social and collaboration capabilities around with SAP Jam, with built-in support for responsive web & mobile access. It also provides ability to measure user interaction and provide real-time analysis for insights to iteratively optimize the experience and adoption. Now, let's review some of the best practices in deploying apps to the SAP HCP.

Best Practices and Build Great Apps

The main objectives of SAP HCP is to provide a consistent look and feel and easy of app access to all users globally across the world. Hence, SAP re-engineered its app suite to defined FIORI, to provide consistent look and feel of all apps, which can be deployed as cloud services in HCP. Thus, it achieves there main objectives:

Creating an enhanced user experience using FIORI using user experience (Ux) methodology

Engaging business suite by extending interfaces into one single platform such as SAP Hybris solution on cloud. For example, SAP Success factor integration in cloud which works as seamlessly as one-unit

In summary, HCP provides robust cloud framework for enterprise solutions from app deployment to extensibilities of apps to various external applications in the cloud framework

Following Figure 5-7 illustrates ADOBE form integration in HCP

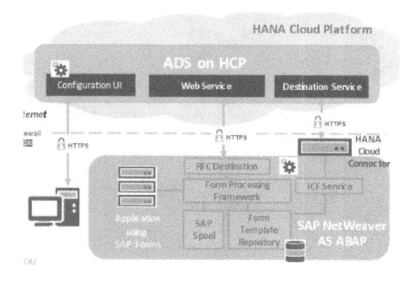

Figure 5-7 Adobe form integration in HCP

Application Development

You can use the following programming models to build highly scalable applications:

SAP HCP is Java EE 6 Web Profile certified. You can develop Java applications just like for any application server. You can also easily run your existing Java applications on the platform.

SAP HANA development tools to create comprehensive analytical models and build applications with SAP HANA programmatic interfaces and integrated development environment.

HTML5 can be used to develop and run lightweight HTML5 applications in a cloud environment.

SAPUI5 is the UI Development Toolkit for HTML5 (SAPUI5) for developing rich user interfaces for modern Web business applications.

Runtime container is used for applications. It provides a secure and scalable runtime environment. One of the key challenges is the connectivity; using the platform services, such as the connectivity services to establish connections to on-premises solutions, enabling integration scenarios with your cloud based applications. The in-memory persistence helps in in-memory computing technology and analytics. Above all data is secured using HCP multi layered security measures. Let's take a quick look at the set of tools used for rapid deployment on cloud.

Tools

Following is a list of useful tools for rapid deployment of apps in HCP as illustrated in Table 5-3 below.

Table 5-3. Cloud Deployment Tools

Tool	Description
Cockpit	Manages account related activities with key inputs about applications
SAP Web IDE	This is an interesting open forum for developers, who can work closely to build new applications to share ideas of rapid prototype implementation techniques.
Maven Plugin	This plugin is used for JAVA applications in the SAP HANA cloud Platform (HCP).
SAP HANA Cloud Connector	It interfaces with the on-demand applications in SAP HANA Cloud Platform and existing on-premises systems. It is possible to control resources availability for the cloud applications in those systems.
SDK	
Eclipse Tools	It contains everything you need to work with SAP HANA Cloud Platform, including a local server runtime and a set of command line tools.
Console Client	Eclipse IDE is a java based toolkit for application development. It helps you to develop and deploy applications as well as perform operations such as logging, managing user roles, creating connectivity destinations.
	It enables development, deployment and configuration of

an application outside the Eclipse IDE as well continuous integration and automation tasks.

Now, let's look at the services provided by SAP HCP.

SERVICES
These services help in rapid deployment of apps in SAP HCP as illustrated below in Table 5-4

Table 5-4. Cloud Deployment Services

Services	Description
Authorization	Effectively managing roles of applications their assignments to users.
Services	You can build services, modules. It can consumed in the SAP HCPSAP HCP provides rob
Connectivity Service	connectivity using secure, reliable and e to consume access to the business. The administrate will have complete control of
Micro Services	technical components exposed to the on dem world.
Document Services	
	SAP HCP offers micro services such as addr cleansing, geocoding services. These mi
Feedback Services	services can be consumed by any application ensure accurate data. Allows you to inspec Java application's runtime behavior and sta
	SAP HANA Cloud Platform provides cont
Gamification Service	repository for unstructured or semi-structu content. It uses OASIS stand
Git Service	protocol *Content Management Interoperabil*
OData provisioning	*Services* (CMIS). The applications consume service using the provided client library.
Internet of Things (IoT) Services	
	SAP HANA Cloud Platform feedback service i platform to consolidate end-user feedback
Lifecycle REST API	their applications to support develope
Monitoring Service	customers, and partners.

OAuth 2.0 Service	The SAP HCP allows gamification services such as online development and administration environment for rapid implementation.
Performance Statistics Service (	
Persistence Service	SAP HCP Git services help you in managing source code versions of applications in the
Profiling	Git repositories.
Applications	SAP HCP can consume data from SAP Business suite backed system by using OData
Remote Data Sync Service	provisioning by connecting between SAP Business suite data to the target clients, platforms within the framework.
SAP Cloud Identity Service	The Internet of Things Services facilitates IoT connectivity to the external interfaces such as registered devices with specific data
SAP Forms as a Service by Adobe	types to be able to transfer data to SAP HCP in a secure manner.
SAP HANA Cloud Platform Mobile Services	The lifecycle REST API provides functionality for application lifecycle management.
	Helps in application monitoring for JAVA applications with metrics gathered for
SAP HANA Cloud Portal	analysis.
	SAP HANA Cloud Platform uses OAuth for authorization and application access.
	Useful in detailed performance analysis by
SAP JamSAP Document Center	monitoring resources
SAP Document Center	SAP HANA Cloud Platform persistence service provides in-memory and relational persistence.
SAP Translation Hub	All maintenance activities, such as data replication, backup and recovery, are handled by the platform.
	Using SAP JVM Profiler helps in analyzing resources issues in JAVA applications regardless of whether the JVM is running locally or on the cloud.
SAP HCP DATA sync	
	SAP HCP remote data sync services supports synchronizing remote dB into SAP HCP dB in the

cloud.

<u>SAP Cloud Identity services</u>	SAP Cloud Identity service is a cloud solution for identity lifecycle management. It provides services for user login, registration, authentication, and access to SAP HANA Cloud Platform applications.
<u>SAP Forms</u>	SAP Forms as a Service is a solution for generating print and interactive forms using Adobe Document Services running on SAP HANA Cloud Platform.
<u>SAP HCP</u>	SAP HANA Cloud Platform is an open, standard-based cloud platform that enables simplified mobile application development, configuration, and management. SAP HANA Cloud Portal is a cloud-based solution for easy site creation and consumption with a superior user experience. Designed primarily for mobile consumption, it runs on top of SAP HANA Cloud and is built to operate with SAP HANA, for in-memory computing.
<u>SAP JamSAP Document Center</u>	SAP JamSAP Document center helps in providing access to the social collaboration that extends across SAP Landscape SAP Document Center helps in content management for mobile applications. SAP HCP provides a common repository for managing documents.

There are various application programing for apps development in HCP. Customers can choose between HANA development tools, JAVA or HTML 5 depending on the requirements. Now, let's explore options of each of these application development tools in the next section.

Develop 'XS' application in HCP

SAP HANA development is used for rapid app deployment. It's easy to build and deploy apps in quick time. It is used for creating comprehensive analytical models, building applications with SAP HANA's program interfaces and integrated development environment.

Benefits and advantages:

- Backup is automatic
- SAP HANA repository and schema packages can be created quickly. It is possible to visualize SAP HANA instances and XS applications in the cockpit.
- Eclipse-based development environment for connecting SAP HANA instances on SAP HCP
- Eclipse-based tools used for data modelling

Appropriate for

- Ease of implementing complex calculation scenarios
- Ease of developing analytic models
- Ready app to implement BIG data scenarios
- Rapid implementation of IoT (Internet of Things) scenarios
- Building XS applications
- Using SAP HANA embedded search capabilities
- Leveraging SAP HANA functional libraries like SAP HANA Business Function Library (BFL) and the SAP HANA Predictive Analytics Library (PAL)
- Developing hybrid applications (native HANA, Java, HTML5, mobile)

Now, let's explore JAVA Development environment for deploying apps in HCP.

JAVA Development

It is easy to deploy JAVA based apps in SAP HANA Cloud platform. The runtime container supports apps runtime with extended capabilities such as API's and JAVA EE API's. For example, Cloud based apps interact at runtime with the respective containers and services using the platform API's as illustrated below in Figure 5-8:

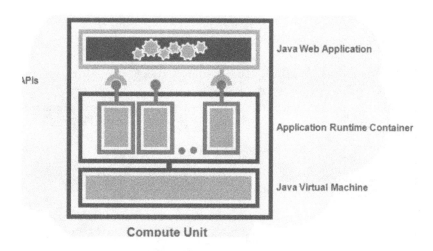

Figure 5-8 JAVA Development in HCP

The Java development process is enabled by the SAP HANA Cloud Platform Tools, which comprise the Eclipse IDE and the SAP HANA Cloud Platform SDK. During and after development, you can configure and operate an application using the cockpit and the console client.

Benefits and advantages

- It offers a standard platform
- Supports a wide-spread Apache Tomcat Web container
- Eclipse IDE with command line tools support
- Supports the platform services APIs

Appropriate for

- Primarily deployment of apps that run Java Web applications based on standard JSR APIs
- Executing Java Web applications which include third-party Java libraries and frameworks supporting standard JSR APIs
- Supporting Apache Tomcat Java Web applications.

Now, let's take a look at HTML5 Development environment in HCP

HTML5: Development

For all static content, you can use HTML5 apps on SAP HCP which consists of static resources. It can connect to on-premises or on-demand service. SAP HCP stores static content in Git repositories. Each HTML5 apps is stored and versioned in the Git repositories. Thus, it helps developers to interact with Git services using a client interface of their choice. For example, you can use EGIT or a native Git implementation to perform Git operations. Then SAP HCP cockpit helps in creating, activating, starting/stopping and test apps. Finally, key users will get an active version that is ready to use as illustrated below in Figure 5-9 REST services.

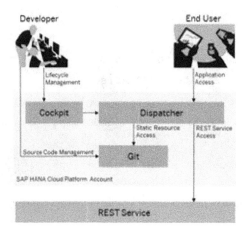

Figure 5-9 REST Service

Extend SAP Cloud Solutions

Let us see the key benefits of extending SAP cloud solutions:

   a. Integrated landscape with external apps. Ease of extensibility with any cloud based apps deployed.
   b. Provides secured app container
   c. Enhanced roles and authorization checks with SSO enablement
   d. Ease of accessing apps within the framework from any external applications
   e. Ease of leveraging apps in the HCP pre-integrated network.
   f. Dynamic UI branding which refers to consistent tile concepts. For example, it also allows the delivery of SAP

solution-specific artefacts, such as navigation exit points, tiles, widgets or external business objects.

- For example, Success Factor, SAP HCP offers out-of-the-box pre-integrated extension accounts. You will be able to leverage all SAP HCP tools for the implementation of these extension applications. You will be able to leverage all SAP HCP tools for the implementation of these extension applications.
- You will be able to leverage all SAP HCP tools for the implementation of these extension applications.

Developing a business record integration in SAP JAM

There are two types of major applications whose content can be integrated into SAP Jam Collaboration in the **Admin** > **External Applications** section:

The SAP JAM collaboration is an initiative from SAP to integration SAP's Enterprise Social Network (ESN) applications to the third-party business critical applications. For example, you can easily present data in the social network structure into SAP using collaboration tools and templates known as work patterns.

The steps for integrating new business records are shown in the following diagram, in the procedure following this figure below 5-10, and in the pages of this section of the *SAP Jam Developer Guide*:

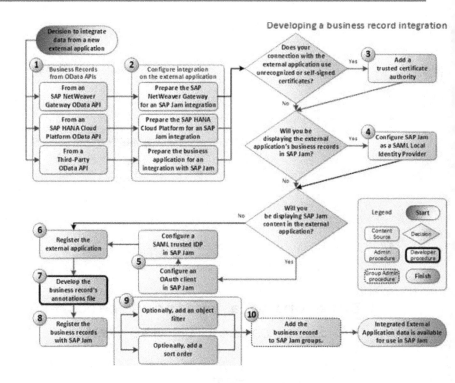

Figure 5-10 Integrating new business records into SAP JAM

Now, let's review the steps involved in integrating in SAP JAM as listed below:

You should select the [App type] for integration using one of the options below:

SAP HCP for cloud based platform using SAP NW gateway for non-cloud or

Using Third-party ODATA API which allows you to direct using the OData API of applications that are readily available to use

In this step, you'll need to configure the app to allow SAP JAM to access the business app's data using secure authorization methods which is a common protocol

Third step is authentication, in this step use a trusted certificate if your network required self-signed (SSL) certificates

In this step, you'll need to configure SAP JAMA as a SAML local identify provider if you want to display external applications data in SAP JAM. For example, users will be able to access data when it is available in SAP JAM

You must register the external business apps into SAP JAM

Also, you can use group admin options to control accessing via SAP JAM.

SAP HANA CLOUD Trial:

You can register for a HCP trial instance for learning purposes. Either you can register using valid SCN user name or create your log as illustrated below in hanatrial.ondemand.com in Figure 5-6:

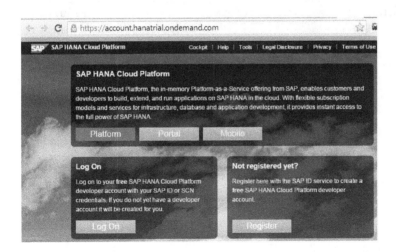

Figure 5-6 SAP HANA Cloud Platform Trial

If you have SCN ID, then log in with SCN credentials to access SAP HCP Trial version. On the welcome page, click [continue] to complete account creation and then launch the cockpit. In case you don't have SCN user id, then register. You'd receive an email with registration details. Now, activate your developer account and then proceed to [Continue] to complete account creation and launch the cockpit. You'll be able to view the cockpit as illustrated below in Figure 5-6

Figure 5-6 HCP Cockpit

Now, you'll be able to create a HANA DB as illustrated below in Figure 5-7 create HANA DB. In SAP HCP account, you can create HANA DB and bind databases to applications running on the cloud platform as show below in Figure 5-7.

Click [Database and schemas] in the left pane as shown below in Figure5-7:

Figure 5-7 SAP HCP Cockpit

Click [New] button and specific database ID/password for the system user. Note once HANA DB is created, you can use this system user to access and manage DB as shown below.

Figure 5-8 SAP HCP Cockpit DB & Schemas

c. Click [Save] button. This will create HANA DB. Now, click [SAP HANA Web-based Development workbench] and user system user to login to HANA DB to create 'myhanddb' as shown below in Figure 5-9.

Figure 5-9 System Logon

Figure 5-10. SAP HANA DB – 'myhanadb'

Finally, you're able to create HANA DB as illustrated above.

Benefits

Rapid deployment to HANA is improving performance to many customers worldwide.

Summary

This chapter described the immediate need for transition your IT landscape to cloud. The trendsetter, SAP has launched its suite of services in SAP HANA Cloud Platform (HCP) to manage your applications end-to-end. It's not just the platform; it provides development environment and options to build custom app on-premises and integrate to cloud or develop agile as on-cloud based on the deployment model customers choose. By leveraging advance in-memory options and its native database, high performance of the apps is guaranteed. In summary, you can run the business as usual without having to worry about the IT infrastructure or software. SAP HCP is a pioneer in PaaS services with extensibility to IoT. The future of gen x enterprise apps can be easily deployed in no time with added value to the customers.

By moving to the cloud, you can focus on business operations rather than worrying about IT spending and ROI. A cloud-based subscription model has no up-front cost. Furthermore, you can avoid risks without investing on a heavy on-premises solution with longer cycle time of implementation. This alleviates problems with operational run costs such as the need to upgrade hardware, operating systems, and databases. The risk to the business is zero when you transition apps to cloud-based services such as IaaS and PaaS. Therefore, you can run your business more efficiently and use a continuous improvement strategy. As discussed in this chapter, the deployment model can use an on-demand, hybrid, or new solution approach. It is up to you to choose the best option for your business.

In my view, new solution is mostly appropriate for start-ups with no upfront capex, however for existing business, you should think about maximizing investments. For example, I would prefer to include Success Factor as on-demand solution available on cloud for employees in an existing landscape, whereas critical transaction data can still reside in the productive environment as on-premises and remaining apps can be deployed on cloud using hybrid solution. In either case, you must plan for a 5-10 years IT transformation strategy to maximize ROI, as IT investment is no longer a commodity. It has to be justified to the business to ensure real value driving the business operations.

■ ■ ■

CHAPTER 6: Migration to SAP HANA

One of the daunting tasks for any project manager is to support a major transformation project from disparate IT systems to the SAP HANA system. During the preparation phase, a lot of due diligence is required to understand the overall IT strategy, to migrate legacy to HANA DB as phased approach or as a big bang. These questions can be answered based on a detailed pre-study and due-diligence phase, where expert IT consultants can investigate key pain points of the customer and recommend it accordingly. There are different strategies to migrate; customers should identify key risks to their existing landscape before staring on the HANA transformation. Once you create a roadmap for migration to SAP HANA DB or the platform migration, you will need to plan the strategy to migrate in phases depending on the criticality of the applications as a set of applications or as a big-bang approach.

The migration procedure of SAP systems to SAP HANA can be on-premises or cloud landscape based on your constraints. Beginning with an overview of available migration path options, we will discuss high level planning and recommendation to identify the best procedure for your requirements. Take these aspects into the discussion with your cross-functional teams and use them as basis for an individual assessment based on the boundary conditions you are facing. It depends on the customers' budget, schedule and release plan of the apps. Without impacting the productive instances, you should plan for a migration by leveraging tools and methods with best practices to ensure smooth migration.

In this chapter, we will look at how to choose a migration path based on your specific constraints, technical approach and best practices with reference links to SAP to help you plan appropriate migration path.

☐ **Note** SAP S/4 HANA aka SAP Business Suite for Hana

Migration to HANA Approach

As illustrated below in Figure 6-1, let's see how to transition your current legacy landscape in to SAP S/4HANA. As briefly discussed, you'll need to plan the migration path as part of pre-study based on the current landscape. For Example, SAP provides addition enterprise mobility capabilities by leveraging Fiori, hence there is an option in HANA to consolidate and optimize your landscape with disparate applications as illustrated below in Figure 6-1 Transition to SAP HANA landscape using Software Update Manager (SUM) with Database Migration Option (DMO).

Figure 6-1 Transition to SAP S/4HANA

Technical Approach

There are three options available to migration to HANA from legacy based on your current installation. The following paths are:

a. New Installation
b. Classic Migration and
c. One-step upgrade and migration with DMO of SUM

Before embarking on the ambitious journey of SAP HANA migration project, you must do a pre-study to understand the current landscape. There are few constraints that you should be aware of and mitigate risks early on in the project. For example, it is essential to understand the changes to the data model, custom extensions, optimization possible and custom code remediation. From hardware perspective, you may want to ask a few questions on reusability o application servers, additional HANA appliance with sizing required etc. as illustrated below in Figure 6-2 Planning SAP HANA Migration.

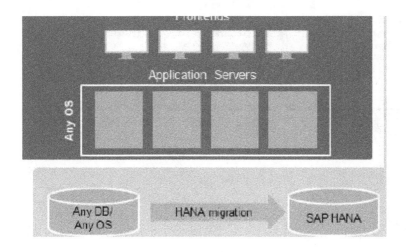

Figure 6-2 Planning SAP HANA Migration Project

Now, let's look at the technical approach in detail.

ABAP-Based SAP Systems

For the migration of ABAP-based SAP systems to SAP HANA, several migration path options are offered as illustrated below in Figure 6-3:

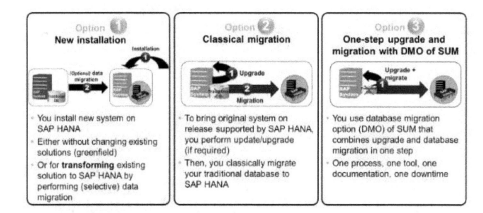

Figure 6-3 Technical Migration Approach

Option 1:

New Installation – Let's say your business is running on SAP landscape which you're planning to migrate to SAP HANA, there are several transformation offerings from SAP Landscape Transformation. There are few options for you to embark on the migration journey. In this option, you'd simply install the new SAP HANA system as illustrated below and then perform data migration which may be required from the traditional db. If it is a green field, this step is not required.

This strategy should be finalized based on the pre-study and the complexities identified in the current landscape. There are various SAP tools available to manage data migration project using tools and accelerators. It is important to engage key users to ensure a perfect migration. For example, in case of finance migration there is a lot of reconciliation required such as closed orders to be moved to the new system if this is a legacy to SAP HANA transition and start opening the accounts in the new system. These are data migration planning that may evolve as part of your pre-study phase. This option is illustrated below in Figure 6-3.

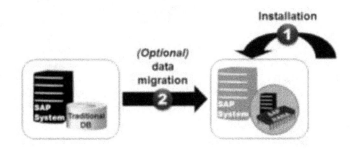

Figure 6-3 Option 1 New Installation

Option 2:

Classical Migration - Applicable for the existing customers First thing is to bring the source release version supported by SAP HANA by performing a version or EHP upgrades as required? Then, you can use the classical migration of SAP systems to SAP HANA (that is, the heterogeneous system copy using the classical migration tools software provisioning manager 1.0 and R3load) to migrated legacy to HANA DB as illustrated below in Figure 6-4. For example, you may run on Oracle DB which can be migrated using this option.

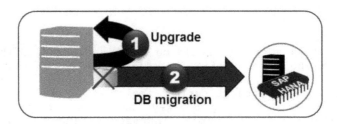

Figure 6-4 Option 2 Classical Migration

In this approach of One-step upgrade and migration using DMO of SUM, you can use database migration option (DMO) of SUM that combines upgrade and database migration in one step. Typically, for database upgrades and migration there may be one or more downtime requirement. However, best feature in this option is to combine both upgrade and database migration in one step using DMO of SUM tool. This is the best part to keep the business downtime minimal without impacting any operations as illustrated below in Figure 6-5.

Figure 6-5 One-step Upgrade and Migration

In addition, see the corresponding End-to-End Implementation Roadmap guides that also outline available migration path options.

Java-Based SAP Systems

For Java-based SAP systems, the classical migration is available, as outlined above.

Now, let's take a look at advantages as listed below in Table 6-1.

Table 6-1 Option 1:

	Advantages	Considerations
	a. No risk for production system with greenfield approach	Greenfield approach unsuited to replace the current production system
	b. Leveraged flexibility since you can	

move only parts of your scenarios	Requires transfer (transport, migration, and load) of relevant business data, if possible at all
c. Results in clean system with no outdated data	
	No real data and performance comparison possible

Let's evaluate merits and considerations as highlighted below in Table 6-2

Table 6-2 Option 2:

Merits	Considerations
Clear separation of tasks – you can first perform an upgrade project and then a migration project Apart from SAP HANA appliance, no additional hardware is required Allows hardware replacement of application server	No data and performance comparison possible between the former setup and the system powered by SAP HANA Typically requires extended downtime of production system and several downtime windows (for example, one for a database upgrade - if SAP Net Weaver ABAP 7.4 or higher does not support your current database release, one for the upgrade of the SAP system, and finally one for the database migration).

Option 3 - One-Step Upgrade and Migration with Database Migration Option (DMO) of Software Update Manager

Today most of the applications are running on a Unicode enabled dB version. Hence, it is essential to combine dB upgrade with Unicode before migration to HANA db. Therefore, database migration option (DMO) of Software Update Manager (SUM) is the standard database migration used for migration in one-step. Essentially, it combines all relevant steps for the in-place migration to SAP HANA including Unicode conversion, system update, and database migration.

For more information about DMO, see:

SAP Community Network (SCN): Database Migration Option (DMO) of SUM - Introduction

For the Database Migration Option of SUM, the following SAP Notes are valid at the time of writing:

SUM SP15 (valid for SAP NetWeaver 7.5): SAP Note 2161396

SUM SP14: SAP Note 2161397

Downtime-Optimized DMO

Anyone who is managing SAP projects would love to hear the downtime minimized option for release or EHP upgrades or migration using downtime-optimized DMO. This features integrated SAP Landscape Transformation technology to enable the migration of selected (large) application tables during uptime processing of DMO, thereby reducing the downtime migration time.

Recommendations

By considering and above merits and considerations, I believe for systems with transactional data (such as SAP Business Suite), the greenfield approach is recommended for testing the overall SAP HANA approach and for gaining initial experience, but not for migrating or replacing your current production system.

If you face new or changed business requirements indicating that your existing solution landscape has to be changed in order to fulfil current objectives, consider performing a new installation to transform your system landscape. This lets you correct corresponding design issues of your SAP landscape, such as consolidating SAP systems or harmonizing data.

In addition, with the option to perform a selective migration, you gain more flexibility since you can migrate; only specific data without business disruption. You can optionally combine this with data cleansing, leaving unused master data behind. This means you can smoothly introduce new business processes as part of your move to SAP HANA. To help you achieve this, SAP Landscape Transformation reduces the effort to build a new targeted landscape such as via shell creation with carve-out options and system consolidation, complemented by corresponding transformation services such as Data Management Services or System Landscape Optimization consulting services. If you have special downtime requirements, you can benefit from DMO migration option.

Landscape Transformation

Customers who want to consolidate their landscape or to selectively transform data into a SAP S/4HANA system; The SAP S/4HANA, on-premises edition 1511 *system conversion* supports one-step procedure (Database, SAP NetWeaver and application transition in one step) for SAP ERP 6.0 EHP x…7 systems. System Conversion requires a Unicode (UC) source system. Non-Unicode source systems will require a two-step approach (first move to Unicode then to SAP S/4HANA, on premise edition 1511) as illustrated below in Figure 6-6.

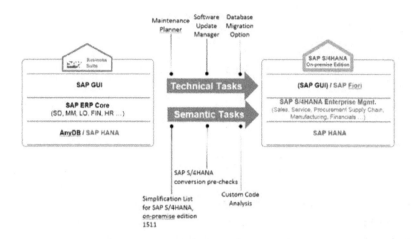

Figure 6-6 Landscape Transformation

Basically it can be distinguished between technical and semantic tasks during the system conversion. The technical installation procedure is based on established lifecycle management tools (Maintenance Planner, Software Update Manager [SUM] and Database Migration Option [DMO]). Due to the fact that SAP S/4HANA is a new product line (and not the successor of SAP Business Suite) things are done differently in SAP S/4HANA. Many of the changes are technical in nature and have no or only limited impact on peoples work and thus do not trigger business change management. Such changes will be mandatory when converting a system to SAP S/4HANA.

Other decisions are more of a strategic nature determining which version of functional support will evolve into the digital era and provide the capabilities demanded from the unstoppable business process innovation. Where those strategic directions demand change management through adoption, SAP at large keeps the traditional capabilities available as compatibility scope enabling a rather technical migration of these processes and leaving the time of change management at customer decision that may well happen when initially converting or at a later point in time.

To allow our customers a better planning and estimation of their way to SAP S/4HANA, we have created the "Simplification List for SAP S/4HANA, on premise edition

1511". In this list we are describing in detail on a functional level what happens in S/4HANA to individual transactions and solution capabilities. In some cases, we have merged certain functionality with other elements or reflected it within a new solution / architecture compared to the SAP Business Suite products. The technical procedure - well established tooling

Maintenance Planner - The Maintenance Planner checks the system with regards to business functions, industry solutions, and add-ons. If there is no valid path for the conversion (for example, the add-on is not released yet), the Maintenance Planner prevents the conversion.

Note: You must run the Maintenance Planner before the SUM. Ensure that the latest version of the Software Update Manager is used:
For all information about using the SUM, please see the document Conversion of SAP Systems to SAP S/4HANA, on premise edition Using Software Update Manager available at: service.sap.com/toolset (LINK)
Software Logistics Toolset 1.0
Section "Documentation"

Project Plan

Ensure you should plan for a detailed pre phase where you'd be able to analyze existing landscape as part of pre-study and ensure the target landscape in HANA addresses key constraints of the business. A sample plan with 4-5 months usually illustrated below in Figure 6-7 for reference.

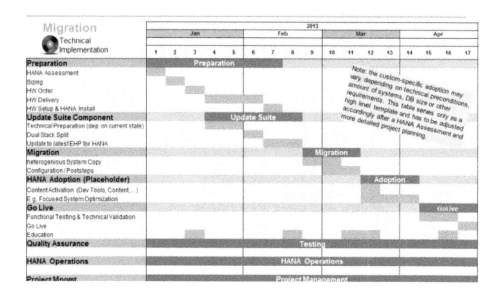

Figure 6-7 Migration Project Plan

Let's take a look at detailed WBS plan as illustrated below in Figure 6-8. The discovery phase would help you identify key constraints such as custom code complexity with test requirements. The technical prep is more in-depth analysis of required sizing of apps server, HANA appliance scalability etc. As you finalize the technical approach, you'd embark on a sandbox upgrade & migrate to ensure systems are upgraded as required for migration requirements to HANA. Following sandbox, you'd repeat similar upgrade and migration procedures in DEV, QAS; where you'd conduct necessary business user acceptance. Finally, you'd plan for a cut-over, post data migration; system will be available for usage in production environment as illustrated below in Figure 6-8 in detailed plan, build and run phases.

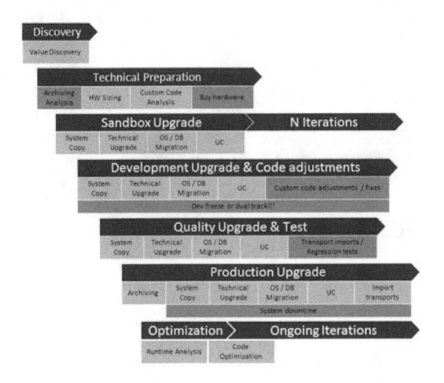

Figure 6-8 Migration Run Task Plan

The design phase is mostly strategizing such as landscape planning, migration and technical approach, planning overall time, schedule and budget.

BUILD

If you chose to run SAP HANA yourself in your own landscape, you can practice the upgrade in a sandbox system. Note this step may not be relevant if SAP HANA is run in a hosted and managed environment. After upgrading your development system, you adjust your custom code to ensure that you fully benefit from the performance improvements of SAP HANA. To achieve the highest efficiency, you need to find out which code is really relevant for the migration process. Smart analysis can save

183

you up to 90% of the migration effort. SAP tools provide you with the necessary functionality to focus on the relevant code objects, and a framework for the overall change management. SAP can also provide you with services to execute the actual migration process. After upgrading your quality system, you perform tests. SAP provides you with a new powerful tool set to automate your tests, thereby increasing their quality and largely reducing manual test efforts for future upgrades. To keep downtime as short as possible, Database Migration Option (DMO) of the Software Update Manager was developed to significantly reduce the required downtime, thereby reducing business cost. In future, DMO tools will be able to keep a downtime near to zero.

RUN

To further improve your system performance, monitor the usage and response times. Using our powerful tool set you can monitor the system and set the focus of improvements to where most value is added to the business. Monitor and back up your system. The following figure illustrates the concept explained above: 1.3 Plan Executive Summary and Key Takeaways ● Start preparing your SAP Business Suite powered by SAP HANA

Finally, plan several cycles in your migration project, so:

- That you can familiarize with the migration procedure and optimize it based on your individual requirements and boundary conditions by performing several test runs with the right grade of realistic hardware and database content you require.

- That you can create, refine and validate your individual migration cookbook.

- That you can perform and validate mandatory code adaptions and simple code optimizations early in the project.

Landscape design

To design the technical system landscape for SAP HANA, follow the steps described in this topic.

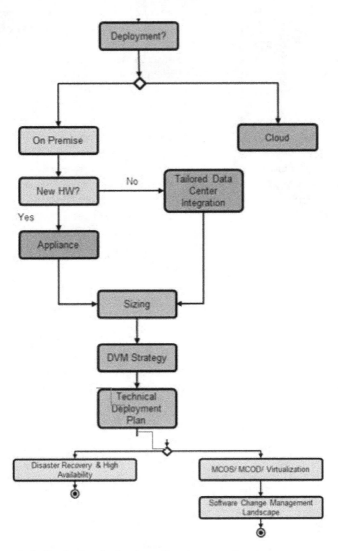

Figure 6-9 Technical System Landscape Design

To develop and implement the future technical architecture for SAP systems with SAP HANA, proceed as follows: Procedure 1. Define the deployment options either in the data centre (on premise) or using a hosted (cloud) solution. 2. Define the hardware (HW) acquisition requirements either by using Appliance or by following the Tailored Data centre integration approach. For Appliance, check partner solutions with customer-specific data centre requirements. 3. Define the general technical architecture, i.e. the components required and the sizing for all applications. Map the sizing results to your hardware using either single-node or scale-out HANA appliances. Bear in mind the SAP HANA architecture, for instance the usage of Master Node. 4. Consider implementing a data volume management strategy if the required DB size is very large. If you cannot reduce your uncompressed data below 4 TB, consider implementing the scale-out approach. 5. Decide on the required number of SAP systems to manage software changes (number of systems in a landscape). 6. Deploy different components, MCOD, MCOS, and virtualization options for setting up each system 7. Define a strategy for high availability and disaster recovery. 8. Define a software change management landscape.

HANA Cloud HEC Architecture

A customer system landscape consists of physical servers running HDB and several virtual machines. For example, SAP Application Server can be set on such a virtualized environment. The HEC customer landscape is completely integrated into the customer corporate network using IPSEC VPN and/or MPLS connections. The concept of an HEC system landscape is shown in the following illustration:

Installation Options In addition to the standard installation option where one application runs on one SAP HANA instance, which in turn exclusively runs on one server, there are other installation options like MCOD, MCOS, and Technical Deployment available for SAP Business Suite powered by SAP HANA systems. With MCOD, you can deploy certain white-listed applications together on the

same SAP HANA database but in different schemas. This
option allows you to perform common cross-schema reporting
on the data of these applications. SAP Business Suite
components like SAP SCM or SAP SRM can be co-deployed with
SAP ERP on one SAP HANA database inside one database schema
with SAP HANA Technical Co-Deployment. For nonproduction
systems like development and test systems you have the
option of installing multiple SAP HANA databases on the
same server with the MCOS scenario.

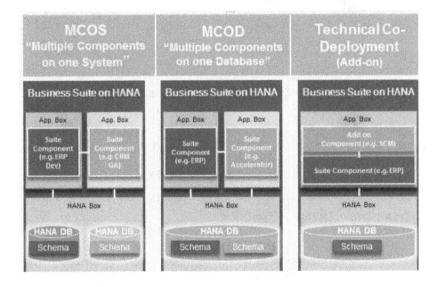

Figure 6-10 HANA Installation Options

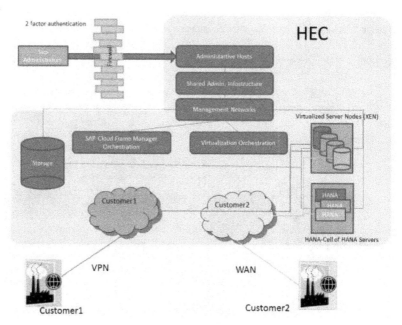

Figure 6-11

Custom Code Checks

These checks are based on the Simplification list concept. Before converting to SAP S/4HANA, on premise edition 1511 you need to check your custom code against the SAP S/4HANA simplifications. These simplifications are loaded into the Custom Code Check Tool. After you run the tool, you obtain a list of instances where your custom code does not comply with the scope and data structure of SAP S/4HANA 1511, on premise edition. For more information about the Custom Code Check tool, see SAP Help Portal: **Link** and the following SCN blog: **SAP**.

188

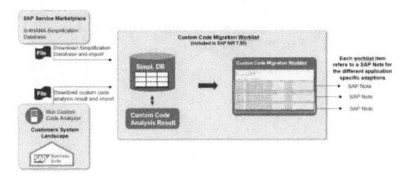

Figure 6-12 SAP S/4HANA Custom code migration work list

Test Management

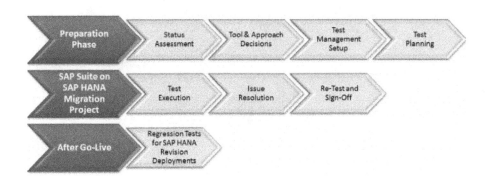

Figure 6-13 Test Management

Test management affects all phases of a migration project - this is also true for a migration to SAP HANA. Be it the decision about testing tools and test planning in the preparation phase, the actual test execution and issue resolving during the migration project, or the later regression tests, like after the deployment of future SAP HANA revisions after the successful migration. To get an overview how SAP Solution Manager Enables test management also for this special use case, see the guide Best Practice: Test Management for SAP Business Suite on SAP HANA Migration Projects.

Related information – at a glance as highlighted below:

SAP S/4HANA, on-premise edition – General Information	
SAP Help	
SAP S/4HANA, on-premise edition 1511 documentation	Link
Getting Started With SAP S/4HANA, on-premise edition 1511	Link
Conversion Guide for SAP S/4HANA, on-premise edition 1511 FPS1	PDF
Simplification List for SAP S/4HANA, on-premise edition 1511 FPS1	PDF
Maintenance Planner – SCN Blog	Link
	Link
Software Update Manager (SUM) for SAP S/4HANA, on-premise edition 1511 Software Logistics Toolset 1.0 –> Section "Documentation" –> System Maintenance	Link
Custom Code Check tool (SAP Help)	Link
SAP S/4HANA Feature Scope Description	Link
SAP SCN	
SAP S/4HANA Cookbook	Link
Simplification List for SAP S/4HANA, on-premise edition 1511 FPS1 – XLS Version	Link
Software Update Manager (SUM) - SCN Blog with more information	Link
DMO Database Migration Option – SCN Blog with more information	Link
SAP SCN - SAP S/4HANA Custom Code Migration Worklist	Link
Custom Code within SAP S/4HANA On-Premise	Link
SAP S/4HANA, on-premise edition: Additional remarks regarding Business Functions (FPS1)	Link
Miscellaneous	
SAP S/4HANA @SAP Learning Hub	Link
S/4HANA Trial	Link
SAP Best Practices for SAP S/4HANA, on-premise edition	Link
SAP Activate	Link
FIORI App Library	Link

SAP S/4HANA, on-premise edition – Important SAP Notes	
General Information	
SAP S/4HANA, on-premise edition 1511: Release Information Note	SAP Note 2189824
SAP S/4HANA, on-premise edition 1511: Restriction Note	SAP Note 2214213
SAP S/4HANA, on-premise edition 1511: supported industry solutions	SAP Note 2214213
SAP S/4HANA, on-premise edition 1511, Country Versions: Release Information & Restriction Note	SAP Note 2228890
Blacklist Monitor in SAP S/4HANA on premise	SAP Note 2249680
SAP Fiori for S/4HANA	SAP Note 2214245
Process integration with other SAP on-premise systems	SAP Note 2241931
Custom Code related information	
Delivery of the S/4H System Conversion Checks	SAP Note 2182725
Custom code check content for SAP S/4HANA on-premise edition 1511	SAP Note 2241080
Running Custom Code Analyzer and Downloading ZIP File(s)	SAP Note 2185390
Business Function related information	
SAP S/4HANA, on-premise edition 1511: Always-Off Business Functions	SAP Note 2240359
SAP S/4HANA, on-premise edition 1511: Always-On Business Functions	SAP Note 2240360
Add-On / Partner related information	
SAP S/4HANA, on-premise edition 1511: Compatible Add-ons	SAP Note 2214409
SAP S/4HANA, on-premise edition 1511: Compatible partner products	SAP Note 2244460
Add-on Product Versions released on SAP NETWEAVER 7.5	SAP Note 2156130
Uninstalling ABAP add-ons	SAP Note 2011192
Conversions to SAP S/4HANA On-Premise with 3rd Party / non-SAP Add-ons	SAP Note 2308014
SAP NetWeaver 7.5	
Additional Information about the update/upgrade to SAP NetWeaver 7.5	SAP Note 2197269
Minimal DB system platform requirements for SAP NetWeaver 7.5	SAP Note 2158828

Figure 6-14

Rapid Data Migration Strategy

SAP S/4HANA, on-premises edition customers will be supported in their implementation project with pre-configuration based on SAP Rapid Deployment Solutions and SAP Rapid Data Migration with SAP Data Services. Additionally, there will be content packages for the implementation and integration with SAP S/4HANA and other SAP cloud solutions, such as SAP Success Factors Employee Central. The following figure 6-15 illustrates the data migration based on SAP Data Services technology at a glance:

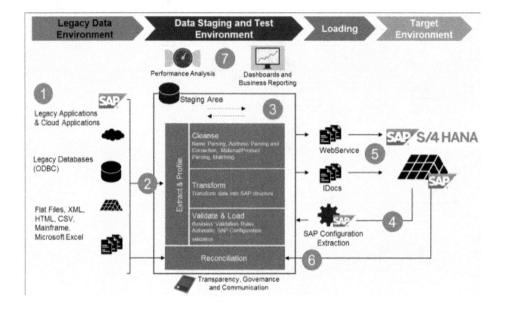

Figure 6-15 Data Migration Strategy

(1) The legacy data environment refers to the source
systems for the migration. It can be any third-party source
system that is supported by SAP Data Services connectivity
(almost everything as SAP Data Services supports ODBC
protocol). SAP systems on a lower release that cannot be
upgraded can be a legacy system as well. The Rapid Data
Migration package comes with pre-built content for SAP
S/4HANA. Extract and profile

(2) Data is extracted from the source and placed in a
staging area in SAP Data Services. At this point, you can
conduct technical profiling with SAP Data Services.
Additionally, you can start profiling very early on the
source systems using SAP Information Steward. The Data
Services environment is used as more information in SAP
Help: Link the Road to SAP S/4HANA 17 staging area that
extracts and profiles the data. The profiling can include
looking at patterns in postal codes. For example, what
percentage of postal codes has 5 digits? It could also be
how many material numbers follow a specific pattern. For
example, you might be interested in how many unique IDs
there are in a certain table. The extraction and profiling

of data is an important first step in a data migration project. The quality of the source data is assessed and the overall risk of data migration is mitigated to ensure overall success of the data migration project. Cleanse, transform, and validate

(3) This includes updating the data so that it meets specific patterns, mapping and transforming the data according to rules, and validating data against the SAP S/4HANA business context. This can involve combining two fields into one, splitting fields, updating the data in a field to match certain rules (for example, telephone number formats), and validating data against required fields and lookup values from the SAP S/4HANA context and configuration. Also, duplicate data records can be eliminated with this step. SAP configuration extraction

(4) Once the data is extracted, it is important to know how the data needs to be prepared for SAP. The solution reads business context and configuration settings in SAP S/4HANA to help map the data. As part of an SAP S/4HANA implementation, the system is configured with many values such as cost centres, company codes and country values. This step enables knowledge of the SAP business context, in order to transform and then validate the data in Data Services against the SAP configuration and customization settings. Mapping of the source data normally requires mapping fields that comply with the SAP configuration.

(5) Once the data is transformed and validated, it is then loaded into the SAP S/4HANA system. This is normally done via IDOCs and Web Services, but can also be done with files & BAPIs. Reconciliation

(6) Reconciliation looks at what was actually loaded versus what was expected to be loaded. This ensures all data was loaded and is ready for use. Dashboards and business reporting

(7) Throughout the process, dashboards are available for the people involved to stay informed about the status of the migration. Additionally, the migration project often sets data quality expectations and governance around data

193

management. The entire process of assessing the data, validating data according to business rules and SAP context lays the ground work for ongoing data governance. For example, if customer records were checked to ensure every customer had at least two contact persons associated with it, then this process can continue to ensure all new customer records have two contact people

One of the common challenges in today's IT landscape is the heterogeneous platforms and the issues of integrating every single component in the landscape. The SAP HANA platform has the solution to integrate all components with one data source. SAP S/4 HANA running on SAP HANA is a next generation business suite. The objective of HANA is to consolidate customer's "IT" landscape and system architecture, thus delivering functional improvements in ERP, and enhancing the user experience seamlessly as one unit. The new principles of User Experience are enhanced in SAP FIORI applications. The SAP S/4 HANA is evolving with the following key aspects in mind:

a) Simplicity of business suite by integration all SAP Business suite under   one roof of HANA

b) Enhance user experience (UX), which is the front-end

c) Ease of Integration in one platform as all products are under one-roof

d) Providing mobile, internet interfaces

e) Enhancements with no major changes as the platform is robust &

f) Provide real time analysis by using in-memory techniques for 365x time's faster access with increased RAM

The above factors indicate how the business will run way forward. With these aspects in mind, if you visualize SAP S/4 HANA, it can provide users a user experience, with simplicity and ease of use business suite. Also, it aids in the instant data analysis for managers to make quick decisions and helps organizations achieve operational excellence such as "quicker MRP runs", "quick month-end account closures" etc. SAP has delivered EHP 7.0 (Enhancement package 7) for SAP ERP 6.0 with lots of simplified financial and logistics transactions readily

available for SAP HANA. It simplifies business
transactions.

SAP S/4HANA Roadmap

The roadmap for SAP S/4 HANA is to provide Simple
Financials, SAP Simple Logistics, and Simple Operations to
benefit from significant functional improvements those
customers can leverage. The Simple financial application on
HANA, enables "on-the fly" month-end closures using the
high performance and agile HANA database. The
simplification of the architecture indicates SAP products
such as SCM, PLM, SRM, EP, and BW will run on SAP HANA as
one source data, instead of multiple databases. Thus,
integration of products is simpler as it sits on one
database, "HANA" and data can be accessed real time, almost
350x times faster, anytime, anywhere. This is the most
exciting news of recent times as a breakthrough in
technology, thus providing real functional and technical
benefits to the customer.

Moreover, SAP IT systems will become lean with the advent
of HANA, with unified landscape with one source of data,
HANA dB, instead of multiple database(s) by applying the
database principles of multiple components in one database
(MCOD). All these SAP applications run on a single SAP HANA
production appliance. There are three options to deploy SAP
business suite on HANA, as MCOS, MCOD or co-technical
deployment as illustrated below. I wondered, how these
applications run on a single source and how are they
deployed. The following Figure 1-2 explains the schema for
each of these applications on the SAP HANA database. If
you're aware of "schema" concept in a dB, you'll be able to
appreciate these ideas. A simple example is how you'd
organize your workplace, a big space or partitions for
different purposes and/or all in one huge conference room.
It is a choice for the manager to support his activities.
In a similar way, SAP offers three options of deployment.
In simple terms, 'MCOS' refers to the multiple components
on one system; each schema uniquely refers to the

corresponding business application. In MCOS, there might be more than one HANA DB. Whereas, in MCOD, components are grouped into schemas. Finally, the co-technical deployment refers to the ADD-ON's on one unified schema of the single HANA DB.

As we keep talking about Big data, enterprise should be able to capture unstructured information such as marketing, sales data or prospect details in a text format from social media analytics. SAP provides integration with HADOOP as well as helping read unstructured data using SAP HANA Text analysis to derive meaningful information from the unstructured data.

How to Choose the Right Option for You?

1. See the Standard Recommendation from SAP

Use the following recommendations as starting point for an individual assessment - that is, take the recommendation and relevant aspects into the discussion with your cross-functional teams and use them as basis for an individual assessment based on the boundary conditions you are facing as illustrated below in Figure 6-7.

For ABAP-based SAP systems, the following recommendation applies:

Figure 6-16 Recommendation

The general recommendation is to use the database migration option of SUM, as it has become our standard procedure for migrations to SAP HANA - with it, you can profit from a simplified migration to SAP HANA, performed by one tool, with minimized overall project cost and only one downtime window.

As reasonable alternative to our standard recommendation, in case the database migration option of SUM does not fit your requirements, consider to use the classical migration procedure with software provisioning manager, which is also continuously improved especially for the migration to SAP HANA. Reasons might be that the database migration option of SUM does not support your source release or if you prefer a separation of concerns over a big bang approach as offered by DMO of SUM.

As possible exception, there are further migration procedures for special use cases, such as the consolidation of SAP systems in the course of the migration project or the step-wise migration to SAP HANA, as outlined above.

For Java-based SAP systems, use the classical migration approach (and skip step 2 below).

2. Individually Assess Your Situation

Based on the standard recommendation from SAP, find the best option depending on your individual requirements and the boundary conditions you are facing. To support you in this process, SAP provides a decision matrix in the End-to-End Implementation Roadmap for SAP Net Weaver AS ABAP guide (SMP login required), which is intended to highlight important aspects for your decision on the right migration procedure, including these key considerations.

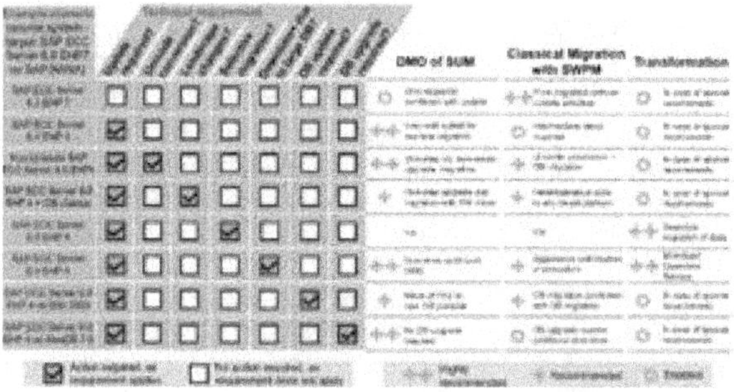

Figure 6-17 Key considerations

What is the release and Support Package level of your existing SAP system? Is an update mandatory or desired as part of the migration procedure?

Is your existing SAP system already Unicode?

Do you plan any landscape changes - such as changing the SAPSID of your SAP system or the hardware of your application server - as part of the migration or do you rather prefer an in-place migration?

Do you plan the migration of your complete system or a partial migration?

Are your operating system and your database versions supported according to the Product Availability Matrix (PAM) of the target release or are corresponding updates required?

Do you expect a significant downtime due to a large database volume?

All these aspects are reflected in the matrix, which is intended as a starting point for your individual assessment as outlined above.

Relevant Aspects for Planning a Migration Project to SAP HANA

As preparation for a lecture about the available migration path options to SAP HANA, my colleague gathered several aspects for the planning of a migration project to SAP HANA. It's not a complete list, some parts might seem trivial, aspects and recommendations are gathered from different documents and colleagues (thanks to everybody that supported us here!), but I wanted to share them with you via this blog nevertheless, and if it is only that you can cross-check your individual project plan.

Project Team

With SAP HANA, several aspects come into play - be it bare metal topics like network and storage, OS, DB, and, of course, the applications running on top of the SAP HANA platform. Therefore, build cross-functional teams right from the start already for planning the implementation of SAP HANA, as you have to come up with ideas concerning such diverse topics like appliance shipment, wiring + setup process, user management, adapting your development process, and operations concept for this platform.

Check Supported Platforms, Releases, Add-Ons, and Possible Restrictions

Make sure your product is released on SAP HANA and restrictions do not apply - see the Product Availability Matrix (PAM) for your product (SMP login required)

Not all add-ons and third-party products are currently supported, so check early. Current SAP Notes that provide corresponding information at the time of writing this blog (SMP login required):

SAP ERP: SAP Note 1820906

SAP CRM: SAP Note 1820903

SAP SCM: SAP Note 1821797

SAP SRM: SAP Note 1820905

SAP Net Weaver AS ABAP 7.4: SAP Note 1826531

For third-party products, see SAP Note 1855666

SAP strongly recommends that all other partner add-on products need to be certified for SAP HANA – for more information, see the Partner Information Center.

Sizing of SAP HANA

It's important to do a proper sizing of SAP HANA systems as part of the pre-study. You can use SAP resources to analyze current Application server reusability, data growth based on the past dB growth rate etc.

Note: See SAP Note 1514966 (*SAP HANA: Sizing SAP In-Memory Database*)

Define Your Overall Target Landscape
There are multiple options of HANA deployment such as virtualization, multiple components on one system (MCOS)

and on one database (MCOD), and the option to run SAP HANA and SAP Net Weaver on one server

---

Note: see for example:
- SAP Note 1826100 (*Multiple applications SAP Business Suite powered by SAP HANA*)
- SAP Note 1661202 (*Support for multiple applications on SAP HANA*)
- SAP Note 1681092 (*Multiple SAP HANA databases on one SAP HANA system*)
- SAP Note 1788665 (*SAP HANA running on VMware vSphere VMs*)
- SAP Note 1953429 (*SAP HANA and SAP Net Weaver AS ABAP on one Server*)

Then, based on the available options, define your overall target landscape such as if you want to put development and QA system on one SAP HANA system or scale up vertically by increasing size of hardware versus scale-out scale horizontally by adding nodes.

Migration Procedure

Besides all the boundary conditions to consider, choose your migration procedure (such as database migration option of Software Update Manager or the classical migration procedure with *software provisioning manager*), as outlined in the Migration of SAP Systems to SAP HANA page.

Critical Success Factors:

You must plan ahead with key constraints as some of the success factors mentioned below:

Platform & Appliance methodology (Installation & Update)

Backup & Recovery (System Copy)

High Availability

- Disaster Recovery

- Monitoring & Administration

- Security & Auditing

- Trigger SAP HANA hardware provisioning in time - lead times can be four to six weeks

- Plan for up-skilling of your database administrators

- Ensure SAP Solution Manager availability for your SAP HANA landscape

Standard maintenance processes apply also for your applications running on SAP HANA like for any other SAP system.

Best Practices

Custom Code Migration

The following Figure 6-18 illustrated managing custom code as part of the migration project. You will need to analyze code optimization with required migration for HANA compliance. There may be inclusions such as Open SQL's to be added to the existing custom code, in any case, you will need to review code optimization to leverage the best performance HANA DB and columnar storage. Once implemented, it will be the RUN cycle to manage the custom code.

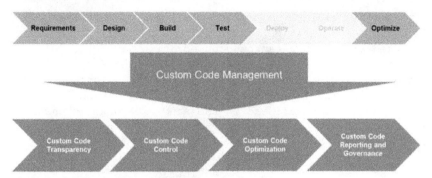

Figure 6-18 Custom Code Migration

One of the key constraints in planning your migration to SAP HANA is a fully-fledged relational database system optimized for transactional (OLTP) and analytical (OLAP) processing. Hence, you'll need to consider recommendations of the in-memory columnar storage in SAP HANA, in order to transition some of custom ABAP developments to SAP HANA. However, by avoiding functional regression during migration, all ABAP code will need to be assessed for implicit behaviour. There are many other aspects such as performance optimization of custom developments is required. In order to leverage SAP HANA completely, data access patterns should be optimized.

Since HANA supports open SQL'S that are not previously taken in to account In particular, it explains the steps that can be followed before a technical migration takes place. It also includes steps that need to be considered independently from SAP HANA. ABAP coding will need to be transitioned to address ABAP coding in combination with standard database access through Open SQL. For some specific environments and frameworks, additional guides and recommendations may exist. For example, Current SAP service offerings for more information see Best Practice Guide - Considerations for Custom ABAP Code during a Migration. Let's look at some of the best practices in optimizing code for HANA transition.

SAP Code Inspector (SCI) / ABAP Test Cockpit (ATC) SCI is the standard tool for analysing ABAP developments to detect potentially critical source code in terms of performance, security, globalization, or quality in general. It looks at selected checks that can be grouped in to variants. SCI is integrated into the test cockpit, a tool used for QA of custom developments. You can also check out external tools available to ensure a robust code optimization and migration is planned ahead in the sandbox system to ensure adequate testing is done prior to moving it to production.

Note: See ABAP Test Cockpit - an Introduction to SAP's new ABAP Quality Assurance Tool

---

Summary

In this chapter, we discussed importance of robust migration strategy and key constraints with recommendations. Basically there are three main options to choose based on existing landscape. You must be cognizant of the downtime constraints, sizing parameters, functional regression and landscape transformation to plan the approach as big bang or phased. In either case, you must do a careful evaluation of various constraints discussed in this chapter to identify and mitigate risks at an early stage of the project. There are key decisions to be made with your business such as on-premises or cloud migration with your near-term or long-term strategy of IT landscape transformation program.

■ ■ ■

CHAPTER 7: SAP HANA Studio

If you're a seasoned developer, who had developed ABAP programs in SAP then you would appreciate SAP's innovation in HANA Studio. I have managed projects involving extensive source code changes as part of upgrade and performance optimization projects with complex integration scenarios. It's hard to maintain source code up-to-date and current. Also, if you have multiple systems, then maintaining a common repository of source code becomes challenging with every change induced in the environment for business reasons or as a system requirements such as patch update, release or enhancement package implementations. If you carefully observe the evolution of ABAP programming, it transitioned from R/2, R/3 classic ABAP to ECC object oriented (OO) ABAP using ABAP workbench (SE80) with enhanced objects orientation provided with changing architecture. Gone are the days of customization taking longer than six months as we are talking about rapid deployment in 4-6 weeks. Eventually development will no longer be a time consuming task. If you observe any implementation project plan, you'd realize a lot of time, resources and efforts are spent during the "Realization" phase of the project. This phase would involve extensive coding, testing and integration activities.

In a classic ABAP workbench, most of these things are manual, whereas in Eclipse it is automated to accelerate app deployment in quick turn-around time which is less expensive with tools for acceleration and helps you be on or ahead of the schedule, which was not the case in most of the implementation projects due to changing requirements and/or less adaptability in the code post integration. These risks are mitigated by using integrated development environment (IDE) such as Eclipse as common platform for both JAVA and ABAP based application development to ensure accelerated code deployment and maintenance. SAP's desktop tooling strategy for SAP HANA and cloud-based development is based on a standard Eclipse environment, where users install development tools in their workspace via plug-ins. Unlike with SAP Net Weaver Developer Studio, however, users can now customize their Eclipse workspace by picking and choosing which plug-ins to install — both those from SAP and those available from external partner sites. They are also not limited to Java development.

Today, it's all about HANA DB; hence the programming has to be rapid, easily customizable and deployed. Keep these caveats in mind, SAP has developed Eclipse based integrated development for HANA server. Eclipse is easy to setup in few steps. One of its nice features is that you can setup multiple "projects", each project means one connection to an SAP system, and in each project you can add different packages. So this means you can have all your SAP systems accessible easily and could make life a little easier for you.
The open Eclipse platform offers first-class user experience, powerful platform capabilities, and a broad and vivid ecosystem contributing enhancements and extensions. Thus, SAP as active contributor and strategic developer of the Eclipse foundation continuously invests in harmonizing design-time and development tools on the Eclipse platform like the ABAP development tools or SAP HANA Studio to increase the developer productivity and enable specific cross-tool interactions.

Eclipse platform Key benefits:

a. The Eclipse platform the ABAP Development Tools offer failover-safe online development in multiple AS ABAP systems, advanced source code editing and

b. Refactoring support, powerful search and navigation capabilities, ideal support for task-oriented and test-driven development, and built-in extensibility by rich extension points.

This is an Eclipse-based integrated development environment (IDE) that is used to develop artefacts in a HANA server. It enables technical users to manage the SAP HANA database, to create and manage user authorizations, to create new or modify existing models of data etc. It is a client tool, which can be used to access local or remote HANA system. It helps developers to build, deploy apps in quick turn-around by providing required tools for deployment. The SAP HANA studio runs on the Eclipse platform 3.6. We can use the SAP HANA studio on the following platforms Microsoft Windows or SUSE Linux or Mac OS.

Note: For Mac OS, HANA studio is available but there is no HANA client for that. Let us explore SAP HANA Studio features in this chapter with easy steps to download, install and include SAP HANA system for usage. SAP provides an update site (https://tools.hana.ondemand.com) from which customers can download and install SAP's various Eclipse plug-ins for SAP HANA and cloud development according to their needs.

Evolution of HANA Studio

Why do you think SAP thought for a better development environment? Today, applications are disparate; as it is required to connect to multiple interfaces, manage integration points developed in ABAP/JAVA programming languages. Basically it has to connect seamlessly as one unit. While SAP HCP is an end-to-end platform, SAP envisaged a complete package as PaaS to support existing and new clientele, hence its strategy to provide an integrated development environment in SAP HANA Studio. Lt's take a look at the Overview screen as soon as you log into SAP HANA Studio as illustrated below in Figure 7-1

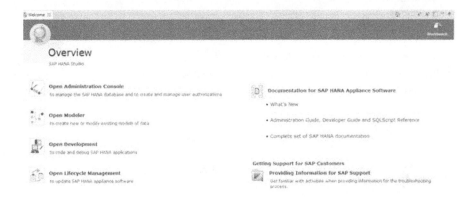

Figure 7-1 SAP HANA Studio Overview

Supported Platforms:

The SAP HANA studio runs on the Eclipse platform 3.6. We can use the SAP HANA studio on the following platforms: Microsoft Windows x32 and x64 versions of: Windows XP, Windows Vista, Windows 7 or USE Linux Enterprise Server SLES 11: x86 64-bit version

System Requirements illustrated below in Figure 7-2: JAVA JRE 1.6 or 1.7 must be installed to run the SAP HANA studio. The Java runtime must be specified in the PATH variable.

Make sure to choose the correct Java variant for installation of SAP HANA studio:
a. For a 32-bit installation, choose a 32-bit Java variant.
b. For a 64-bit installation, choose a 64-bit Java variant.

Illustrated below in Figure 7-2.

SAP Development Tools for Eclipse

HOME   ABAP   BW   CLOUD   GATEWAY   HANA   HCI   SAPUI5

ABAP Development Tools for SAP NetWeaver

This site describes how to install and update the front-end components of ABAP Development Tools for SAP NetWeaver (ADT).

It also provides you with detailed information on how to prepare the relevant ABAP back-end system for working with ADT.

Prerequisites

Eclipse Platform	Luna (4.4) or Kepler (4.3)
Operating System	• Windows 7 32- or 64-Bit, or • Apple Mac OS X 10.8, Universal 64-Bit, or • Linux distribution * The compatibility is no more tested by the Eclipse Community since Eclipse Kepler (4.3)
Java Runtime	JRE version 1.6 or higher, 32-Bit or 64-Bit
SAP GUI	• For Windows OS: SAP GUI for Windows 7.30 • For Apple Mac or Linux OS: SAP GUI for Java 7.30
Microsoft VC Runtime	For Windows OS: DLLs VS2010 for communication with the back-end system is required. NOTE: Install either the x86 or the x64 variant, accordingly to your 32- or 64-Bit Eclipse installation.

Figure 7-2 System Pre-requisites

SAP HANA STUDIO PERSPECTIVES

The SAP HANA studio provides an environment for Administration, Modelling and Data Provisioning. There are several predefined User Interface layouts addressing several applications types called 'Perspectives'. In HANA Studio every HANA system has two main sub-nodes, Catalogue and Content as illustrated below in Figure 7-3.

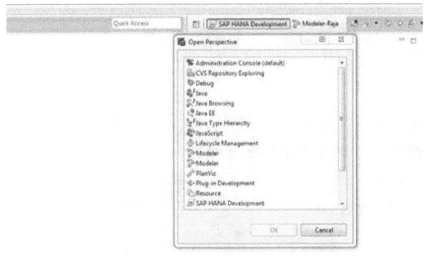

Figure 7-3 Open Perspective

Modeller perspective:
It provides views and menu options that enable you to
define your analytic model, for example, attribute,
analytic, and calculation views of SAP HANA data.

a. SAP HANA Development perspective:
It provides views and menu options that enable you to
perform all the tasks relating to application development
on SAP HANA XS, for example: to manage application-
development projects, display content of application
packages, and browse the SAP HANA repository.

b. The Debug perspective:
It provides views and menu options that help you test your
applications, for example: to view the source code, monitor
or modify variables, and set break points.

c. Administration Console perspective:
It provides views that enable you to perform administrative
tasks on SAP HANA instances.

d. Catalogue and Content:

211

In HANA Studio every HANA system has two main sub-nodes, Catalogue and Content as illustrated below in Figure 7-4 in order to manage data dictionary objects.

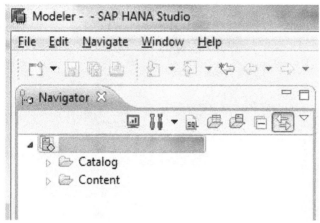

Figure 7-4 Modeller

e. Catalogue:
The Catalogue represents SAP HANA's data dictionary, For all data structures, tables, and data which can be used. All the physical tables and views can be found under the Catalogue node. This node contains a list of Schemas which a used to categorize tables according to user defined groupings.

f. Content
The Content represents the design-time repository which holds all information of data models created with the Modeller. Physically these models are stored in database tables which are also visible under Catalogue. The Models are organized in Packages. The Contents node just provides a different view on the same physical data.

Now, let's understand how to download, install SAP HANA Studio with including HANA system to the studio.

Download & install SAP HANA studio

Gone are the days of searching for your admin to install software app for you. Nowadays, it's as easy as installing an app in your mobile. SAP HANA Studio is no different from the mobile app installation. The process is simple and transparent and anyone can do without dabbling through the complex installation manuals. You can use the S-USER ID to download from SAP HANA STUDIO from the SAP Service Market place or you can install it from the Eclipse portal. In this section, let's explore both these option how to download and install SAP HANA Studio and how to add SAP HANA system to the SAP HANA Studio.

SAP HANA Studio installation is done in 2 steps:

a. [Download] and [Install] Eclipse

b. [Install HANA software] (plugin) in Eclipse

Option 1 - Let's assume you don't have S-USER ID. Now this option covers detailed steps of installation from the Eclipse.org site for external users:

Step 1: Download and install Eclipse

Download and install eclipse from Eclipse Mars or Eclipse Luna. For example, go to [Eclipse Mars site] and download Eclipse as per your operating system as illustrated below in Figure 7-x.

Eclipse IDE for Java EE Developers

Package Description

Tools for Java developers creating Java EE and Web applications, including a Java IDE, tools for Java EE, JPA, JSF, Mylyn, EGit and others.

This package includes:

- Data Tools Platform
- Eclipse Git Team Provider
- Eclipse Java Development Tools
- Eclipse Java EE Developer Tools
- JavaScript Development Tools
- Maven Integration for Eclipse
- Mylyn Task List
- Eclipse Plug-in Development Environment
- Remote System Explorer
- Code Recommenders Tools for Java Developers
- Eclipse XML Editors and Tools

Download Links

Windows 32-bit
Windows 64-bit
Mac OS X (Cocoa) 64-bit
Linux 32-bit
Linux 64-bit

Downloaded 1,445,431 Times

▸ Checksums...

Bugzilla

▸ Open Bugs: 48

▸ Resolved Bugs: 137

File a Bug on this Package

Figure 7-5 Eclipse IDE

As soon as [Eclipse] is installed, open it as illustrated below in Figure 7-6.

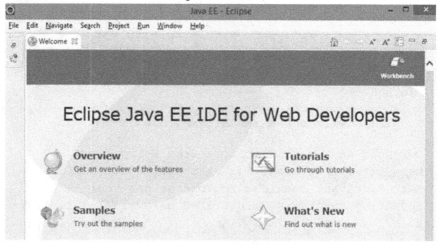

Figure 7-6 Eclipse Java EE IDE

Step 2: Install HANA software (plugin) in [Eclipse]

In Eclipse, choose in the menu bar Help – [Install New Software] as illustrated below in Figure 7-7.

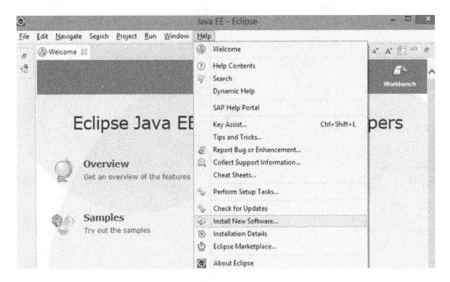

Figure 7-7 Java EE - Eclipse.

For Eclipse Mars, add the following URL:
https://tools.hana.ondemand.com/mars

For Eclipse Luna, add the following URL:
https://tools.hana.ondemand.com/luna

Press [Enter] to display the available features.
Select [SAP HANA Tools] and choose [Next] as
illustrated below in Figure 7-8

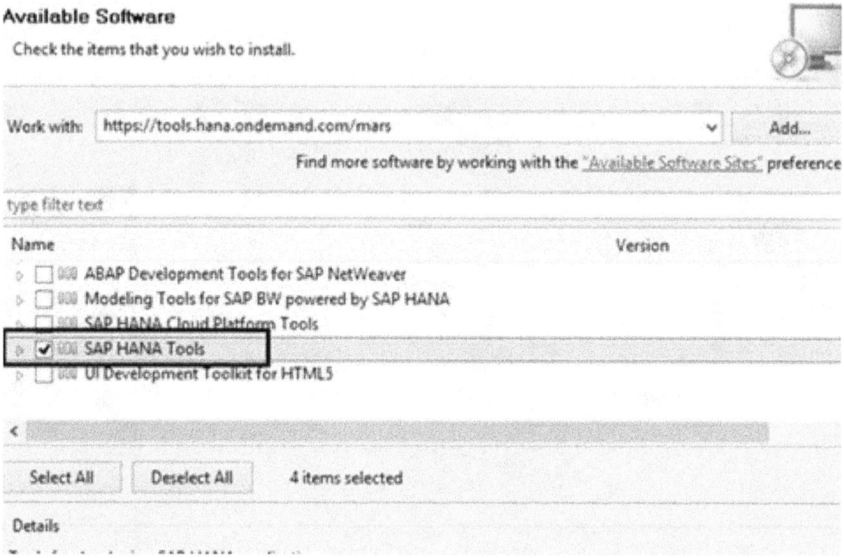

Available Software

Check the items that you wish to install.

| Work with: | https://tools.hana.ondemand.com/mars | ∨ | Add... |

Find more software by working with the "Available Software Sites" preference

type filter text

Name	Version
▷ ☐ ▒▒ ABAP Development Tools for SAP NetWeaver	
▷ ☐ ▒▒ Modeling Tools for SAP BW powered by SAP HANA	
▷ ☐ ▒▒ SAP HANA Cloud Platform Tools	
▷ ☑ ▒▒ SAP HANA Tools	
▷ ☐ ▒▒ UI Development Toolkit for HTML5	

| Select All | Deselect All | 4 items selected |

Details

Figure 7-8. Tools for developing SAP HANA apps

Note: In case you want to work with HANA Cloud Platform, also select the [SAP HANA Cloud Platform Tools].

In the next [wizard page] – you'll get an overview of the features to be installed. Choose [Next] and confirm the license agreements and choose Finish to start the installation as illustrated below in Figure 7-9.

Figure 7-10 Review Licenses.

This may take several minutes as illustrated below in Figure 7-11. In case you get a warning message, click on Yes. Finally, restart your eclipse.

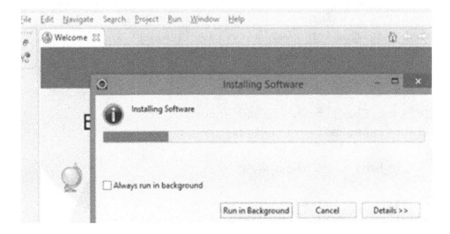

Figure 7-11 Installation Software
Hurray!!! You have successfully installed SAP HANA
Studio.

Option (2) - Download SAP HANA Studio from the SAP
Service market place. Now, let's assume you have a
valid S-USER ID to login to SAP Service market
place, you can download [HANA Studio] from SAP
Service Market Place. In case you have valid
license, you may download HANA Studio from SAP
Service Market Place. This is paid version and you
need user in Service Market Place.

a. Go to [SAP Service Market Place]

b. Choose [Support Packages and Patches] - A-Z
Index: H - [SAP HANA Enterprise Edition] - [SAP
HANA Enterprise EDIT 1.0] - [Comprised Software
Component Versions] - [SAP HANA STUDIO 1.00] -
[your operating system]

c. Run the [SAPCAR] executable to download the SAR
file. Extract this SAR file.

d. Use command [SAPCAR -xvf] - <your-SAR-file> to
extract the file. Run the 'HDBSETUP' executable to
install and update HANA Studio. When prompted, use
option Install new SAP HANA Studio to proceed with
the installation. Let's review detailed steps of
installation process as described below.

Detailed step-by-step Installation process:

Select [File] to download according to your OS as
illustrated below in Figure 7-12:

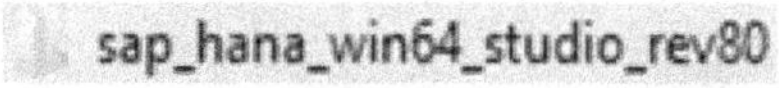

sap_hana_win64_studio_rev80

Figure 7-12 install file

Installation on Microsoft Window - Install SAP HANA
Studio in the default directory with administration
privileges or in user home folder without
administration privileges.

Click on [hdbsetup.exe] for installing SAP HANA
studio as illustrated in Figure 7-13.

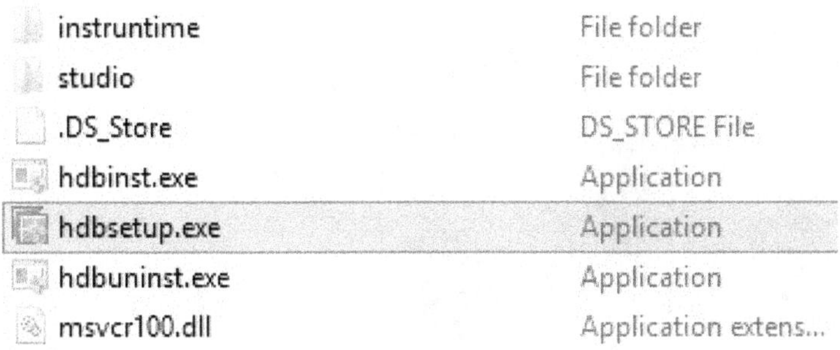

instruntime	File folder
studio	File folder
.DS_Store	DS_STORE File
hdbinst.exe	Application
hdbsetup.exe	Application
hdbuninst.exe	Application
msvcr100.dll	Application extens...

Figure 7-13 Install exe file

SAP HANA Lifecycle Management Screen appears as
illustrated below in Figure 7-14 Intro screen.

SAP HANA
Lifecycle Management

Version 1.09.80.00.391861

Figure 7-14

Default installation folder is C:/Program Files /
SAP / hdbstudio.

Steps 1 - Define Studio Properties as illustrated
below in Figure 7-15

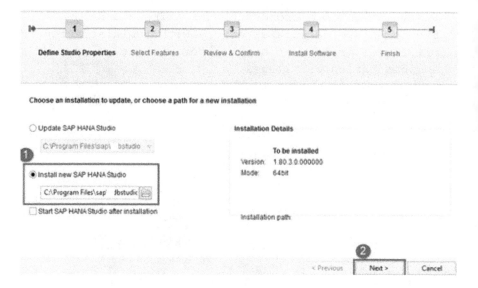

Figure 7-15 SAP LCM Install screen

Select install new SAP HANA Studio. Click [NEXT] bottom, Select Features screen appear as below –

Step 2 - Select features as illustrated below in Figure 7-16

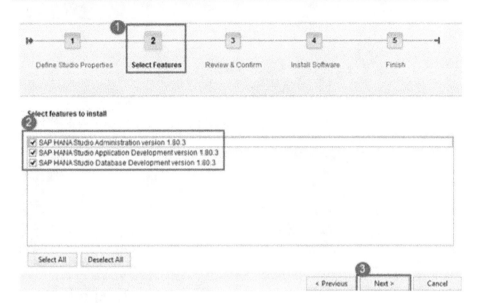

Figure 7-16 Select Features

Select Features screen are used to select features below:

a. SAP HANA Studio Administration – Toolset used for various administration tasks, Excluding Transport.

b. SAP HANA Studio Application Development – Toolset used for developing SAP HANA native Applications (XS and UI5 Tools excluding SAPUI5).

c. SAP HANA Studio Database Development – Toolset used for content development and click [NEXT] button.

Step 3 - [Review and Confirm] as illustrated below in Figure 7-17

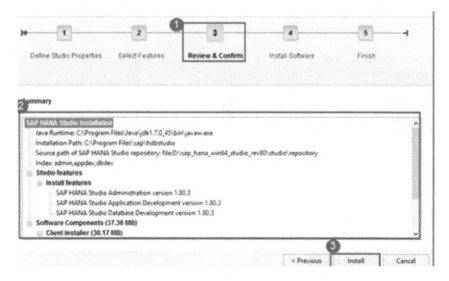

Figure 7-17. Review and Confirm

Review & Conform Screen appears. Summary of SAP HANA Studio Installation display. Click [Install]

Step 4 & 5 - Install Software and Finish. Installation Progress screen appear and after it goes to [Finish] page as illustrated below in Figure 7-18.

Figure 7-18. SAP HANA Studio Install complete screen

ADD SAP HANA system into HANA STUDIO

In this section, let us explore how to add HANA system into HANA Studio. In order to connect to a SAP HANA system we need to know the Server Host ID and the Instance Number. Also we need a Username & Password combination to connect to the instance. The left side Navigator space shows all the HANA system added to the SAP HANA Studio.

Steps to add new HANA system:

a. Right click in the Navigator space and click on [Add System] as illustrated below in Figure 7-19:

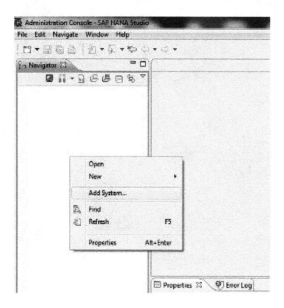

Figure 7-19 Administration Console

b. Enter [HANA system] details - [Hostname & Instance Number] and click [Next] as illustrated below in Figure 7-20

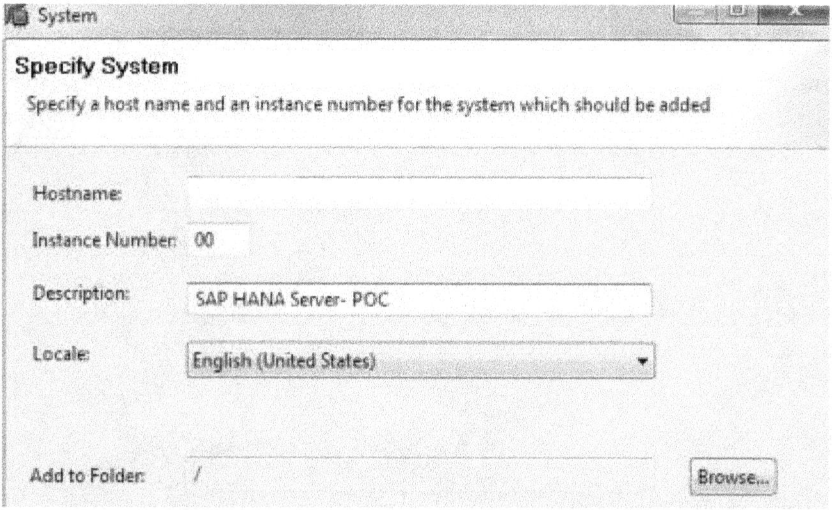

Figure 7-20 System screen

c. Enter the [database username & password] to connect to the SAP HANA database. Click on [Next] and then [Finish] as illustrated below in Figure 7-21

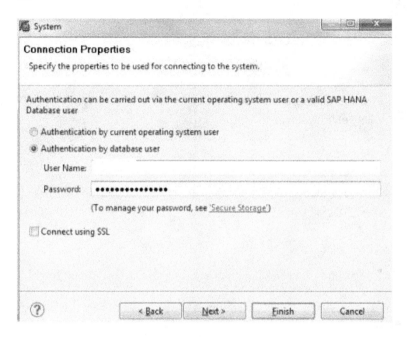

Figure 7-21 System Authentications

d. The SAP HANA system now appears in the Navigator as illustrated below in Figure 7-22

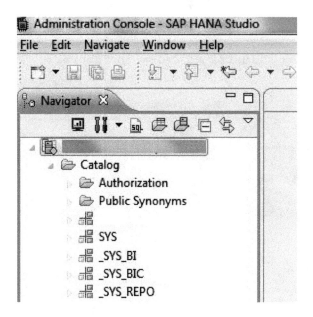

Figure 7-22 SAP HANA Studio Admin Console

Detail steps to add HANA system to the HANA Studio:

a. Run SAP HANA Studio. Now, go to Default installation folder is "C:/Program Files / SAP / hdbstudio". There is hdbstudio.exe file, by right clicking on it; you can create a shortcut as illustrated below in Figure 7-23.

| hdbstudio.exe | 5/21/2014 8:44 AM | Application |

Figure 7-23 app exe file

When you click "hdbstudio.exe" file, it will open Workspace Launcher screen as illustrated below in Figure 7-24.

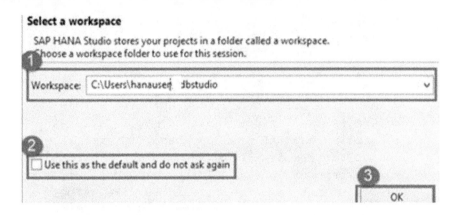

Figure 7-24 Workspace Launcher.

Workspace is selected by default. We can change Workspace location by Browse option. Workspace is used to store studio configuration settings and development artifacts. Select [Use this as the default and do not ask again] option to prevent popup this screen every time for workspace selection when we open SAP HANA Studio. Click [OK]. SAP HANA Studio Welcome screen appear as illustrated below in Figure 7-25

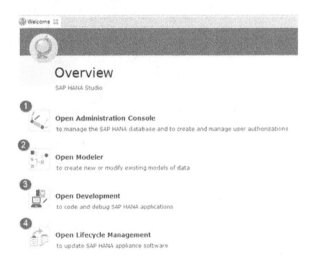

Figure 7-25 SAP HANA Studio Welcome Screen. In the Welcome screen different perspective is displayed, Detail of each perspective is as below:

a. Administration Console Perspective - This screen is used to configure, administration and monitoring the SAP HANA Database. Several View and editor are available in SAP HANA Administration Console. System View Toolbar is used for Administration; it looks like as below:

Below is a Table 7-1 illustrates System-level editors and views available in SAP HANA Administration Console.

Table 7-1 System Level Editors

Editors/Views	Detail
Systems	System view provides hierarchical view of all the SAP HANA System managed in SAP HANA Studio with their contents (catalog, content, etc.)
System Monitor	System Monitor is an editor which provides an overview of all SAP HANA Database at one screenshot. We can see the detail of the individual system in System Monitor by drill down.
Administration	This is used for performing administration and monitoring task.
Admin diagnosis mode	This editor is used in case of emergency to perform monitor and operation on the system in which either No SQL connection available or the SQL

	connection overload.
SQL Console	Used for Entering, Executing and analyzing SQL statement in SQL Console.

b. Modeller Perspective - This perspective is used to create modelling objects, database object management in SAP HANA System. This perspective used by modellers for the following activity – Create / Modify Tables, Functions, Indexes, View, Sequences, Synonym, Trigger, Views. Create Modelling object like Attribute View, Analytic View, Calculation View, Analytic Privileges, Procedures and Decision Table. Data Provisioning to SAP HANA database from SAP / NonSAP Source through SLT, BODS, and DXC.

c. Development Perspective - This Perspective is used to develop an application on HANA for the web environment. In this Perspective programming language is used – JAVA Script, J Query, ODATA, etc.

d. Lifecycle Management Perspective - This screen is used to Install and Update software regarding SAP HANA Database and SAP HANA Studio. Lifecycle management is also used to transport an object from one HANA system to another HANA System.

You'll need to authenticate user name/password to connect to the HANA system as illustrated below in Figure 7-26.

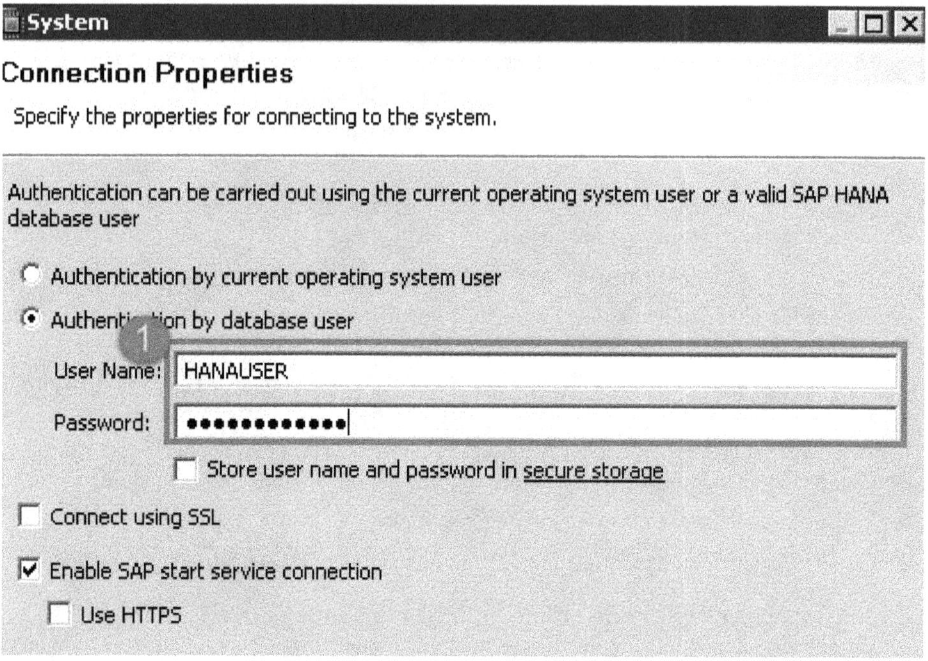

System _ □ ✕

Connection Properties

Specify the properties for connecting to the system.

Authentication can be carried out using the current operating system user or a valid SAP HANA database user

○ Authentication by current operating system user

◉ Authentication by database user

User Name: HANAUSER

Password: ●●●●●●●●●●●●

☐ Store user name and password in secure storage

☐ Connect using SSL

☑ Enable SAP start service connection

☐ Use HTTPS

Figure 7-26 Connection Properties. Enter Username and Password for SAP HANA Database for access it from SAP HANA Studio and click [Finish]. Now, let us explore the options of working with SAP HANA Studio.

Work with SAP HANA studio

To login in SAP HANA Database through SAP HANA Studio, follow below steps as illustrated below in Figure 7-27:

Figure 7-27 SAP HANA Studio Login screen. Click on Added System. Here [DB (HANAUSER)]. A popup screen for User Name/ password. Enter User Name and Password for HANA Database. Click [Ok] button. After Login to SAP HANA Studio, We get below screen for selected HANA System as illustrated below in Figure 7-28 HANA System.

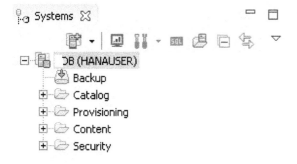

Figure 7-28 HANA Systems. In Hana Studio under HANA System following sub-nodes exits-

Catalogue - SAP HANA Studio Catalogue node
represent SAP HANA data dictionary, in which
Database object (Table, View, Procedure, Index,
Trigger, Synonyms, etc.) stores in Schema Folder.
When the user is created in SAP HANA, Schema of the
same name will be created in SAP HANA Database by
default. This is a default schema of user when a
user creates any database object. Schema is used to
group database object.

Schema defines a container that hold database
objects such as Table, Views, Trigger, Procedure,
Sequence, Function, Indexes, Synonyms, etc. Schema
can be created in SQL Editor by below SQL:

1   CREATE SCHEMA "SCHEMA_NAME" OWNED BY "USERNAME".

Here "SCHEMA_NAME" AND "USERNAME" Should be
changed according to Requirement. After Refresh
Catalogue Node Newly Created Schema will be
displayed.

I have created Schema "APRESS_SCHEMA" by it in-front
SQL as illustrated below in Figure 7-29.

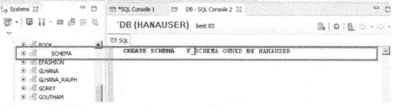

Figure 7-29 Create Schema

All Database Object are stored in respective folder of
Schema as illustrated below in Figure 7-30

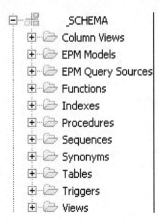

Figure 7-30 DB objects in Schema

Provisioning is used for selecting source Meta data and importing metadata and data into SAP HANA. There are two categories of provisioning, they are SAP HANA In-Built Tool (Flat file, Smart Data Access, Smart Data Streaming, etc.)

External Tools (SLT, BODS, DXC, etc.)

In SAP HANA Studio Provisioning node, SAP uses a new feature called, "Smart Data Access" which is Built in Tool. Smart Data Access combines data from heterogeneous data sources like Hadoop, Teradata, Oracle, and Sybase as highlighted below in Figure 7-31.

Figure 7-31 Provisioning

Data from different sources will store in SAP HANA database as "Virtual Table". The restriction with virtual tables is, it can be only used to build calculation views in SAP HANA.

Content - Content Node is Design Time Repository, which hold all information of data models in the

package. All information view e.g.(Attribute View,
Analytic View, Calculation View, etc.) will be created
in Package under Content Node.

The package is used for grouping related information
object in a structured way. The package can be created
by clicking right click on [Content Node] -[New]-
[Package] as illustrated below in Figure 7-32:

Figure 7-32 Package creation

a. Security - Security Node in SAP HANA Studio contain
3 Sub-node, they are used for Create User Audit
Policy, Password Policy, etc.

b. Users - Used for create/Modify/Delete user. Role
and Privileges will also grant to user from this
screen.

c. Roles - Used for Create/Modify/ delete Roles.
Privileges are added/deleted from here to Role.

Summary

In this chapter, you have learned the basics of SAP HANA
studio, which is the integrated development environment for
developing HANA apps. This is the future strategy of SAP to
support an integrated development platform to build apps
using JAVA/ABAP programming languages for multiple systems
in one integrated environment. Now, you have understood the
basic know-how of using SAP Eclipse in SAP HANA Studio
development environment for building and deploying the next
generation SAP HANA apps with tools, perspectives, which
are new ways to manage administration and authorization
controls all in one place. Also, you've learnt the basics
of installation SAP HANA studio using S-USER ID in SAP
Market Place or using an Eclipse.org site to download and
install SAP HANA STUDIO software step-by-step and you've
observed how to add SAP HANA system to the Studio with
basic work ways using perspectives.

CHAPTER 8:
SAP HANA Administration Basics

The objective of this chapter is to help you understand the basics of SAP HANA administration and how it helps you run it faster and effectively. SAP HANA Studio is an advanced tool available in HANA to support administration of SAP. Basically it consists of administration tasks to manage and development studio to maintain code progression. Typically, HANA uses SQL as a standard database query language with additional engines to support Java program or any external coding. It's easy to use SAP HANA Administration tools and masters it with least learning curve. Another feature is that SAP HANA studio can add more than one HANA systems to manage. It is one repository for administration of multiple instances. The activities include a) DB maintenance b) backup, c) Backup and Restore d) upgrade dB and patches e) Execute SQL f) Table level display, monitoring tasks and more administrative tasks etc.

As you know SAP HANA is integrated with Sol Man. Thus, there is a tight integration of SAP HANA based systems in to service management and ALM (application lifecycle management) managed in one repository. For example, the technical monitoring of the database is embedded into the monitoring solution landscape. It helps in managing stack, thus enabling operation control from a technical perspective as well as from an end-user point of view. The DBA cockpit is used for support and troubleshooting. It also helps in quick processing using guided procedures and knowledge documents. Thus, it helps in segregation of duty such as administering changes and troubleshooting.

Note: You can refer to the

www.saphana.com/community/resources/hana-academy

SAP HANA Landscape

Why do you think customer should switch to SAP HANA? There are critical factors such as increasing profit, TCO and analysing sales & market trend is critical for any business. One of the primary reasons is the ease of managing the HANA landscape with reduced administration tasks. Now, let's see core features of SAP HANA as illustrated below in Figure 8-1 Landscape

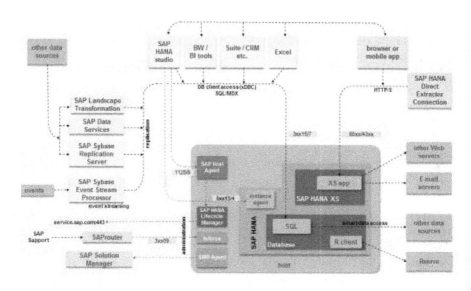

Figure 8-1 illustrates the connections that exist to various components, applications. These entities present in the extended SAP HANA Extended System Landscape. Details are provided about the nature of the interface, and the relevant port number ranges are visible as well. For more information about the details about the various components and connections in the extended SAP HANA system landscape, see the SAP documentation SAP HANA Master in the standard help page in SAP. SAP HANA box contains database which can run SQL, application server known as XS and Linux operating system with SAP specific software's. For data replicating (into HANA) the data various methods are available of which SLT and data services are popular choices. In our experience Sybase replication server was found to be very costly. SAP AG support specialist can login to system using SAP solution manager and SAP router.

SAP HANA Scenarios:

Based on the requirements, HANA can be tailored into landscape in four different ways which we call as scenarios. Depending on the system architecture we generally distinguish it as two. They are side-by-side scenarios and integrated scenarios. Side-by-side scenarios are used when SAP HANA is required as an additional component to an existing landscape to facilitate analytical features or accelerate processed. In integrated scenarios SAP HANA is used as primary database as illustrated below in Figure 8-2 below.

Data Mart Scenarios:

Agile Data Marts - As illustrated below in Figure 8-2 Enterprise data warehouse model (EDW/ETL model).This is for no-time critical data and already transformed data. SAP HANA as core value proposition is flexibility i.e. its ability to connect to multiple technologies.

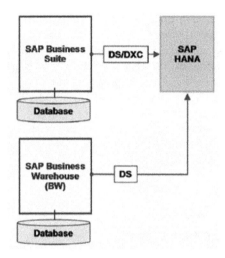

Figure 8-2

Operational Data Marts - As illustrated below in Figure 8-3, Operational data marts are for real-time data. SAP HANA acquires data via real-time replication. The core value proposition is to report the real time data.

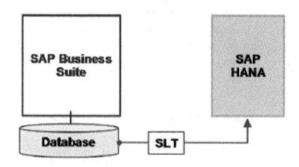

Figure 8-3

SAP HANA Accelerators - As illustrated below in Figure 8-4, SAP HANA uses accelerators to improve performance such as critical ABAP reports and business process running within HANA.

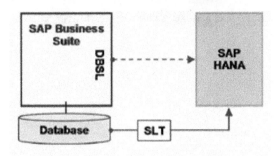

Figure 8-4

    SAP HANA as Primary Persistence - As illustrated below in Figure 8-5, HANA uses SAP ABAP application server runs on HANA DB. Moreover, all ABAP object uses in-memory database to store its tables. This allows speed and simplification of BW/Business suite.

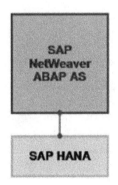

Figure 8-5

Examples for SAP applications that have been optimized to use SAP HANA as primary persistence are:

a. SAP BW 7.30 SP05
b. EHP 7 for SAPERP6.0
c. EHP 3 for SAP CRM 7.0
d. EHP 3 for SAP SCM 7.0
e. EHP 3 for SAP SRM 7.0 &
f. SAP Portfolio and Project Management 6.0

DOWNLOADING THE SAP HANA SOFTWARE

Now, let us explore steps for downloading migration information from Service market place of SAP.

SAP HANA Software in Service Marketplace:

1. Open the SAP Software Download Centre in the Service Marketplace

2. Navigate to the SAP HANA Platform Edition Software: SAP Software
Download Centre - [Support Packages and Patches] - [A-Z Index] - [H] -
[SAP HANA PLATFORM EDITION] - [SAP HANA PLATFORM EDIT. 1.0]
-
[Comprised Software Component Versions]

3. Show the different components included in the Platform Edition

Opening SAP HANA Administration Console

In order to access the DB admin and monitoring features of the SAP HANA studio, you open the SAP HANA Administration Console perspective. Let's review the procedure.

Procedure:
From the file explorer, start hdbstudio.exe. On the Welcome page, choose Open SAP HANA admin Console as illustrated below in Figure 8-6.

Figure 8-6

Let us look at the screen Areas of the SAP HANA
Administration Console as illustrated below in Figure 8-7.

Figure 8-7

Managing SAP HANA Systems in the SAP HANA Studio. The SAP
HANA studio allows you to work efficiently and conveniently
with SAP HANA systems.

Systems View:
As illustrated above in the system view helps in managing
systems in SAP HANA studio and its contents. It is the
central access point for performing system-specific
administration and monitoring activities as illustrated
below in Figure 8-8:

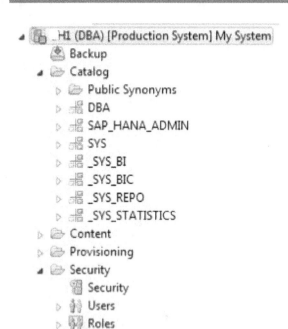

Figure 8-8 Administration and Monitoring

In order to do better admin and monitoring, you must be aware of the following: The Catalogue folder contains all activated database objects such as objects under one schema. The Security folder consists of all DB users with activated roles.

Toolbar Options in the Systems View as illustrated below in Figure 8-9:

Icon	Option
	Add System...
	Add System Archive Link...
	Open System Monitor
	Open Default Administration
	Open Diagnosis Mode
	Open SQL Console
	Find System
	Collapse All
	Link with Editor

Figure 8-9

Add an SAP HANA System:

In order to connect to a SAP HANA system we need to know
the Server Host ID and the Instance Number. Also we need a
Username & Password combination to connect to the instance.
The left side Navigator space shows all the HANA system
added to the SAP HANA Studio.

Steps to add new HANA system:
You can view from the [Systems] view toolbar, choose [Add]
system. Now, the [System wizard] opens. You can then right
click in the navigator space and click on [Add System] as
illustrated below in Figure 8-10:

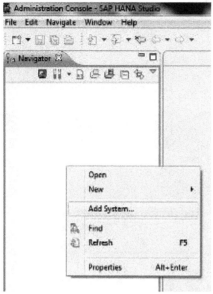

Figure 8-10 Add System

Enter HANA system details, i.e. the [Hostname & Instance Number] and click [Next] as illustrated below in Figure 8-11 specify system.

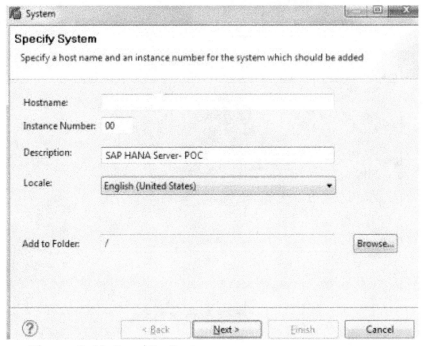

Figure 8-11 Specify System

Enter the database [username & password] to connect to the SAP HANA database. Click on [Next] and then [Finish].

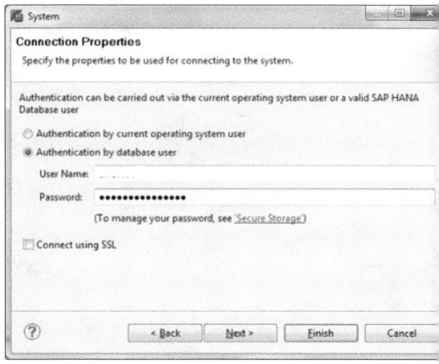

Figure 8-12 Connection Properties

A. log off and log in to the sap Hana system

b. In order to [log off] from the system, just right click in system view and select [log off] and finally,

c. In order to log on to Hana system, you can double click in systems view and select [Log on]. Alternately, you can also do it from the context menu. Now, let's see how to start and stop individual dB services.

Start and stop db. SERVICES:

Now, let's explore the steps to start and stop individual dB services. Let us [Stop] and then [Start] individual database services such as [Name server], [Index server], [xsengine] and so on running on an SAP HANA host or hosts. Let's review the step-by-step procedure.

You can stop a few services without having to stop the entire DB in order to save you from downtime of the system.

This would have least impact to the production users. For example, you can select [Admin] - [Open landscape] - [services] tab. In this tab, you will see all the DB services, just select the appropriate ones and right click the service, choose the required option as illustrated below in Figure 8-13.

1. In the Administration editor open the ▶ *Landscape* ❯ *Services* ▤ tab.
2. Right-click the service and choose the required option:

Option	Description
Stop...	The service is stopped normally and then typically restarted.
Kill...	The service is stopped immediately and then typically restarted.
Reconfigure Service...	The service is reconfigured. This means that any changes made to parameters in the system's configuration files are applied.
Start Missing Services...	Any inactive services are started.

Figure 8-13 Services. Let's review HANA licenses part of how to manage it.

SAP HANA licenses management

As you know, license keys are important for SAP as files. It is no different from any SAP systems. In HANA also, you'll need the keys to change standard code. SAP will provide this file to ensure your SAP HANA version is registered such as MS Office applications. There are two ways to import license keys; one way is to use the SAP HANA studio. The other option is using the SAP HANA HDBSQL for those who are familiar with the command line. As discussed there are two licenses available, one is the temporary license keys, for example, immediately after installation, you can for the temp licenses. However, at some point after a certain number of days (<=90 days) you will need permanent license keys. This can be automatically installed with a new SAP HANA dB, whereas for perm. Keys, Install number, system id, type, product information with HW and OS key details etc. It will be processed within few hours (<= 3 man days).

2) Now, let's see how to determine the HW key and System Identification. From the SAP HANA STUDIO - Select [SID] and then right click, properties - License Tab. In the

navigation area, choose the option to display the license information. You may need [license] admin privileges to access this page.

3) Now, let's see how to request for a license key. Go to online service marketplace, then request for the license key specifically in the [request] page. Now do a [Search an installation] or [select it from a list] and search for an ERP or an SAP NetWeaver installation. You can enter the install no. in the blank field for installation. You may choose the other option using install search option, where the system displays all installation numbers to select the license key.

4) Now, let's see the inputs required to request for license key for a new SAP HANA database. [New system] option and enter all required details such as sys id, prod type, version, hostname and system details including system usage type (SAP HANA BI, SAP HANA PI etc.) and OS system type like SUSE LINUX or RHEL etc. Then, select Continue to precede to the HW data and enter details such as HW key, License type with quantity such as GB size and validity period.

Choose "Save" to save your entries. Choose "Continue" to display all the system data again. Enter your e-mail address and choose "Send". There is an option to split SAP HANA licenses by number of instances. You can request license keys for Test and Development systems.

5) Downloading the license key by logging into market place and navigate to requests - license keys - select as highlighted below:

[SAP License Install] Overview screen - select [Installation] - then click sys id and choose [Display system] - [Continue] - [Display License script] - [Download]

Finally, select [Open - File - Save as] to save the license key file directly to your host.

6) You can install a permanent license key received by e-mail or by means of a download in your SAP HANA database only by using the SAP HANA studio. As pre-requisites for this option, you'll need system authorization LICENSE ADMIN as highlighted below:

[SAP HANA Studio] - Navigate to the properties page of the relevant database for which you have requested the license key. Select [Installing the license key] in the properties page. Finally, [Navigate to license file] - [Select]. After a successful confirmation, the properties page of the system is updated with the new license information if this is valid for the database.

You may need a temporary license key to manage creating an immediate request to the SAP support team. For example, if a production failure stopping key activities, then you can raise a priority 1 message for issuing a temporary license key that is valid for one week. However, you'll need the following data to proceed with the request, such as sys id, how key and install number. The key will be issued quickly. Request a permanent license key within this week. In the next section, let's evaluate various options provided by HANA to monitor system performance. It is a very complex task to assess performance in the legacy databases using command line to identify performance bottlenecks, which may stem from application, hardware capacity or anything hampering the overall system performance. However, these issues are mitigated in HANA by providing a simple user friendly system monitoring via HANA STUDIO. It's simple to use the tools to identify performance bottlenecks. It is self-explanatory to identify performance bottlenecks due to long running jobs, or hardware capacity or lack of memory issues or logs etc. as discussed below.

Monitoring System Performance

As explained HANA helps in managing key system monitor activates such as threads, session control, transactions that are blocked etc. It helps you in monitoring work load in the system to improve performance bottlenecks that may occur from time-to-time. Furthermore, you can take a look at frequently used transactions and queries in the SQL Plan cache, to identify any scope of fine tuning performance parameters such as identifying expensive statements etc.

Also, you'll be able to check status of running batch jobs to assess overall load in the system.

Thread Monitoring

This option helps you to manage all processes that are running the system. You might be familiar with a list of process in [Task Manager] as an example in windows. Similarly, you'll be able to monitor active threads in the system in the [Administration editor] on the [Performance] →[Threads]. It helps you to assess scope of processes running longer and you may need to check if it blocked beyond a certain amount of time.

Session Monitoring

Similar to thread monitoring of your core processes, you will be able to monitor all active sessions in the landscape in [Administration editor]-[Performance]→ [Sessions] sub-tab.

Monitoring SQL Performance with the SQL Plan Cache:

As discussed, in order to gain insight of the work load analysis in the system, The SQL plan cache will help you to analyze the system by analyzing frequently run SQL. You can view the plan cache in the [Administration editor] - [Performance] - [SQL Plan] Cache sub-tab.

Expensive Statements Monitoring:

Most of the issues are primarily due to the expensive statements, which mean it takes a lot of memory with intensive computing hogging the system performance. These expensive statements could be an invalid query to a huge table resulting in performance bottlenecks. This is expensive statements monitor helps you to assess performance of the SQL's. Go to [Administration editor] - [Expensive Statements Trace] sub-tab. You can see a detailed tree structure with details of aggregate statement executed.

The following information may be useful, a. Query start time, b. How long it takes in micro sec and c. Object name

Job Progress Monitoring:

It is essential to analyze batch jobs that are running too long. You can view in [Administration editor] - [Job Progress] sub-tab.

Load Monitoring

It is a graphical display of a range of system performance indicators. You can view in [Administration editor] - Load] sub-tab.

Monitoring Disk Space

It is essential to monitor available disk space to ensure the dB can be restored from the most recent commit state. In other words, you always want to be able to recover your data from the most recent commit state. In order to ensure the DB can be restored, there is a lot of disk space required for volume log information. Hence, you must ensure that there is enough space on disk for data and log volumes. There is a possibility to monitor disk usage, volume size, and other disk activity statistics by viewing volume details in the [Administration editor].

Service

It helps you analyze the various storage types such as logs and traces

Resolve Disk-Full Events:

For example, let's take a typical case study. Now, let see how a customer recovers in case of the disks are full. On which the database data and log volumes are located run full, the database is suspended, an internal event is triggered, and an alert is generated. A disk-full event must be resolved before the database can resume, that is, space on the volumes has to be freed. If a disk-full event occurs, the database is suspended and a Disk Full Event field is displayed on the Overview tab of the Administration editor. To resolve the event and allow the database to resume, you must make space available on the full volumes.

Procedure:

On [Volumes tab] - [set the Show filter] to Storage. Now, check whether it is the database that is using all the space or additional files. There is an option move or delete any files that are not needed, or add additional storage space. The disk-full event will be handled automatically using log volume checks.

Starting and Stopping SAP HANA Systems

The SAP start service (sapstartsrv) is the standard SAP mechanism for starting and stopping an SAP HANA system. In the Systems view, right-click the system you want to start and choose Configuration and Monitoring →Start System...

In the Systems view, right-click the system you want to stop and choose Configuration and Monitoring →Stop System...

Restart a system

In the Systems view, right-click the system you want to start and choose Configuration and Monitoring→Restart System as illustrated below in Figure 8-14

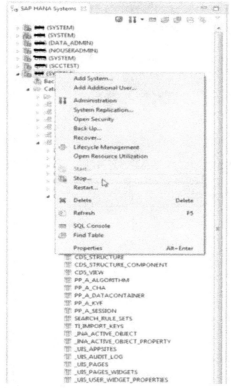

Figure 8-14 Restart System

Let's see a quick snapshot shot of SAP HANA Systems in HANA Studio as illustrated below in Figure 8-15

Figure 8-15 HANA System in HANA Studio

The SAP HANA Platform provides the following services as highlighted in Table 8-1 below:

Description	Services highlight
1. Application Services	Java script, Graphic Modeler, ALM
2. Processing Services	Spatial, Graph, Predictive, Search, Function Libraries, Data Enrichment, Planning, Text Analytics Series Data
3. Database Services	OLAP+OLTP, Multi-core/parallelization, Advanced compression, Multi-tenancy, Multi-tier storage, Data model, open standards, high availability, disaster recovery
4. Integration Services	Data Virtualization, ELT & Replication, Streaming, Hadoop Integration, Remote Data Sync.

Table 1-1. Services Provided by SAP HANA

SAP HANA Studio

Now, let's see how SAP's vision came true. The following Figure. 8-x illustrates SAP S/4 HANA architecture. As illustrated above in the SAP HANA Studio architecture, the objectives of SAP HANA client are to make a connection to the SAP HANA one DB. You can install HANA studio and client in your laptop to connect to the SAP HANA one db. The SAP HANA Studio was developed using Java Language in Eclipse platform. It is used of central development environment and main administration tool for admin purposes. The following admin tasks can be done using SAP HANA Studio as illustrated below in Figure 8-16:

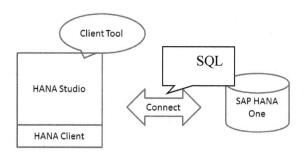

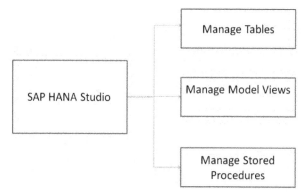

Figure 8-16

The above development tasks such as managing tables, creating, modifying the model views and managing stored procedures can be done using SAP HANA studio. The repository helps in source control. The SAP HANA Studio can be used for various purposes such as perspectives, which are views on-screen such as administration and development consoles.

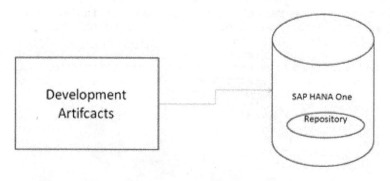

Figure 8-17

Now, let see the administration activates such as Db monitoring and admin console part of SAP HANA Studio as illustrated below in 8-17.

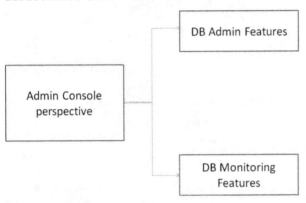

Figure 8-18

There are other perspectives to support you in development such as:

a. Modeller perspective

b. Development perspective &

c. Debug perspective.

Now, let's see administration console perspectives. SAP HANA studio talks to SAP HANA DB using SQL. You may interact with Studio using SQL directly or other features in the screen. Whenever SAP HANA Studio talks to database using SQL.

SAP HANA Studio Workbench and Perspectives

Now, let us understand deeper into the concept of perspectives in HANA as illustrated below in Figure 8-18:

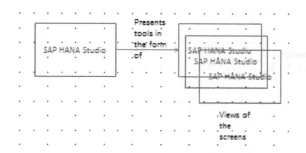

Figure 8-19 SAP HANA Studio

SAP HANA quick sizing

Now, let's review case study of sizing HANA using SAP Quicksizer method. The QuickSizer method is useful for the customers who will be implementing SAP HANA instance as a standalone instance or performing the implementation from scratch with limited details about the data models for SAP BW scenario. In QuickSizer there are three scenarios:

A. Standalone HANA

b. SAP NetWeaver BW powered by SAP HANA &

c. HANA Rapid Deployment Solutions

Description	Screen Shots
1. Start the QuickSizer as highlighted in the screen shots on the right.	Japanese Customer no. 334646 Project Name SAP HANA Create Project — Change Project Create with ref. — Display Project Show my Projects — Show Examples Quick Sizer for beginners

2. Select standalone option for memory sizing

as illustrated. [Run] the sizing script attached to [SAP note 1514966] for detailed view of sizing information. Quick size checks for the CPU required for HW configurations as illustrated in the screen on the right.

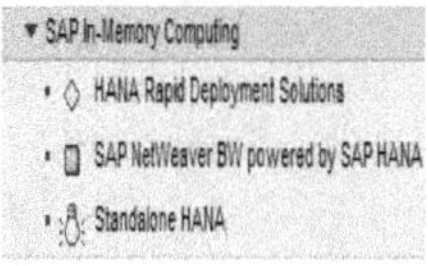

3. Specifics for Standalone HANA

As illustrated below provide details of no. of concurrent users, compression factor which is the evaluation of uncompressed data tables without index as illustrated in Figure 8-20.

Input:

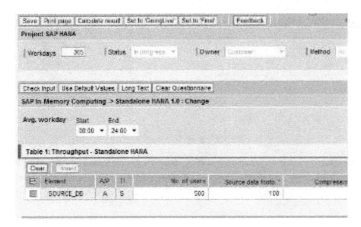

Figure 8-20 Input screen

4. Specifics for SAP NetWeaver Powered by SAP HANA
As an input, you will be required to provide average workday, load time to calculate sizing details as illustrated below in Figure 8-21.

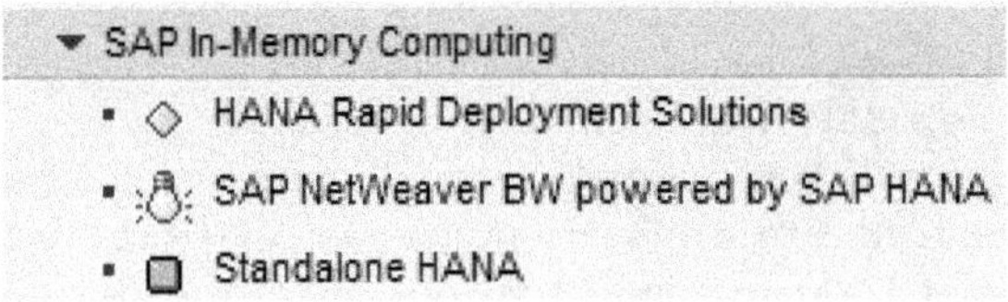

▼ SAP In-Memory Computing

- ◇ HANA Rapid Deployment Solutions

- ⚙ SAP NetWeaver BW powered by SAP HANA

- ▢ Standalone HANA

Figure 8-21 In-Memory Computing

259

4. Integration Services

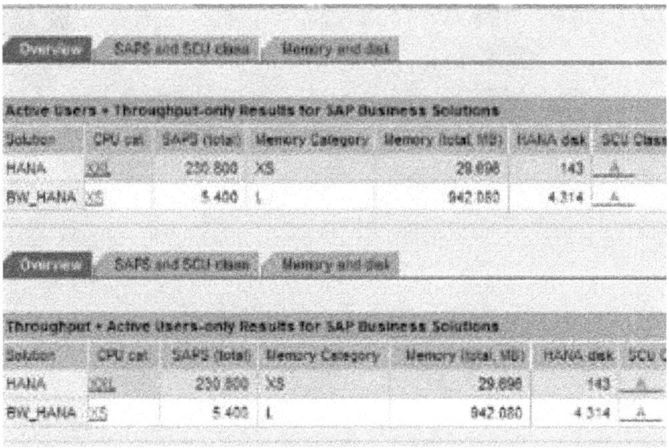
Overview | SAPS and SCU class | Memory and disk

Active Users + Throughput-only Results for SAP Business Solutions

Solution	CPU cat.	SAPS (total)	Memory Category	Memory (total, MB)	HANA disk	SCU Class
HANA	XXL	230.800	XS	29.898	143	A
BW_HANA	XS	5.400	L	942.080	4.314	A

Overview | SAPS and SCU class | Memory and disk

Throughput + Active Users-only Results for SAP Business Solutions

Solution	CPU cat.	SAPS (total)	Memory Category	Memory (total, MB)	HANA disk	SCU C
HANA	XXL	230.800	XS	29.898	143	A
BW_HANA	XS	5.400	L	942.080	4.314	A

Figure 8-22 Integration services

The above detailed evaluation of sizing parameters will help you decide on required sizing for your specific requirements.

Note: You may check online help in sap Hana platform site for more details of Quick Size services provided by SAP.

Summary

To summarize, SAP HANA Administration is relatively easy to manage without having to worry about the performance bottlenecks. SAP's investment is well justified with a robust platform to manage application suite, monitoring tools as discussed using SAP HANA STUDIO.

Moreover, it has further simplified usage and a central monitor options for monitoring multiple SAP instances in one place. The entire gamut of managing the SAP HANA landscape from application life cycle management to suite of products to support performance is simplified both for the administrators and the managers to understand issues and implement steps proactively. As discussed, Quick size tool as described in the chapter helps you in sizing HANA DB requirements.

■ ■ ■

CHAPTER 9: SAP HANA Modelling

If you had experience in designing complex relational database systems, then you'd really appreciate the myriads of simplicity in HANA data process for designing complex enterprise applications with analytical capabilities. As you know one part is to design a robust online transaction processing application (OLTP) and the other part is to build database that can support analytics (OLAP). Since, HANA supports both these two options, instead of building separate databases. Typically, in OLAP, you would focus on data model such as schemas for extensive analytical capabilites. For example, sales volume analysis for 5 years, which means a lot of data need to aggregated to build a report to support your business decision. Whearease OLTP is predominanly focussed on run-time and transaction available real-time, which means a lot of data in-memory to support real time processing. Now, HANA combines both of the above capabilities into one huge database running on SAP HANA platform with in-memory capabilities. Gone are the days of extensive batch processing to refresh your data marts that supports analytical requirements of your organization. Instsead of designing legacy database design projects from scratch, customer's are selecting HANA option to quickly implement SAP HANA enterprise suite for both analytical and transaction purposes with capability of the user to quickly model as per analytical requirements of the enterprise.

If you had designed a relational dB, you would be really concerned about the normalization-which follows rules to eliminate data redundancy or cardinality process-meaning unique values in the database. If you had run month-end processing, you would realize the complex process that updates, inserts Finance tables to ensure on-time closure with a lot of batch processing. Eventually, this may lead to certain inconsistencies as data is not real-time. Today, it's all consolidated into one HANA dB, hence you have a responsibility to model dB to leverage the best practices of HANA. HANA takes care of all these contraints of the yester years of realational database. HANA provides with in-memory options for faster data access as it stores data in columnar structure. Overall SQL, view

The objective of this chapter is to help you understand the various modelling techniques in SAP HANA and how to leverage SQL for database queries and working with 'VIEWS'. In this chapter, let's explore the concept of HANA data modelling and how to create modelling views on top of the database tales, schemas to implement the business logic, such as an analytical reporting. It is possible to consume views using SAP HANA native or HTML or even JAVA based applications. You can also use SAP tools like SAP Lumira or Analysis Office to directly connect to HANA and report modeling views. Now, let's start from the schema design, tables, and then discuss attributes, measures, views and types of join in HANA that supports your volume of data processing using in-memory capabilities. It's made simple for anyone interested in learning the HANA data modelling concepts.

Introduction to Star Schema

It is a best practice for any data warehouse application to design star schema, which illustrates fact and dimension tables. Well, fact is the core contains primary keys and the dimension is around it with measures such as quantity; hence the structure looks like a star.

Perhaps, this is the reason why they named it as 'star schema'. In order to meet business logic, fact tables are joined with dimension tables in HANA. The Fact Table is a collection of primary key for dimension tables and measures. Therefore, they are joined with respective dimension to fetch data in views. Whereas, the dimension table consist of master data and it is connected with one or more fact tables. Thus, these dimension tables are used to create schemas with fact tables and can be normalized.

For Example, Customer, Product, table etc.

Let's say for example, a company sells products to customers. Every sale is a fact that happens within the company and the fact table is used to record these facts as illustrated below in Table: 9-1 PRD-CUST Dimension Table which illustrated a product table with list of products sold to respective customers with total units sold as a measure unit:

TimeID (Day)	ProductID	CustomerID	Units Sold
1	P01	C001	2
2	P02	C002	3
4	P03	C003	4

Table: 9-1 Fact (Product) table

Now, let's see the dimension table

Table: 9-2 Dimension (Customer) Table

265

CustID	Name	Gender	Region	Income
C001	Pradeep	M	TN	2
C002	Suma	F	KA	3
C003	Supriya	F	KA	4

For example, in the above example, we have fact table that records details of the customer named Supriya as illustrated above. It indicates the details of the customer and region where the customer belongs to with sales data. Also, we have a product table and a time table that highlights details of the purchases. Thus, schemas are created by joining multiple fact and Dimension tables to meet business requirements. The database uses relational model to store data. However, Data Warehouse uses Schemas that join dimensions and fact tables to meet business logic. There are three types of Schemas used in a Data Warehouse –

a. Star Schema

b. Snowflakes Schema

c. Galaxy Schema

As discussed, in a typical star schema, Each Dimension is joined to one single Fact table, which is represented by only one dimension and is not further normalized. The dimension Table contains set of attribute that are used to analyze the data.

For Example, We have a Fact table as 'Fact Sales' that consist of Primary keys for all the Dim tables such as time, item with location key information, which are further linked to the dimension tables as illustrated below in Figure 9-3 start schema model.

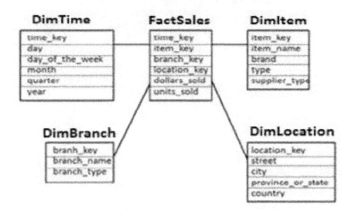

Figure 9-3 Star Schema Data Model

Each Dimension table is connected to Fact table as Fact table has Primary Key for each Dimension Tables that is used to join two tables. The facts/Measures in Fact Table are used for analysis purpose along with attribute in Dimension tables.

Whereas in Snowflakes schema, it goes deeper in normalizing dimension tables at second level for one fact table to ensure less data redundancy as illustrated below in Figure 9-4.

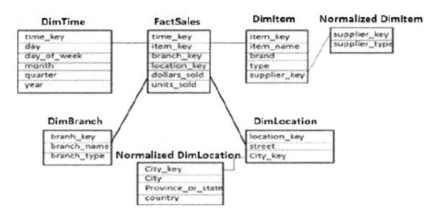

Figure 9-4 Snowflakes Schema Data Model

As illustrated above in Figure 9-4, in snowflakes schema data model, fact sales table is linked to the branch, location dimension tables as in a typical star schema. In addition, dimension table, such as location is further normalized by having another dimension underneath to provide additional details of the city details to ensure least data duplicates.

Further to the above model, in a galaxy schema goes another level deeper by further normalization process with number of facts and dimension. As illustrated in Figure 9-4, we have multiple fact tables such as sales and shipping with primary keys. Now, the dimension tables are linked to this schema, however the point is that the time-dimension table is linked to more than one fact table which forms the complex galaxy for increased normalization process.

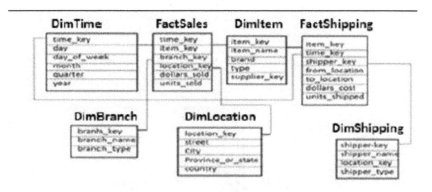

Figure 9-4 Galaxy Schema Data Model.

In the next section, let us analyze tables, attributes and measures.

Tables, ATTRIBUTES and measures

As illustrated below in Figure 9-5 SAP HANA Info view, we can connect to the SAP HANA information model from third-party applications such as MS-Excel, office etc.

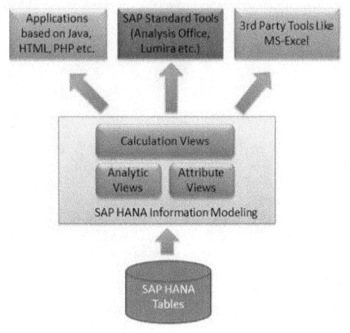

Figure 9-5 SAP HANA Info view

These modelling SAP HANA views can be classified into the following:

Attribute, Analytic and Calculation Views. These views effectively use in-memory technique to optimize query processing at run-time using the calculation engine for optimized performance as illustrated below in Figure 9-6 SAP HANA Info views.

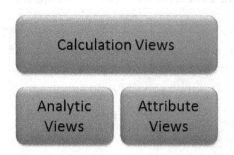

Figure 9-6 SAP HANA Info Views

As discussed as an example of attribute view which represents master data details. For example, 'Product' details with ID, description and delivery data can be combined into one data object. These attribute views can be used in analytic and calculation views depending on the requirements. Whereas, analytic views are primarily used for detailed transaction data analysis such as sales volume analysis of all stores for 5-10 years etc.

Now, let's understand view processing in HANA.

SAP HANA Attribute View - You can join multiple master tables and use this view effectively. Now, let's explore creation of standard attribute views as illustrated below in Figure 9-7 Attribute view creation flow.

Create Standard Attribute View

Standard view creation has pre-define step as illustrated below-

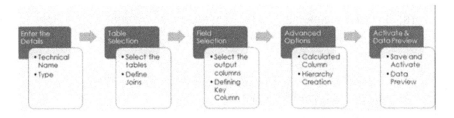

Figure 9-7 Attribute View creation flow

Table Creation for Attribute View

Here we are going to create Standard Attribute View for product table, so firstly we create "PRODUCT" and "PRODUCT_DESC" Table.
SQL Script is shown as below for table creation –
Product table Script –

```
CREATE  COLUMN TABLE "APRESS_SCHEMA"."PRODUCT"
(
"PRODUCT_ID" NVARCHAR (10) PRIMARY KEY,

"SUPPLIER_ID" NVARCHAR (10),
"CATEGORY" NVARCHAR (3),
"PRICE"        DECIMAL (5,2)
);

INSERT INTO "APRESS_SCHEMA"."PRODUCT" VALUES
('A0001','10000','A', 500.00);


INSERT INTO "APRESS_SCHEMA"."PRODUCT" VALUES
('A0002','10000','B', 300.00);


INSERT INTO "APRESS_SCHEMA"."PRODUCT" VALUES
('A0003','10000','C', 200.00);
```

```
INSERT INTO "APRESS_SCHEMA"."PRODUCT" VALUES
('A0004','10000','D', 100.00);


INSERT INTO "APRESS_SCHEMA"."PRODUCT" VALUES
('A0005','10000','A', 550.00);


Product Description table Script-
CREATE COLUMN TABLE "APRESS_SCHEMA"."PRODUCT_DESC"

(
"PRODUCT_ID" NVARCHAR (10) PRIMARY KEY,

"PRODUCT_NAME" NVARCHAR (10),
);

INSERT INTO   "APRESS_SCHEMA"."PRODUCT_DESC"   VALUES
('A0001','PRODUCT1');

INSERT INTO   "APRESS_SCHEMA"."PRODUCT_DESC"   VALUES
('A0002','PRODUCT2');

INSERT INTO   "APRESS_SCHEMA"."PRODUCT_DESC"   VALUES
('A0003','PRODUCT3');

INSERT INTO   "APRESS_SCHEMA"."PRODUCT_DESC"   VALUES
('A0004','PRODUCT4');

INSERT INTO   "APRESS_SCHEMA"."PRODUCT_DESC"   VALUES
('A0005','PRODUCT5');
```

Now table "PRODUCT" and "PRODUCT_DESC" is created in schema
"APRESS_SCHEMA".

Attribute View Creation

STEP 1 - In this step,

a. Select SAP HANA System.
b. Select content Folder.
c. Select Non-Structural Package Modelling under Package
APRESS_SCHEMA in the content node and right click->new.
d. Select Attribute view option as illustrated below in
Figure 9-8.

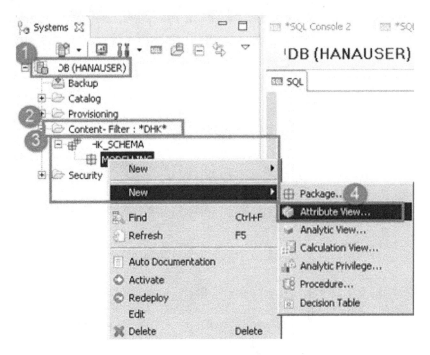

Figure 9-8 Attribute view creation

STEP 2 - Now in next window,

Enter Attribute Name and Label.
Select View Type, here Attribute View.
Select subtype as "Standard".

Click on Finish Button.

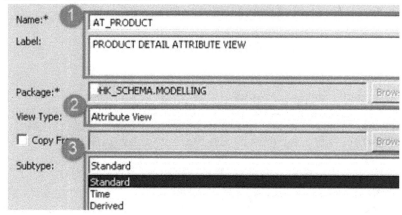

Figure 9-9 Standard Attribute

STEP 3 - Information view editor screen will open.
Detail of each part in Information Editor is as below
-
Scenario Pane: In this pane the following node exists-
Semantics
Data foundation
Detail Pane: In this pane following tab exists -

Column

View Properties

Hierchery
Semantics (Scenario Pane): This node represents output
structure of the view. Here it is Dimension.
Data Foundation (Scenario Pane): This node represents
the table that we use for defining attribute view.
Here we drop table for creating attribute view.
Tab (columns, view Properties, Hierarchies) for
details pane will be displayed.

Local: Here all Local attribute detail will be
displayed.
Show: Filter for Local Attribute.
Detail of attribute.
This is a toolbar for Performance analysis, Find
column, validate, activate, data preview, etc.

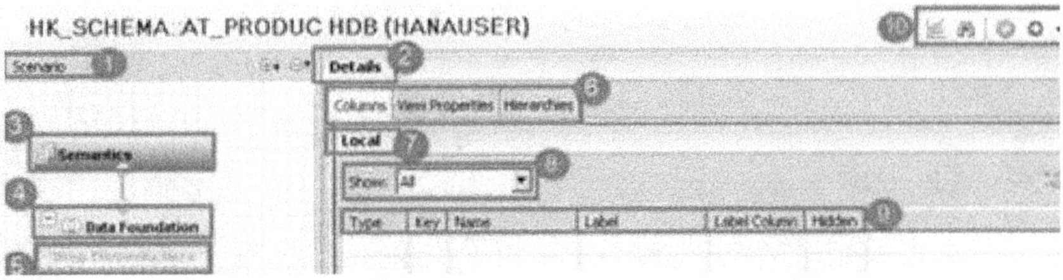

Figure 9-10

STEP 4 - To include database table for creating attribute view, click on data foundation node and follow the instruction step by step as below - Drag table "PRODUCT" and "PRODUCT_DESC" from TABLE node under APRESS_SCHEMA

Drop "PRODUCT" and "PRODUCT_DESC" to data foundation node.
Select field from "PRODUCT" Table as Output In detail pane. Field icon color changes from grey to orange.

Select field from "PRODUCT_DESC" Table as Output in the detail pane. Field Icon color change from grey to orange.
The field selected as output from both the table appear Under Column list in Output Pane.

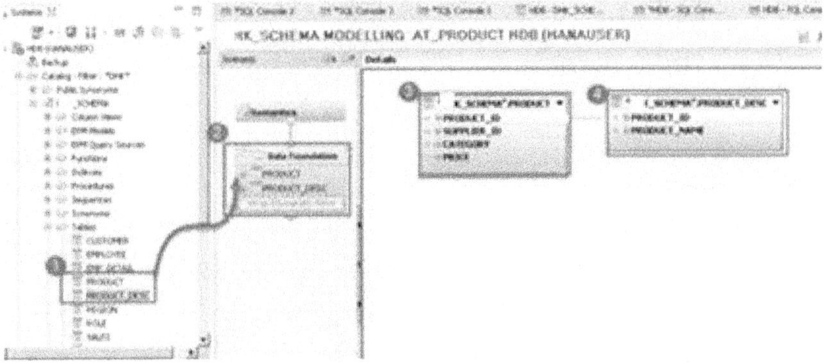

Figure 9-11 Schema Modelling

Join "PRODUCT" table to "PRODUCT_DESC" by "PRODUCT_ID" field.

STEP 5 - Select Join path and Right Click on It and choose Edit option. A screen for Edit Join Condition will appear
Select Join Type as Type "Inner".
Select cardinality as "1..1".

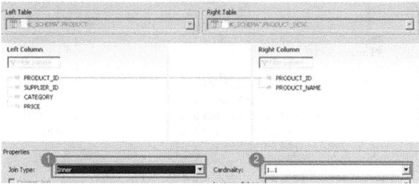

Figure 9-12 Edit Join

After selecting join type click on "OK" button. In next step, we select the column and define a key for output.

STEP 6 - In this step, we will select column and define the key for output
Select Semantic Panel.
Column tab will appear under Detail pane.
Select "PRODUCT_ID" as Key.
Check Hidden option for field PRODUCT_ID_1 (PRODUCT_DESC table field).
Click on validate Button.
After successful validation, click on activate Button.

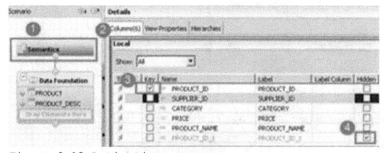

Figure 9-13 Activation

Job Log for validation and activation activity is displayed on bottom of screen on the same page, i.e. Job Log section as below:

☑ Job Log ☒ ⊙ History ⬛ Progress

Current | History

Job Type	System	User	Submitted At
Activation	HDB	HANAUSER	Sun Sep 06 17:20:26 IST 2015
Model Validation	HDB	HANAUSER	Sun Sep 06 17:20:24 IST 2015

Figure 9-14   Job selection

STEP 7 - An attribute view with name "AT_PRODUCT" will be created. To view, refresh the Attribute View folder.
Go to APRESS_SCHEMA->MODELLING Package.
AT_PRODUCT Attribute view display under Attribute view folder.

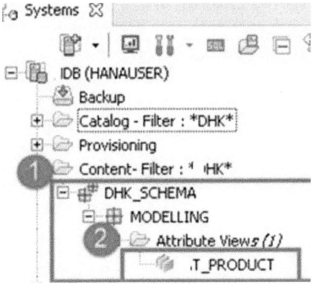

Figure 9-15 attribute view

STEP 8 - To view data in Attribute view,
Select data Preview option from the toolbar.
There will be two option for data view from attribute view -

277

Open in Data Preview Editor (This will display data
with analysis option).
Open in SQL Editor. (This will display output as only
SQL query Output).

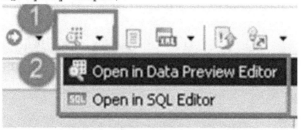

Figure 9-16 Data preview editor

STEP 9 - To see View Attribute data in data Preview
editor -
There are 3 options - Analysis, Distinct and Raw data
Analysis: This is a Graphical representation of the
attribute view.
By selecting Analysis tab, we select Attributes for
Label and Axis format view.
Drag and drop attribute in label axis, it will display
in Label axis(X Axis).
Drag and drop attribute in value axis, it will display
in value axis (Y Axis).
The output will be available in the format of Chart,
Table, Grid, and HTML.

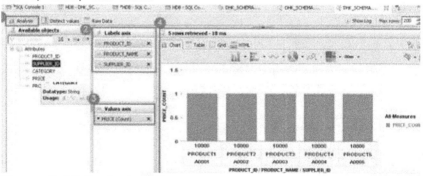

Figure 9-17 Product view

Distinct Values: The distinct value of the column can be displayed here. This will show total no. records for selected attribute.

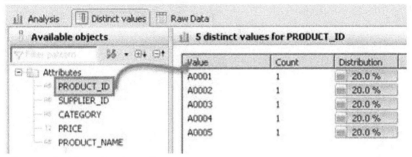

Figure 9-18 Column values

Raw Data tab: This option display data of attribute view in table format.
Click on Raw data tab
It will display the data in table format

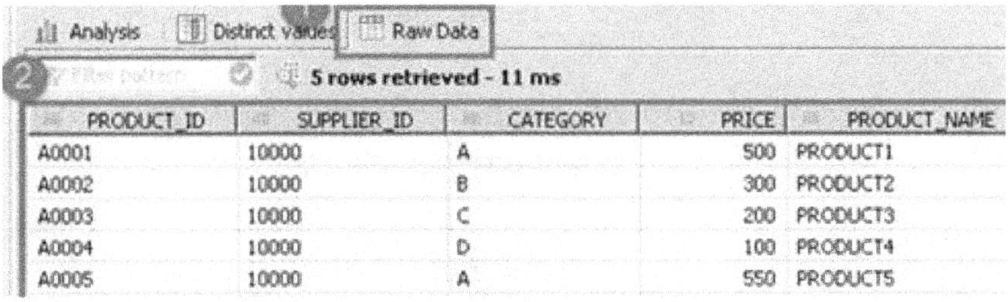

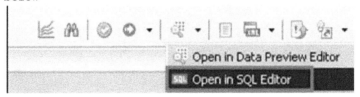

Figure 9-19 Row data

STEP 10 - View Attribute data in from SQL editor as below -

Open in Data Preview Editor
Open in SQL Editor

Figure 9-20 SQL Editor

This option display data through SQL Query from the column view under "SYS_BIC" schema. A column view with name "will created after activation of attribute view

"AT_PRODUCT". This is used to see SQL query used for displaying data from the view.
Display SQL Query for data selection.
Display output.

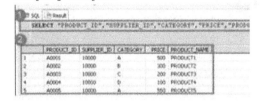

Figure 9-20

Attribute View when activated, a column view under _SYS_BIC schema is created. So, when we run Data Preview, system select data from column view under a _SYS_BIC schema.
Screen shot of column view "AT_PRODUCT" under "_SYS_BIC" Schema of catalog node is as below -

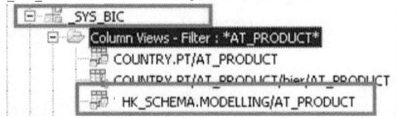

Figure 9-21 Column View

Raw Data - It will show in Table format from Raw Data tab as below:

PRO...	SUPPLIER_ID	CATEGORY	P...	PRODUCT_NAME	PO_NUMBER
A0001	10000	A	500	PRODUCT1	1000001
A0002	10000	B	300	PRODUCT2	1000002
A0003	10000	C	200	PRODUCT3	1000003
A0004	10000	D	100	PRODUCT4	1000004

Figure 9-22 Raw Data

280

Note: SAP HANA Analytic view can contain only Attribute view and does not support Union.

WORKING WITH TABLES

There are different types of joins available in HANA. These are inner, left outer, right outer, full outer, and referential and text joins as illustrated below in Table 9-1 Joins.

Tables, Attributes and Measures

Join Type	Uses
INNER	Records selected based on join criteria matching in both tables a, b
LEFT OUTER JOIN	Records selected from table a with matching record from the table b.
RIGHT OUTER JOIN	Records selected from the table b with matching record from the table a.
FULL OUTER	All records selected from

```
JOIN                    both tables a, b.
```

Let's see an example of joining two tables to explain the join types. You may call it Customer and Sales Order tables as illustrated below in Table 9-2 Customer and Table 9-3 Sales Order.

CustID	Name	Gender	Region	Income
C001	Pradeep	M	TN	2
C002	Suma	F	KA	3
C003	Supriya	F	KA	4

Table 9-2 Customer

TimeID (Day)	ProductID	CustomerID	Units Sold
1	P01	C001	2
2	P02	C002	3
4	P03	C003	4

Table 9-3 Sales Order

Now, let's explore options to create tables using SQL Script as highlighted below:

```
CREATE COLUMN TABLE <Schema_Name>."CUSTOMER" (
      "CustomerID" nvarchar(10) primary key,
      "CustomerName" nvarchar(50)
);
INSERT INTO <Schema_Name>."CUSTOMER" VALUES ('C001',
'Pradeep');
INSERT INTO <Schema_Name>."CUSTOMER" VALUES ('C002',
'Suma');
INSERT INTO <Schema_Name>."CUSTOMER" VALUES ('C003',
'Supriya');
```

```
CREATE COLUMN TABLE <Schema_Name>."SALES_ORDER" (
        "OrderID" integer primary key,
        "CustomerID" nvarchar(10),
        "Product" nvarchar(20),
        "Total_Units" integer
);
INSERT INTO <Schema_Name>."SALES_ORDER" VALUES (1,
'C1','P01', 2);
INSERT INTO <Schema_Name>."SALES_ORDER" VALUES (2,
'C1','P02',3);
INSERT INTO <Schema_Name>."SALES_ORDER" VALUES (3,
'C2','P03',4);
```

Now, you have tables created. Let's see how the join works.

Inner Join:
The INNER JOIN selects the set of records that match in both the Tables.

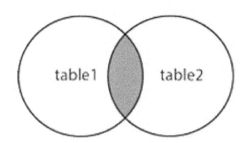

Syntax
```
SELECT T2."Time ID", T1."Cust ID", T1."Name", T2."Product",
T2."Units Sold"
      from "CUSTOMER" AS T1
           INNER JOIN
      "SALES_ORDER" AS T2
           ON T1."CustID" = T2."CustomerID";
```

The result of Inner Join will be like this in Table 9-3
Inner join output:

Time ID	Cust Id	Name	Product	Units Sold
1	C001	Pradeep	P01	2
2	C002	Suma	P02	3
4	C003	Supriya	P03	4

Table 9-3 Inner Join Output.

As discussed inner joins are very effective to fetch
records that match primary key criteria. For example,
Customer ID in the above example. Hence, it is faster to
retrieve data than the outer joins. For example, Inner
joins can be used in a real time analytical views by
joining different master tales.

Now, let's review Left Outer join, which is predominantly
used for fetching "all" record set from the first table
(Table 1) as illustrated below in Figure 9-24, even if
there are columnns with null columns.

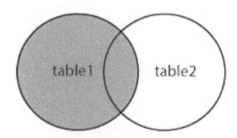

Figure 9-24

Syntax

```
SELECT T2."TImeID", T1."CustID", T1."Name", T2."Product",
T2."Units Sold"
      from "CUSTOMER" AS T1
          LEFT OUTER JOIN
      "SALES_ORDER" AS T2
          ON T1."CustID" = T2."CustomerID";
```

The result of Left Outer Join will be like this in Table 9-3:

Time ID	Cust Id	Name	Product	Units Sold
1	C001	Pradeep	P01	2
2	C002	Suma	P02	3
4	C003	Supriya	P03	4
5	C004	Jason	P04	NULL

Figure 9-3 Left Outer Join

The Right outer join is similar to the left outer join with the only difference being all record set from the second table which is Table 2, even there are null values in the left table as illustrated below in FIgure 9-26.

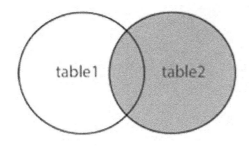

Figure 9-26 Right Outer Join

Syntax

285

```
SELECT T2."Order ID", T2."Customer ID", T1."CusT Name",
T2."Product", T2."Total_Units"
      from "CUSTOMER" AS T1
           RIGHT OUTER JOIN
      "SALES_ORDER" AS T2
           ON T1."CustomerID" = T2."CustomerID";
```

The result of Right Outer Join will be like this in table
Figure 9-27:

Order ID	Customer ID	Cust Name	Product	Total UNITS
101	C01	Jay	Camera	100
102	C01	Jay	Television	200
103	C03	Shiva	Ipod	300
NULL	C04	Krishna	Laptop	NULL
105	C05	NULL	Mobile	500

Figure 9-27 Right Outer Join

Wherase the full outer join will fetch the complete set of
records from both tables as illustrated below in Figure 9-

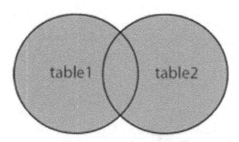

28.
Figure 9-28

Syntax:
```
SELECT T2."Order ID", T1."Customer ID", T1."Cust Name",
T2."Product", T2."Total_Units"
      from "CUSTOMER" AS T1
           FULL OUTER JOIN
      "SALES_ORDER" AS T2
           ON T1."CustomerID" = T2."CustomerID";
```

The result of Full Outer Join will be like this in Table 9-4:

Order ID	Customer ID	Cust Name	Product	Total UNITS
101	C01	Jay	Camera	100
102	C01	Jay	Television	200
103	C03	Shiva	Ipod	300
NULL	C04	Krishna	Laptop	NULL
105	C05	NULL	Mobile	500

Table 9-4 Outer Join Example

Now, let's see text joins.

Text Join

Text Join is used for language-specific data access. These text tables consist of texts to fetch records with specific language keys as illustrated below in Figure 9-29 Text Join sample. Let's say you want to join two tables, a. PRODUCT b. PRODUCT Text

a. PRODUCT

Product ID	Name
1	PRD A
2	PRD B

b. PRODUCT_TEXT

Product ID	Name	Languag	Description
1	PRD A	DE	Description in German
2	PRD A	ENG	Description in English
3	PRD B	DE	Description in German
4	PRD B	ENG	Description in English

Join these two tables as illustrated below:

Product ID	Name	Languag	Description
1	PRD A	DE	Description in German
2	PRD A	ENG	Description in English
3	PRD B	DE	Description in German
4	PRD B	ENG	Description in English

Product ID	Name
1	PRD A
2	PRD B

Figure 9-29 Text Join sample

As illustrated above in the text join sample, the table product is joined with product text table for language English based on user log on session say English. The above sample will fetch description of products in English. Hence, it is easy to identify a specific language description based on the logon, where there is multi language maintained.

Let's see an example of implementing text joins using graphic interface as illustrated below. Right click on your schema and refresh to see the 2 tables created as illustrated below in Figure 9-30 Table join illustrated.

*Sample Code for creating Product, and Product Text tables
with insert values:*

```
CREATE COLUMN TABLE "SAP_HANA_APRESS"."PRODUCT"(
      "PRODUCT_ID" INTEGER,
      "PRODUCT NAME" VARCHAR(2),
       primary key("product_id"));
CREATE COLUMN TABLE "SAP_HANA_APRESS"."PRODUCT_TEXT_TABLE"(
      "PRODUCT_ID" INTEGER,
      "LANGUAGE" VARCHAR(1),
      "PRODUCT_DESCRIPTION" VARCHAR (50),
       primary key ("product_id","language"));
INSERT INTO "SAP_HANA_APRESS"."PRODUCT" values(1,'shirts');
INSERT INTO "SAP_HANA_APRESS"."PRODUCT"
values(2,'trousers');
INSERT INTO "SAP_HANA_APRESS"."PRODUCT_TEXT_TABLE"
values(1,'E','Hawai  Shirts');
INSERT INTO "SAP_HANA_APRESS"."PRODUCT_TEXT_TABLE"
values(2,'H','Houston Trousers')
```

Text Joins and Engine

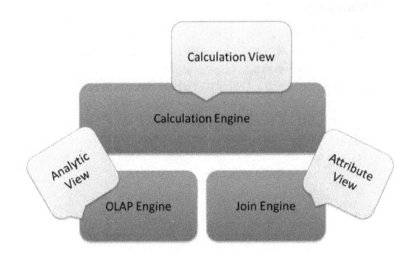

Figure 9-40 SAP HANA Engines

Join Engine is used for attribute views, where OLAP engine is used for analytic views without any calc. columns. There is another option for calculations where in HANA user's calculation engine for analytic views with calc. attributes and views, which is primarily sued for analytical purposes.

You can run the plan visualization on query to identify the engine.

Note: You can visit SAP HANA page for more details of SPS details with offerings such as SaaS offerings. SAP HANA SPS 10 Online Help and Release

---

Summary

In this chapter, we discussed elaborately on SAP HANA DATA Modelling concepts involving creation of tables, schemas, views with different types of views, joins and schemas for a robust data warehouse model to analyses data. Now, you're familiar with types of joins with its usage to build an effective data model for your application.

CHAPTER 10:

Methods and Tools for HANA Implementation

Primary focus in this chapter is to discuss transformation of legacy applications to SAP HANA with mitigated risks. The methods and tools described will help you understand the current situation of legacy applications with the ability to transform to the high performance HANA database using simple tools and techniques discussed throughout this chapter. This may involve custom code changes with necessary hardware change requirements. Needless to say there are lots of challenges in transforming custom code from legacy SAP systems to S/4HANA due to changes in the data structures. I have managed projects with thousands of custom code changes required as part of R/3 upgrade to ECC, which involved hours of manual and automatic code checks to remediate and test non-compliant code. Now, HANA is no exception. A transformation project to HANA may involve analyzing custom code in the repository to check the usage and compatibility in in S/4HANA. Hence, this may be a challenging project to embark for any project manager. I would recommend usage of tools to expedite the remediation process. I have used proprietary tools for quick remediation of custom programs in R/3 to ECC for large Oil & GAS clientele. The situation is no different in an S/4HANA transformation project. Hence, a lot of due diligence is required by the project managers to study the current situation of custom code in the repository, its usage and finally a transformation plan to use a combination of manual and automated checks, remediation to ensure S/4HANA transformation is successful.

Similar to projects in the past where new technology was used for an existing application or an application was upgraded implementation projects can be a risky endeavour. While an implementation of a new application can follow agile development methods, all developers should be familiar with the techniques to be used in order to reap the benefits of an in-memory columnar data store. The bigger issue that follows, for development teams, is the transformation of existing applications to HANA or S/4 HANA. Applications designed to run with a relational data store in a heterogeneous environment are not taking advantage of the features and benefits of a HANA or S/4 architecture and simplification through a pure lift and shift approach. While SAP has done a great job that companies can get going on the new technology, the benefits are only achieved after the recommended changes have been performed.

This chapter focuses primarily on the changes needed to transform existing systems to HANA. We will describe some useful tools to reduce the risk of a transformation project and describe what to look for.

Path to a HANA Transformation

The following section describes the path to transform an existing system to HANA. To be correct, the HANA transformation is a technical upgrade followed by waves of functional improvements to take full functional advantage. We only focus here on the functional upgrade. The typical steps SPDD, SPAU and tools such as SUM, DMO (Reference: DOC-49580 in SCN) will be used. The following high level task list describes a typical implementation from the technical preparation all the way to a go live. Looking at all the components one can identify many of the tasks that are needed with any upgrade tasks. It is therefore also recommended to start with a thorough analysis and a sandbox approach for the upgrade.

We will focus in this chapter on the analysis components to be considered and the optimization of the existing system to leverage the advantages of the new architecture. Before you start on the path to SAP HANA, a Proper analysis of all custom code aspects is necessary. A major transformation is always a good opportunity to clean up the system, make it more maintainable, retire code, improve the quality, perform a custom code impact analysis. SAP offers a variety of tools that are coming with the license. Before a transformation is started, the existing landscape can be used for preparatory steps. It is advised to look at the following:

Housekeeping Jobs

It is essential to get an overview of all your custom code and analyze which custom code (known as "Z" ABAP programs in SAP) is really necessary for your business. Typically, over time a lot of unnecessary components have been accumulated. This has two main reasons. On the one side it is the project teams and the constant need to perform projects under time pressure. On the other side the ABAP language and the technical evolution and capabilities are always evolving. As a fact with the transformation to HANA you are facing such a major technology improvement. A landscape that has evolved over the years collects a lot of the issues which are called Technical Depth. It helps you to analyze technical depth to be able to clean it.

The need from business users to enhance systems periodically will not change since writing custom code transactions is the only way to map the process that distinguishes you from the competition. Buying any ERP system or off the shelf App in general does not help you to be the leader in your market if your competition buys the same system. Only the strategic processes reflected in custom code, which indicates your specific logic implemented in the programming are giving you the competitive edge. Turnaround of the projects are often business crucial and the developers are getting it to work. They are artist and very creative when it comes to finding solutions. Similar code is copied and adjusted, the quick development short cuts are taken, I would argue most of the time with the best intentions to try something out, get feedback improve the results. Once it is working and the business users have seen it the obvious happens, they want the feature now. So often the developers are not given the time to clean up the code, look at this performance glitch and finish the error and exception handling the way it should. Even worse when security issues are going in production like that debugging breakpoint that the developer put in with an 'if' clause to only use it with his SY-UNAME. For example, as key pointers such as missing authority checks is a non-compliance, etc. Another fact is that experienced developers are hard to change, if they know it works this way they continue to use the constructs that are actually obsolete. Fortunately, the times of unstructured programming is gone, we know though from our analysis the undefined identifiers are still used and often lead to run time errors. All this is technical depth that comes from the development teams.

ABAP first appeared in 1983 and is a cross platform language. SAP has done a great job to keep it always downward compatible. This bears, however, also the disadvantage that a lot of old coding constructs will accumulate since there is no need to clean it up and companies will "not touch a running system" unless it is necessary. ABAP is one of the few languages that allow different programming paradigms to be mixed. One can use unstructured, structured and object oriented language constructs. With the evolving technologies companies are faced with modernizing the source code since well written object oriented functionality will have problems in dealing with memory management.

With about 10 times more possible ways to implement business functionality, and programs that have been developed 15-20 years or longer ago there is a high likelihood there is a lot of unnecessary coding.

SAP continues to renew the language. New method calls replace obsolete function calls, new source code syntax takes advantage of new technology and perform faster, more stable and are easier to maintain. SAP's Code Inspector tool often brings up hundreds of thousands issues. Not all of them need to be fixed, it actually bears a high risk, cost and time component that outweighs the benefits of having clean code. However, it is strongly advised to take a closer look before a transformation.

Before transforming the system to HANA it is advised to eliminate unused objects. Get an overview of your custom code and analyze code which is not necessary to run your business. SAP offer in the newer version UPL, it is a reliable tool and you can create a custom code directory containing only the objects used in production. The other objects can be retired; there are many ways to phase them out since most business users have a hard time to make the decision functionality is not needed anymore. One example is to comment transactions out of bring up a message when it is called.

Another good housekeeping advice is about performance. All the custom code you have in your systems and the thousands of objects is not running with the same priority and to the same amount. As a fact, often only as little as 20% is frequently used based on the industry standards. Programs that run once a quarter or even once a year are typically not in the focus of performance improvement since they run in batch jobs anyhow. It is the transactions that are called daily thousands of times that matter. SAP's SQL monitor will give some insight to find those programs. Measure your old productive system for 2-4 weeks, sort the results in transaction SQLM by "number of execution" and you have your candidates. You might ask yourself the question, why is this necessary? SAP HANA will not always perform faster. At the end it is different database architecture and goes from a relational to a column based access.

Technical Preparation and Analysis

The technical preparation is split in the following tasks:

- Repository Analysis
- Code reduction Analysis
- Hardware sizing
- Custom Code Analysis

Repository Analysis

An object repository analysis will show all the objects that need to be moved to the new environment. It is important to decide which objects are not necessary, or objects that are clones of standard that are bound to use inefficient coding. The former can be archived; the latter can be evaluated for possible rewriting or replacement through new standard programs or processes.

Once all objects have been identified it is important to find out what changes the objects need to not only run but also use the new architecture in the best way. The changes are primarily in the way the source code accesses the database. For some companies, Business Suite on HANA or S/4 HANA offers business benefits through consolidations of multiple systems since the data reside in one HANA instance. ABAP code is running on SAP HANA just like on any other database. Due to the architecture some SQLs run faster on e.g. when selecting columns without an index. However, ABAP code which relies on specific capabilities or features of the database used in the existing system must be corrected. The following areas need to be analysed:

a. Mandatory corrections of code to avoid functional issues

All ABAP code, SQL code or database calls which build on specific features of the predecessor database like native SQL, assumptions on sort order of OpenSQL queries, etc.

b. Recommended SQL performance optimization

In order to avoid performance degradation there are a few obvious areas that one can analyze in advance. Often this optimization is not specific to HANA and will also bring results in the existing system. There are "Golden Rules" where SQL performance can be accomplished.

4. Reduce the amount of data exchanged by retrieving only the records needed

5. Minimize the amount of transferred data by getting only the fields needed

6. Reduce the number of data transfers with less queries

7. For data that are accessed very frequently, enable buffering at the application serve

c. HANA Code Pushdown techniques (or code-to-data)

To speed up custom code processes significantly, code pushdown techniques exploit the features of the new database paradigm in the best way. The fundamental concept behind moving code to data is that access and light preparatory processing is done in memory in the database server instead at the application layer (application server). The database layer has been optimized for parallelization, in memory operations for sorting, filtering and organizing of data results. This brings not only the advantage of faster in-memory processing, but also reduces data transfer between application layer and the database layer, if used judiciously of course. To achieve this, ABAP code segments can be created as CDS or HANA Views and AMDP procedures.

Performance improvement of 100 or 1000 times faster and more can be achieved.

Please note that the application re-architecting requires a new approach in ABAP application coding. SAP has evolved the ABAP language to use new features that enables succinct coding and faster access to data. Most important new features are meshes and OpenSQL improvements. The most important aspect of the new programming paradigm is however the adoption of a coding style where batches of data are fetched from the database server. The old style of coding where data are fetched as single rows from the database, in loops is obsolete and inflexible. Such a change in the programming paradigm will also improve performance in any enterprise database environment, not only in in-memory databases.

Archiving Analysis

A transformation to a new system is always a good opportunity to archive a lot of the data and processes used in the existing system. Reducing the size of the system and throwing out what is not needed or duplicate is the easiest way to reduce a systems total cost of ownership. Any line of code needs maintenance and costs money for an organization.

A usage analysis is the first and obvious way to reduce unnecessary code. Analysis of various systems shows that often less than 50% of the custom transactions are used. SAP is offering various tools to look at the usage of custom code transactions. The transaction ST03 which runs in all the common releases that is out today. The logging has to be switched on ideally for 12 months so you are covering also end of quarter and end of year programs. The results need to be handled with caution and cannot be taken easily to retire an object. The reason is simple, if a program calls another program, the second program will not be in the list of used programs. With a dependency analysis of programs one can catch the remaining programs, so it requires still manual work.

Another way more accurate way to find out about the usage is UPL. UPL is clearly the superior technology for tracking which code is being executed on a system which is done at the kernel level since it records which objects are being executed at a more granular level. The prerequisite for using UPL is that the system has to be at a relatively new Support pack level while being available in latest

NetWeaver 7.0 and above releases. All new SAP tools rely on UPL rather than ST03 data such as the Solution Manager Business Process Change Analyzer (BPCA) and Scope Estimate Analyzer (SEA). For a useful sample size, it is recommended to have at least had 12 months of usage data available. So plan accordingly and start the usage collection as soon as possible.

Identified transactions and associated artefacts (source code, DDIC objects) can be retired. That will reduce the source code in many systems by 50% or more.

Key benefits:
+ Low CPU / runtime and memory overhead
+ Fine level of granularity
+ captures dynamic code execution
+ supported on most NetWeaver systems
Minor drawbacks as following:
- No runtime / DB information is captured
- Not capturing entry points such as transaction or batch invocation

Another area of reducing source code that goes to the new environment is clones. Many custom transactions have been copied from standard transaction and adjusted. Developers like to do that when a customer transaction covers most of the functionality a user likes but not all. There is a chance that in the following version of SAP and specifically in new S/4 functionality the adjustment is not needed anymore since the new standard functionality offers all that is needed.

Similar to the source code one should also look at the data.

Hardware Sizing

Basic step is to execute the HANA Sizing Report (reference: OSS note # 1872170)

This will create ABAP reports /SDF/HDB_SIZING (or ZNEWHDB_SIZE if done manually); the results should be cross referenced with sanity check as outlined in OSS note 1793345. This will also give sizing information relevant for S/4HANA.

New option not only Intel Xenon but also IBM Power (OSS Note 2218464).

Naturally you need to consider virtualization, such as VMWare vSphere (OSS Note 2315348)

Consider data growth and future uses that are currently unknown.

For SoH and S/4HANA you can still only use Scale Up vs. Scale Out (which is an option for BW). So giving you some headroom or choosing expandable HW seems wise. Other aspects to be thought of are the balance of execution between application and database layer. Inefficiently coded applications do not experience processing spikes, since they mainly wait for data from the database layer. Should the code become efficient by retrieving and processing large data chunks, one will notice that the application server will experience a heavier load and spikes in it. On top of that, an in-memory database will deliver the data very fast, so the wall time on the application side will be minimized.

Extensibility will also drive HW sizing, HCP can be used to innovate in modern languages not relying on SAP NetWeaver. Questions remain about why not use a stable environment that powers your core business for innovation, licensing might play a significant role if SAP does not see the light an offers reasonable licensing term for native and mixed used (SAP core apps but customer applications).

Data archiving strategy must be reviewed (or established). You don't want to buy more than you need. Not all customers are comfortable buying a database license based on data volume, since it a change from known licensing models.

Dynamic tiering and automatic data aging …

Technologies that are emerging as complimentary to pure HANA are Hadoop, SAP VORA (Apache Spark ++) which can provide cheaper and fast processing on larger scale than HANA alone.

Changes to the Existing Source Code

In order to take full advantage of the HANA features the existing code needs to be changed. One can categorize these changes in the following areas

- HANA Code Compliance (HCC)

- HANA Performance Optimization (HPO)

- HANA Code Pushdown Techniques

- S/4 HANA specific rules

- Modernization of source code

To each of these areas the following changes will bring the best results.

HANA Code Compliance

HANA code Compliance actually starts with having a Unicode enabled system. From EHP 8 onwards (NetWeaver 7.50), SAP supports only Unicode. While many systems are already Unicode enabled, the once that are not need to do this the latest when they move to EHP 8 / NetWeaver 7.50 or HANA.

Non-determination execution of queries without explicit ordering.
This come in two flavors, since most Cluster and Pool Table will be converted to regular Transparent Tables SAP no longer guarantees the implicit ordering of data by primary key. In cases where the code actually depends on the ordering of the data it is required to enforce ordering of the result set (either in OpenSQL or in ABAP) to retain function operation. SAP's Code Inspector provides detection capabilities for this case as illustrated below. Let's look at the code sample illustrated below in Figure. 10-1 code sample.

```
814    SELECT bukrs belnr gjahr
815           buzei bschl koart
816           shkzg mwskz dmbtr
817           pswbt pswsl zuonr
818           sgtxt kostl aufnr
819           hkont kunnr lifnr
820           prctr anlnl umskz     "31.01.2012 gerhardt
821    INTO CORRESPONDING FIELDS OF TABLE pt_table
822    FROM bseg
823    FOR ALL ENTRIES IN lt_bkpf
824    WHERE bukrs = pa_bukrs
825      AND belnr = lt_bkpf-belnr
826      AND gjahr = lt_bkpf-gjahr.
```

Figure 10-1 Code sample before transformation

```
1058   SELECT bukrs belnr gjahr
1059          buzei bschl koart
1060          shkzg mwskz dmbtr
1061          pswbt pswsl zuonr
1062          sgtxt kostl aufnr
1063          hkont kunnr lifnr
1064          prctr anlnl umskz     "31.01.2012 gerhardt
1065   INTO CORRESPONDING FIELDS OF TABLE pt_table
1066   FROM bseg
1067   FOR ALL ENTRIES IN lt_bkpf
1068   WHERE bukrs = pa_bukrs
1069     AND belnr = lt_bkpf-belnr
1070     AND gjahr = lt_bkpf-gjahr ORDER BY PRIMARY KEY.           "$smart: #600
```

Figure 10-2 Code Sample after transformation to HANA

The second case is an optimization done post transformation process. The ordering of the result set from SELECT statements that SAP explicitly stated to not be guaranteed.

These cases are much harder to find and Code Inspector does not in all cases provide a complete coverage.

These are coding best practices to follow as part of HANA transformation project such as the following:

    a. Direct write access to the underlying physical table of Cluster and Pool Tables.

    a. Native SQL must be eliminated since it will not be compatible with HANA in most cases. ADBC based access should also always be reviewed to assure compliance with HANA.

    b. Code that checks the existence of indexes required in production to assure proper execution will fail since HANA does not require indexes for fast access.

Let's review best practices as part of HANA transformation project in terms of hardware sizing with specific custom code optimization.

HANA Performance Optimization

The following rules highlight the custom code best practices to ensure high performance of custom applications, which is the ABAP custom code running on HANA system. Users do have options to checkout proprietary tools that are capable of automatic execution such as smart shift proprietary tools to execute the rule based options discussed in this chapter as illustrated below in Figure 10-3.

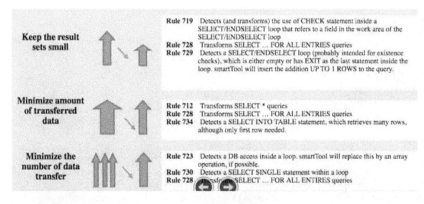

Figure 10-3 HANA Performance Optimization for custom code

SAP's recommended approach of fixing the HCC issues and then performing performance testing to identify performance bottlenecks seems outdated (SQL/Performance monitoring based). The execution of this trial and error based approach seems risky in disappointing users that test the system and experience potentially significantly slower execution that can/will then be remedied later. We recommend a source code centric approach that identifies areas of improvements and in the best case automatically adjusts the code to take advantage of HANA's capabilities (see section with Golden Rules) and prevents the users from being upset with a non-optimized system that cost the business a lot of money.

There are many different patterns where ABAP code (including OpenSQL) can be optimized, below are some common patterns:

A very common pattern is the use of SELECT *, which selects all the columns from the DB table but in most cases only a small subset of the columns are used. In this case HANA and the ABAP runtime waste resources and time in processing the unused columns on the database, transferring them over the network and instantiating records on the application server.
In order to correct this problem it must be determined which columns are required, which is needless to say a very difficult task if done manually (CI offers some support but is not perfect). The quick and "dirty" fix is to just change the query to select the required columns but that still wastes resources in instantiating the resulting records. The proper but more time consuming approach is to change the data structures that hold the data to only contain the required fields. Special case needs to be taken when a query is reused in multiple cases or if the query is embedded in a method or function group where developers have an expectation that the content of an entire table records is being returned.

Reducing complexity – Repository simplification

A complex repository has a large impact on a smooth transformation to business suite on HANA or S/4 HANA. To analyze and remediate the existing source code, the involved resources need to spend quite more time on source code that is not used anymore. In addition, the maintenance effort is higher for all the objects that are kept in the repository. Clones and similar objects that address changing business requirements can be consolidated. Obsolete functionality is not kept up to date and often calls obsolete functions and includes obsolete source code syntax. The complexity hinders organization changes and consolidations become more difficult.

Therefore the tracking and visibility into the repository needs to be increased to reduce this complexity.

Revert Clones and use standard

This is a process business analysts need to perform since there is a limit for automation. While clones and similar objects can be identified it cannot be decided with a rule based approach whether custom code objects that describe a business process and a standard business process are identical. A CRUD Analysis (Change, Read, Update, and Delete) can illustrate what tables, fields and files are accessed but only a human with knowledge about the process can make the final decision whether the custom process can be replaced by a standard process.

Outlook to S/4HANA

We are changing functionality based on the business requirements. It might be too frequent depending on the changing business needs from time-to-time. Hence, it makes sense to assess compatibility in mind. But we are changing the solution. This implies that you need a simplification item DB, which is the content of the database for custom code check tool. The custom code check tool helps you to get an overview of the current solution scope and also the SAP Business suite release that does not match to the scope and data structure of SAP S/4HANA. Now, let's take a look at the SAP HANA simplification DB to support in the transformation as illustrated below:

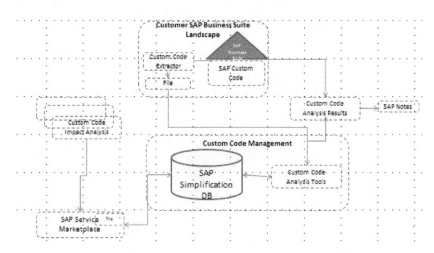

Figure 10-4 Simplification Item Database

Simplification-DB overview

A dedicated simplification item database (S-DB) is available for NW 7.5, which is primarily used for custom code management to gain insights about the usage of customer code. The content of the S-DB is based on the application specific lists about changed entities which development will constantly maintain and update. This tool checks compliance of custom code with SAP S/4HANA data structures and scope. It highlights the differences between the classical business suites with S/4HANA.

The following figure 10-5 describes basically the supporting custom code management approach related to SAP S/4HANA.

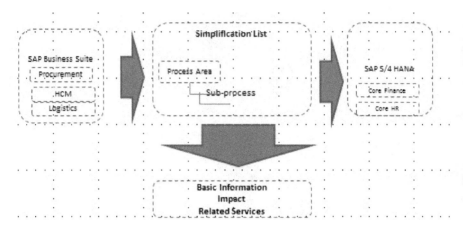

Figure 10-5 Simplification List

A simplification item contains different detailed information about simplifications, impact and related services such as basic information of the technical and functional implementation details.

The Simplification-Items are edition/release dependent. In the first collection round we are focusing on SAP S/4HANA, on premise edition 1511.

Simplification Category

We have the following categories of simplifications:

8. Change of existing functionality

Functionality which is adapted in detail (e.g. data model changes removal of aggregates or the Material Master Field length extension) / required primarily technical migration. From a business process and end user point of view, basically stays the same as before - but might come with custom code adaption effort on customer side.

9. Consolidation of existing functionality

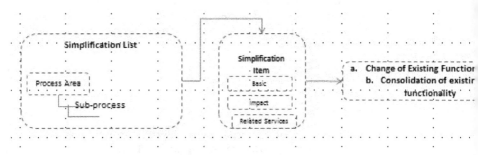

Figure 10-6 Simplification Item List

10. Simplification Items:

    a. Impact Analysis - In the impact section the technical and the business impact will be described with the following categories

    b. Technical Impact - analysis of the technical architecture, stack details &

    c. Custom Code Impact - analysis of custom code and its impact

Here we mentioned if we have custom code impact. In this case the objects which are adapted are listed and additionally included in the Simplification Database as basis for the custom code check tools (executed on customers on premise installation). These changed entities are maintained in appropriate item lists (transaction SE01)

System Conversion Pre-Checks

Here application specific checks are listed which will be provided to check the "readiness" of the appropriate start release.

XPRA

Here automated program logic is listed, which need to be executed within the system conversion steps (Software Update Manager, Maintenance Planer)

Business Impact

Here the business impact on business processes and user interfaces are described in Table 10-1 S/4HANA simplification list.

Note: In the current phase the customer need a NW 7.50 installation to execute the custom code check. In future cloud based code analysis are planned.

Table 10-1 S/4HANA Simplification List – E.g. Sales & Distribution

Topic	Description	Pre-Check	Impact
Data Model in Sales Order	Simplified	Yes	No
Data Model in pricing	Simplified	Yes	No
Foreign Trade	Replaced with GTS	Yes	Yes

Figure 10-6 Simplification List - Example

The customer can extract his customer code from source system and create a similar file with this information (see SAP note # 2185390 for further details). This custom code extractor file can be imported in the NW7.50 custom code check tool, it checks for the code compatibility in target instance. Best part is that the tool analyses core modifications, Z-custom code with usage analysis and provides recommendations to either reset it to standards.

Pre-checks to S/4HANA

Transition path to HANA is illustrated below in Figure 10-8:

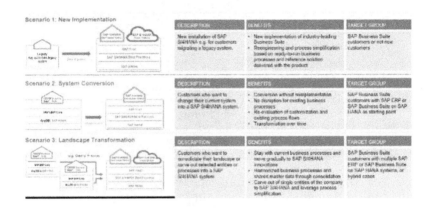

Figure 10-8 Transition path to HANA

If it is migration using System conversion or Landscape transformation, then probably all old (and redundant) custom codes, existing order types also will be carried over without much of transformation process. Perhaps a hybrid approach using System conversion for core ECC functionality and then a partially new implementation is a better option to resolve most of the conflicts. For example, you may find restrictions for specific countries such as Brazil, Portugal, Russia, and Chili. Refer SAP Note # 2228890 S4H 1511 Country specific version release info and restriction lists for specific details. You may want to check prior to the migration in terms of the functional impact as well in specific modules such as Finance, Supply Chain, Manufacturing and project systems relevant to your configuration. You may want to evaluate specific constraints in BOM, MRP areas of impact as well to ensure a clean migration strategy to HANA. For example, classic G/L migration to new G/L is mandatory. Similarly, customer and vendor master will be replaced by the business partner. There are changes in the material master CHAR length and Sales data model, Foreign trade, hence each of these areas have to be planned as per the migration strategy. There are changes to the SD credit management which his replaced by financial supply chain (FSCM) with rebate processing replaced by settlement management etc.

BEST PRACTICES OF HANA IMPLEMENTATION

Coding best practices:

a. Join on key columns or index columns. Hence, you must avoid calculations before aggregation on line item level
b. Prefer column reads for reporting to increase query performance
c. Use filter data amount as early as possible in the lower layers (For example. constraints, where clause & analytic privileges)
d. Reduce transfer between views such as using 'CE' functions instead of SQL
e. Aggregate data records using groups, thereby reducing columns
f. Avoid large data results sets between HANA database and client applications

Recommendations

The below points should be considered during development process for enhanced performance experience:

a. Use pre-defined parameters available at Universe layer to avoid performance bottlenecks, thereby reducing records fetched at universe level.

a. Enable END-SQL paramter in the business layer, therby restricting the universe to fetch only 50k records at a time as illustrated below in Figure 10-9 .

Edit Query Script Parameters

Add, delete, or change the value of query script parameters.

Parameters

Name	Value
AUTO_UPDATE_QUERY	No
CHECK_INTEGRITY	false
CUMULATIVE_OBJECT_WHERE	No
DISABLE_ARRAY_FETCH_SIZE_OPTIMIZATION	No
DISTINCT_VALUES	DISTINCT
END_SQL	50000
EVAL_WITHOUT_PARENTHESIS	No
FORCE_SORTED_LOV	No
THOROUGH_AGGREGATE_AWARE	Yes
TRUST_CARDINALITIES	No

Figure 10-9 SQL Query script parameters

- Use table partitioning to distribute rows across partitions.
    - Load balancing – to distribute the load across servers
    - Parallization – operations can be run in parallel as threads
    - Partion Pruning – To speed up query run-time, queries are analyzed to see if they match the partition specification of a table.
    - Explicit partition handling – It indicates applications can actively control partitions

    - for example by adding partitions that will hold the data for an upcoming month such as huge volume sales data as illustrated below in Figure 10-10.

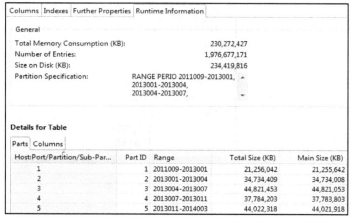

Host:Port/Partition/Sub-Par...	Part ID	Range	Total Size (KB)	Main Size (KB)
1	1	2011009-2013001	21,256,042	21,255,642
2	2	2013001-2013004	34,734,409	34,734,008
3	3	2013004-2013007	44,821,453	44,821,053
4	4	2013007-2013011	37,784,203	37,783,803
5	5	2013011-2014003	44,022,318	44,021,918

Figure 10-10 Run Time information

- Visualization plan — SAP HANA comes with in-build perspective called Plan Viz perspective, this should be used for creating and evaluating the SQL queries, so that maximum performance can be achieved as illustrated below:

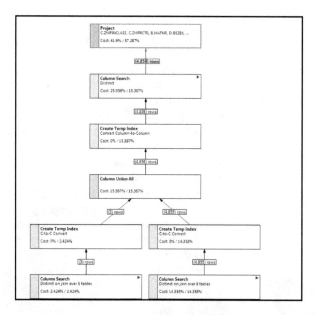

Figure 10-9 Visualization Plan

- Scheduling procedures in off peak hours - Stored procedures should be scheduled during off peak hours as these can impact the system performance by using the maximum amount of available memory.

  Below figure shows memory usage during stored procedure run.

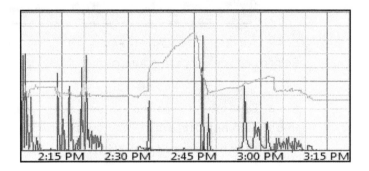

Figure 10-10 Memory Usage Analysis

- Keep tables as narrow as possible. HANA has a cost for columnar inserts, so you get a reduction in data load performance with an increase in the number of columns.

- Use Intelligence assistance provided in SQL editor and function editors to Provides both the function Syntax details and code Examples in SAP HANA SPS 7.02

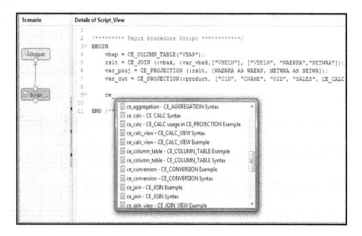

Figure 10-11 Sample SQL Script for Performance Improvements

Below points should be kept in mind as they can hinder the HANA performance:

- Running reports with huge data volume

- Reports that are run without any filters can get unexpected no of rows as a results from HANA system and that can cause performance issues.
- Scheduling stored procedures at on peak hours as illustrated below in Figure 10-12

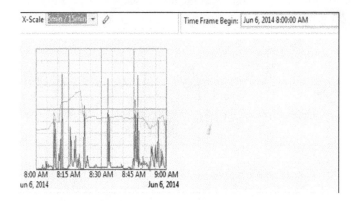

Figure 10-12 Peak load memory utilization

- Table replication (tables having larger amount of dataset) and stored procedures should not run at same time.

    - Whenever initial load for the large table is done it can take ample amount of time as for larger tables we could be having multiple partitions. Merge operation requires some CPU time as well as resident memory. Hence can interfere with the stored procedure run.

Thread Type	Thread Method	Thread Detail
LogBackupThread		
BackupExe_LogWaitForBackintConn		
MergedogMonitor	merging	1 of 1 table(s): _SYS_SPLIT_CE12000~14
SaveMergedAttributeThread	prepareDeltaMergeSave	IndexName: PE2_PH2:_SYS_SPLIT_CE12000~14en Attribute: 266/RAUBE
MergeAttributeThread	prepareDeltaMerge	IndexName: PE2_PH2:_SYS_SPLIT_CE12000~14en Attribute: 268/WWSST
MergeAttributeThread	prepareDeltaMerge	IndexName: PE2_PH2:_SYS_SPLIT_CE12000~14en Attribute: 267/EXTWG

Figure 10-13 CPU Thread Details

- Proper HANA sizing needs to be done for better performance results as illustrated in the Table 10-2 HANA sizing parameters.

315

Table 10-2 HANA sizing parameters

- HANA creates the backup files regularly hence consuming memory, these backup files should be deleted regularly after taking them on external drives.

- SAP Notes should be implemented for proper utilization of the HANA performance.

- Partitioning of table should be done for faster query results. Consider your partitioning strategy. On a single node appliance 3-5 partitions is normally a good number for optimal insert performance.

- When data is replicating in SAP HANA then Date field data type is changed from DATE to NVARCHAR.

- Avoid using VARCHARs if you don't need them. Fixed width CHAR is better for smaller fields, and INTEGER fields are even better.

Table 10-2: Coding best practices

Good	Bad
CREATE COLUMN TABLE "SCHEMA"."TABLE" ("TIME" TIME, "FIELD1" CHAR(1), "FIELD2" CHAR(16), "FIELD3" CHAR(4), "MEASURE1" INT, "MEASURE2" DECIMAL(7,4)) PARTITION BY ROUNDROBIN PARTITIONS 12;	CREATE COLUMN TABLE "SCHEMA"."TABLE" ("TIME" TIMESTAMP, "FIELD1" VARCHAR(255), "FIELD2" VARCHAR(255), "FIELD3" VARCHAR(255), "MEASURE1" BIGINT, "MEASURE2" DECIMAL(15,7) "UNUSED_FIELD" VARCHAR(2000));

The adoption trend for software-as-a-service (SaaS) is significant for SAP's business. They have more than $1 billion in subscription now and they want to grow it over the next five years at a much faster rate.

SAP HANA SPS 10 Online Help and Release notes: http://help.sap.com/hana_platform/

Summary

To summarize, you have learnt the best practices of transforming legacy databases to HANA DB, the high performance is guaranteed with custom code changes as described in this chapter. Moreover, a careful planning and execution of hardware sizing can help in eliminating performance bottlenecks. In order to leverage the best performing HANA database, you must embark on a custom code clean-up and performance optimization of the existing hardware and infrastructure in order to ensure high performance of applications. We have elaborately discussed the strategy for transformation with best practices.

■　■　■

Chapter 11:
SAP Business Suite - S/4HANA

The key objectives of this chapter are to walk you through the maze of SAP Business Suite S/4 for HANA to discuss roadmap of S/4HANA and deployment strategy. Let's take a minute to appreciate SAP's evolution till-date since 1972 started from R/1, then progressed to R/2, R/3 and finally HANA was launched by SAP in the year 2011 with In-memory Computing. HANA was born based on the extensive research, innovation and development to re-build its technology to the next generation HANA platform, thus providing platform as services with the power of HANA DB in a robust architecture as illustrated below in Figure 11-1 with over 74% of world's transaction revenue touches on SAP system with over 282k customers as on 2015.

With the forecast of 9B mobile users all over the World, SAP has extended its portfolio into enterprise mobility by leveraging mobile platform with front-end using FIORI. Now, you have one SAP HANA cloud platform providing all the benefits to the customers never than before. You've the consolidated platform that offers robust architecture with consumable services for the current and next generation enterprises with analytics running 1800x times faster than ever before. For example, an existing organization with huge investments done in on-premises solution can perhaps consolidate using HANA benefits on-cloud as well as on-premises. As an alternative solution customers can exhaust benefits by directly launching into HANA Cloud without any capital expenses.

Figure 11-1 Evolution of HANA

S/4HANA Roadmap

Thus, HANA has transitioned from shop-floor based software with an image of complex and expensive software to a lean platform that runs on HANA. It's made simple for complex solutions as illustrated below in Figure 11-2, thus encompasses Application, database and integration services offered by HANA platform expanding into BIG data and enterprise mobility as illustrated below.

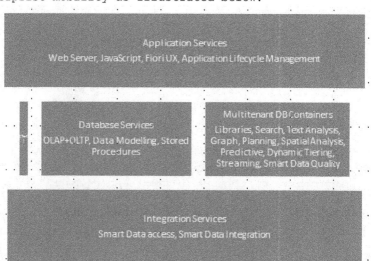

Figure 11-2 SAP HANA, In-memory platform

The future roadmap of HANA is illustrated below in Figure 11-3. The evolution of HANA started as an in memory platform and then extended in to business warehouse. Now, it has expanded as S/4HANA that is the future ERP suite for business with simplified data model.

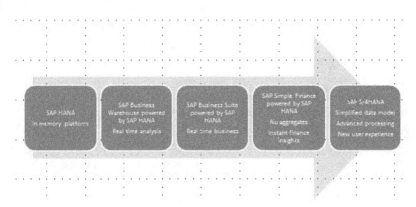

Figure 11-3 SAP HANA Roadmap

The overall SAP's strategy has changed to a simplified data model with new user experience and advance process. Customers have choice of deployment such as on-premises, on-cloud or hybrid etc. Let's look at the future strategy as illustrated below in Figure 11-4 SAP HANA Evolution

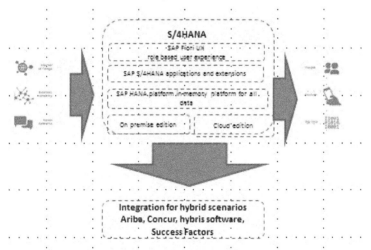

Figure 11-4 S/4HANA Evolution

Eventually, SAP had transitioned its data model into simple structure for high performance as illustrated below in Figure 11-5 with SAP Finance with aggregates and indices

of 10-Inserts, and 5-updates to 5-Inserts and 0-Updates in the new SAP HANA data model.

Figure 11-5 Core Data Model changes in Simple Finance

Some of the features in Simple Finance in HANA are a near real-time period closing, with better oversight through new dashboards. It's easy to analyze profitability and cost analysis with project forecasts in the new data model saves turn-around time in data processing. With the new arrival of logistics and manufacturing enables faster decision support, KPI-driver process control and real-time execution. Now, let's see the roadmap of SAP S/4 HANA as illustrated below in Figure 11-6 SAP S/4 HANA Roadmap which is a clear indication of its strategy on-cloud for analytics and enterprise mobility platform on HANA.

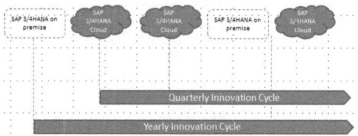

Figure 11-6 SAP S/4HANA Roadmap

Let's observe S/4HANA deployment options as illustrated in Figure 11-7 S/4HANA Deployment options

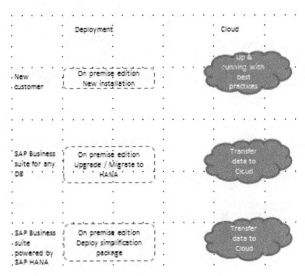

Figure 11-7 S/4HANA Deployment options

As per plan (1), new customers can choose on-premises or cloud options by using a simple installation and migration planning in three steps a. Plan, b. Install and c. Import done with SAP consulting. Plan (2) is for customers those who're already running SAP ERP on any database. The additional step will be migration from legacy DB to HANA DB using tools as illustrated below in Figure 11-8 Migration as 'one step migration' plan offered by SAP.

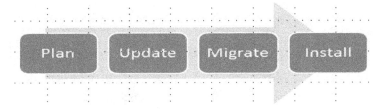

Figure 11-8 Legacy DB to HANA Migration

Plan (3) is for customers who run SAP Business suite. Migration to S/4 HANA for Plan (3) customers can be done in two steps: 1. Plan (Identify key scenarios) and 2. Install (Install exchange innovation) with a detailed deployment options illustrated below in Figure 11-8 Detailed Deployment Options.

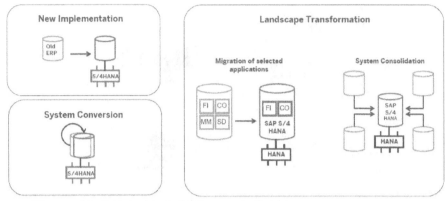

Figure 11-8 Detailed Deployment Options

Each of the above scenarios is possible via rapid deployment model. For example, a green field implementation can directly venture in

Option (1) - New Implementation as illustrated above. Second option is to install S/4HANA using software provisioning manager (SWPM) and migrate legacy data using migration server/migration workbench as illustrated below

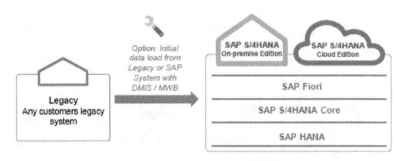

in Figure 11-8 Option (1) New Implementation

Figure 11-8 Option (1) New Implementation

Option (2) - System Conversion

Those who are already running SAP ERP or Business suite can do a direct migration to the S/4 HANA can transition in one step as illustrated below in Figure 11-9 Option (2) Migration using rapid database migration of SAP business suite to SAP S/4 HANA in one step using SUM with DMO.

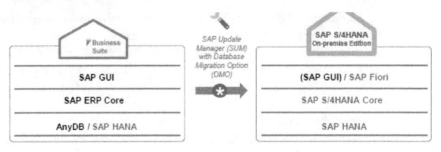

Figure 11-9 System Conversion (One Step Migration)

Option (3) - System Conversion & SAP S/4HANA Finance

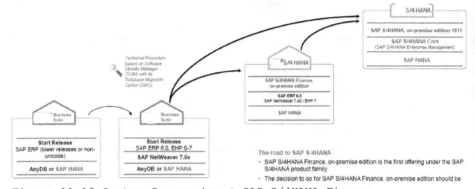

Figure 11-10 System Conversion & SAP S/4HANA Finance

Option (4) - Alternatively, customers have the option
(4) for a landscape transformation as illustrated below in
Figure 11-11 Landscape Transformation

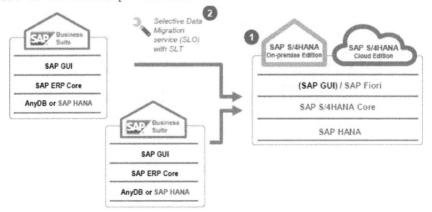

Figure 11-11 Landscape Transformation

The above Figure 11-11 illustrates system conversion and S/4HANA migrations to the on-premises edition 1511 for customers who want to consolidated their landscape or carve out selected processes in to SAP S/4HANA. Perhaps this is based on the business benefits and decision by the IT management of the business. For example, those who have fragmented landscape can ease the maintenance by consolidating into S/4HANA as illustrated below in Figure 11-12 Consolidated Landscape

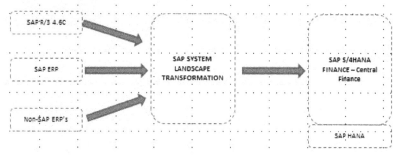

Figure 11-12 Consolidated S/4HANA Landscape

A snapshot of what you get as part of the S/4 HANA package is illustrated below in Figure 11-13 SAP S/4 HANA suite.

Figure 11-13 S/4HANA Suites

S/4HANA Implementation Approach

During the preparation and blueprint phase, customer will discuss with the implementation partner regarding the business processes and customization requirements. This required. This requires detailed technical know-how. Customers coming from SAP Business Suite can move to SAP S/4HANA, on premise edition basically in a one-step-technical procedure using SAP Update Manager with Data Migration Option (DMO) as discussed in the technical deployment approach.

On the contrary, if customer chooses to go for S/4HANA Cloud edition, then the customer will be following the best practices offered by SAP with standardized business processes. In addition, customers will get an option to fine-tune requirements to participate in innovative business processes. The cloud edition can implement the solution with key user business know-how. During this process, limited technical know-how is required. Customers coming from SAP Business Suite can move to SAP S/4HANA, cloud edition by implementing the SAP S/4HANA cloud system using the guided configuration functionalities plus (if required) data migration functionality technically based on SAP Landscape Transformation

---

Note: Refer sap.com/s4hana or sap.com/s4hana-trial also refer scn.sap.com/community/s4hana for more pointers to decide on S/4 HANA right now.

SAP S/4HANA Editions

There is a compelling reason why customers would like to switch to SAP S/4HANA. A few deployment options are available such as on-premises, cloud or hybrid. In each of the model, customer has the ability to carefully assess pros and cons of migrating the I.T landscape based on detailed pre-study. Once done, customers can leverage tools for rapid deployment. The SAP Business Suite customers will need to procure the S/4HANA foundation promotion licenses to run the new SAP S/4HANA. However, for the SAP S/4HANA Cloud edition the pricing is based on the subscription model, which is the pay-per-licenses, which might be very cost effective. In my view, there is a significant benefit in moving over to the cloud landscape, since SAP takes care of all necessary updates to the HANA software without customer having to pay anything extra. The only caveat is that customer may not have the entire flexibility of custom specific changes in the landscape as in a typical on-premises landscape.

To mitigate the above risks, customers can raise requests to participate in the innovation packages released by SAP. In summary there is a very low IT spending due to running enterprise applications on S/4HANA if you do not have too many custom specific requirements. In a way this would control customer's behaviour of frequently changing the application landscape and help you consolidate I.T spending. In my view, this is the best way forward. It's rather easy to start planning on Cloud with the plethora of SAP on-cloud framework encompassing best-in-class enterprise landscape for HR, Payroll, Manufacturing all end-to-end operations managed on the cloud such as Ariba, Success Factor for HR etc.

The following Figure 11-14 illustrates the innovation packages released by SAP.

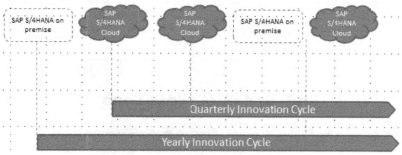

Figure 11-14 SAP S/4HANA Innovations

THE ROAD TO SAP S/4HANA

S/4HANA is the next generation business suite on HANA. It is primarily focussed on run simple in the digital economy. There are various options available for the customers such as a. On-premises, b. Cloud c. Hybrid. Customer can evaluate the best choice that will suit the requirements. It offers a personalized experience with SAP FIORI as the front-end. The simple Finance on HANA replaces classic Finance. Simple Logistics is also catching up as more and more customers sign-up for the pre-study using simple logistics. Further enhancements will be delivered by SAP in innovation packages. The roadmap of S/4HANA is clear with simple apps that will help you run business in the digital economy with lean IT investments and support model required.

SAP S/4HANA Finance Benefits:

1. Financial consolidation,

2. Financial statements,

3. Business planning and simulation,

4. Central Ledger/Central Finance system,

5. Delivers daily, global pre-consolidation statements in real-time,

6. All key finance and accounting functions in one global system,

7. Supply chain systems of record &

8. Integrated business processes with automatically generated finance transactions

In case of legacy systems, which rely on complex models with low performing computations? SAP HANA and SAP Simple Finance is agile to financial management and planning. It eliminates the need of aggregates, complex month-end process and duplication is avoided. This is done by precipitation of data which clogs other systems; hence it has taken care of the cost of managing financials without disruption to the business. Thus, financial analysis is QuickC without the analysis of what-if models to ensure quicker month and quarterly closure process.

Let's understand a little bit more on S/4HANA suite. The extensive computing is what is causing performance bottlenecks. For example, Aggregates such as the materialized aggregates. These issues have been eliminated by revising the data model in S/4HANA. For example, it does all calculations in accounting without any materialized views, thus eliminating performance issues. These materialized aggregates are no longer necessary. Therefore, by removing redundant data storage in a non-disruptive manner improves transactional throughput. It also eliminates high storage costs. The data model in simple finance removes data redundancy, thus increasing transaction throughput.
Components of controlling, General Ledger data model have been optimized for high performance.

There are phenomenal key benefits of leveraging S/4HANA as discussed below:

1. Optimized data model in HANA by removing redundant data which is common in the legacy predecessors of SAP dB

2. Zero redundancy - It refers to eliminating unnecessary data storage. Hence, there is zero redundancy using in-memory techniques. For example, tables such as BSID, KNC1, LFC1 has improved by multi-fold.

3. Innovation - The replacement of materialized views in ERP with compatibility views in S/4HANA is paying high dividends. Yes, today customers can migrate their legacy ERP systems and migrate data into S/4HANA. This switch from usage of materialized views has significantly improved

performance. Further innovation packages are delivered for
S/4HANA in simple finance and simple logistics to run apps
simple and agile.

4. Reduction of data footprint - As you know in ERP, most
of the performance issues are due to intensive usage of
material view usage. Thus, it holds the system resources.
Now, in S.4HANA, good news is that there are no
materialized views. Hence, performance has improved
significantly especially due to optimized tables such as:
a. BKPF,
b. BSEG,
c. BSID,
d. BSIK

As illustrated below in Figure 11-14 postings are made
simple in SAP S/4HANA Simple Finance

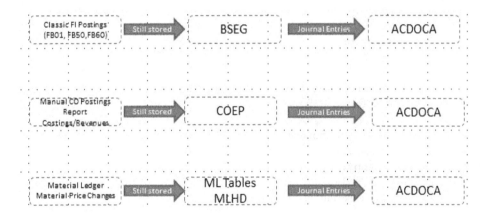

Figure 11-14 Journal Entries postings in ACDOCA

The classic FI postings are costly in terms of resource
utilization, whereas in S/4HANA these journal entries are
maintained in ACDOCA tables. As you know in FI postings,
'Prima Nota' refers to the source document which triggers
journal entries. For example, FB50 tcodes are used for
invoice postings. These are all prima nota stored in BSEG
the old line item table; however journal entries are
actually stored in ACDOCA table. For example, manual CO
postings using KB transactions such as costings/revenues

which are all manual 'prima nota' postings stored in the COEP line item tables, however journal entries are stored in the ACDOCA tables. Next, let's look at the material ledger postings such as price changes, which are stored in MLHD tables; however journal entries are actually stored in ACDOCA tables. Therefore, all postings such as FI, CO and Material ledger journal postings are stored in ACDOCA tables. However, allocation posting are not prima nota postings as illustrated below in Figure 11-15, which are directly written in to ACDOCA tables without any intermediate tables.

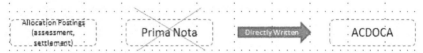

Figure 11-15 Allocation postings in ACDOCA

The real time data is read from the ACDOCA tables using the System landscape transformation replication server (SLT). The key components of SAP Central Finance are:
   a. SAP HANA DB
   b. SAP Business Suite
   c. SAP Landscape Transformation Replication server (SLT)
   d. SAP Simple Finance

The optional components of SAP Central Finance includes:
a. SAP HANA Live,
b. Fiori Apps,
c. SAP BI Tools,
d. SAP Cash Management

Due to the above tables optimized, query processing is much faster than the classic ERP system.

5. Faster transactional processing - It's quick in data processing due to in-memory and data model. For example, there is an intensive G/L posting which happen frequently. However, this is reduced by a factor 0f 2.5 by using the main document posting with associated line items without duplicate processing. In Simple Finance, posting is done by inserting the actual document and its line items. Based on observation, end-to-end transaction processing time is significantly optimized.

Faster transactional throughput

In Simple Finance, posting is done by inserting the actual document and its line items.

Benefits

With the advent of in-memory with high powered HANA dB, the Finance applications have changed. Your month-end closures will run faster without an extensive overload in the system. The need for storage is reduced as it supports dynamic computation. Thus, it eliminates expensive statements, materialized views and aggregates that are time consuming from an end-user perspective. Moreover, removal of materialized view concepts have eliminated data redundancies, thus providing an option to compute much faster than the legacy systems. This helps in analytics and furthermore into the batch process with quick information accessible via multiple devices regardless of huge concurrent users accessing the system. There had been obvious data model changes in the general ledger, accounting modules to optimize table structure for high performance.

Key points of simple finance

Let's analyze key points of SAP S/4HANA simple finance strategy. Now, it's clear you can choose the best deployment options. For example, S/4HANA can be deployed as on-premises or on-cloud. It is clear that is uses advanced in-memory capabilities to amplify performance and ease of data processing. Especially, finance includes complex accounting rules and month-end reconciliation, postings etc. These are taken care in the simple Finance with a simplified version of the data model to ease complex computations. Further, SAP FIORI helps you ease of navigation and information in quick turn-around, without having to search for information details.

From a technical stand-point, SAP Simple Finance is an add-on to ERP,

Simple Finance includes accounting module in SAP powered by HANA. The Cash Management and Integration Business Planning for Finance are included. Hence, it is easy in HANA to quickly access information in BW reporting such as Trial Balance report, P&L information etc. These reports are available as pre-packaged services without having to develop new reports. Further innovations deliver Treasury and Financial Risk management operations and more. If you observe in HANA, SAP FI and CO modules related backend tables had been integrated into on.

Key know-hows before starting Simple Finance implementation:

1. Technical Impact Analysis:

Asses' technical impact such as tables impacted. For example, 'Totals' and index tables have been replaced with HANA views with same technical names. Hence, it is recommended to analyze custom objects for detailed impact.

2. Pre-requisites:

      a. Assess necessary pre-requisites such as SAP ERP 6.0 EHP 7.0 to ensure all required support pack is available as per recommendations in the administrator's guide.

      b. Ensure necessary compatibility checks with external interfaces and integration within SAP IS-solutions.

      c. Prior to the Simple Finance add-on activation, ensure necessary master data migration activity is complete.

d. Install necessary tools for update such as Software Update Manager tool known as 'SUM' tool from the SAP service market place. In addition, you must install packages such as SAP HANA Life Cycle Manager (LCM) tool as a mandatory pre-requisite...

3. Enhanced User Experience (UX):

Assess scope of changes to the user interface to ensure adequate change management and key user training is done. For example, FIORI provides an enhanced user experience; however ensure key users are comfortable navigating through the new interface. Plan for required number of key user training to ensure all your site users are comfortable with new look and feel.

4. Migration:

Ensure migrating the application data first. For specific support pack stacks such as SPS 02, SPS 03, and SP04 there might be few additional configuration requirements.

Note: Refer release note information for SAP Business Suite powered by SAP HANA (# 192590)

To conclude, make sure you understand the scope. The key tables had been replaced in General Ledger accounting such as GLT0 and BSIS for example. Further application index tables of Accounts Receivable and Accounts Payable (KNC1, KNC3, LFC1, LFC3, BSID, BSIK, BSAD, and BSAK) have reduced. Remember Controlling, Material Ledger and Asset accounting tables have been revised.

SAP services as SaaS is increasing with over several thousand customers subscribing for this model.

SAP HANA SPS 10 Online Help and Release

Summary

In this chapter, we have explored the evolution and benefits of SAP S/4 HANA. With this evolution, SAP Business Suite S/4 HANA with inclusions of Simple Finance and Logistics have ventured in to the most ambitious plan of automating your business suite in less time and trouble free. Hence, customers gain ROI quickly. Furthermore, options such as Cloud enablement provides support in terms of low capex. A lot of innovations in terms of technology, ease of use and software maintenance and functionalities simplification are constantly added as part of the HANA package as we speak. Thus, business will benefit most whilst increased customer services and employee satisfaction as organizations can leverage existing resources for more value added activities such as product strategy to move up the value chain. It also would help them venture in to new areas of analytics, enterprise mobility by expanding its footprint in digital marketing.

■ ■ ■

CHAPTER 12:
Authorizations concept in HANA

The objective of this chapter is to help you understand the authorizations model in SAP HANA. Without this knowledge, SAP Project Manager's and/or consultants cannot comprehend the benefits of enhanced authorization in HANA. Now, let us understand the authorization concepts and how it is different from the classic authorization in ERP.

You can authorize users by granting those privileges either directly or through roles. Now, let us understand the concept of roles. For example, you'd have many key users such as Purchaser, Sales Engineer, and Manager etc. using the SAP HANA system. Each of them have set of responsibilities, hence they need a specific set of privileges to access sales information or purchase information that is relevant in the respective domain area. Hence, these roles indicate a collection of specific set of privileges that can be granted to users or other roles, which enables you to create a hierarchy of roles. Basically, you'll need to understand the users, what do they do and how are they going to use the system. You can use roles to assign privileges for different areas to users. For example, a role can enable you to grant analytic privileges, system privileges, package privileges, and so on. To create and maintain artefacts in the SAP HANA repository, you can grant application-development users pre-defined roles that provide access to the areas and objects they require.

SAP HANA with its unique approach to provide users management & Authorization to users using simple authorization mechanism. Perhaps, most of you have developed some kind of authorization matrix to collect information about the client authorization requirements and then use this matrix for the authorization build.

The authorization model might vary from one client depending on the number of users. Hence, you should strategize authorization model based on the requirements with key factors such as considering the upgrade. In some cases, custom roles require additional testing as part of the upgrade as these roles may be impacted by the upgrade.

In this chapter, you will learn how to implement authorization model for the enterprise customers with a case study.

■ **Note**   SAP S/4HANA aka SAP Business Suite for HANA

Authorization Model

The main objectives of authorization model are to ensure the users can perform set of activities that are relevant and assigned to them. As discussed in the example. Sales information should be visible to sales department; hence the sales team will have a specific authorization. Hence, authorization model helps in setting up mechanism of the SAP HANA database to specify who can access information pertaining to the relevant area that is applicable. Also, this mechanism helps in controlling access such as who can create documents or post or even view sales information. Moreover it can help in technical activities for IT admin such as execute stored procedures and functions or perform system-level activities, for example, making backups, creating schema, users, roles, and so on. A simple authorization component with relationship is illustrated below in Figure 12-1.

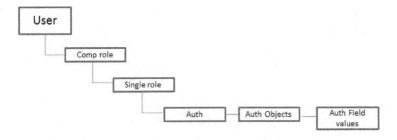

Figure 12-1

Roles

In SAP HANA, as in most of SAP's software, authorizations are grouped into roles. A role is a collection of authorization objects, with their associated privileges. It allows us, as developers, to define self-contained units of authorization. In the same way that at the start of this book we created an attribute view allowing us to have a coherent view of our customer data which we could reuse at will in more advanced developments, authorization roles allow us to create coherent developments of authorization data which we can then assign to users at will, making sure that users who are supposed to have the same rights always have the same rights. If we had to assign individual authorization objects to users, we could be fairly sure that sooner or later, we would forget someone in a department, and they would not be able to access the data they needed to do their everyday work. Worse, we might not give quite the same authorizations to one person, and have to spend valuable time correcting our error when they couldn't see the data they needed (or worse, more dangerous and less obvious to us as developers, if the user could see more data than was intended).

SAP HANA provides you with pre-defined roles as templates that are applicable in respective areas. Hence, at the time of configuration, users can be grouped by respective domain areas with specific roles assigned with certain privileges such as view, edit etc. These roles can be assigned at runtime. The authorization mechanism of the SAP HANA database is used to specify who can access information in the SAP HANA database based on the privileges.

The authorization model
The authorization mechanism of SAP HANA database can help in aligning relevant access for users that are eligible. Authentication setup

Authentication setup is done to ensure users are eligible to access the information relevant to specific area. A classic example is user entering his username and password with access verified in the backend in order to authenticate user access to the system.

Database roles
Roles are assigned either to users or to other roles at runtime. The assigned roles ensure that data, applications, and functions can only be accessed by the users with the required privileges.

Database Privileges
SAP HANA provides a selection of pre-defined privileges that can be assigned to users. Privileges can be assigned to users, roles, or both.

Application Access

The application access is a way to control users accessing application, which is allowed by using appropriate access framework. If there is a specific action to be performed is required in the application, it is controlled via privileges assigned to the roles.

It is always a much better idea to group authorizations into a role and then assign the role to users, than assign authorizations directly to users. Assigning a role to a user means that when the user changes jobs and needs a new set of privileges; we can just remove the first role, and assign a second one. Since, we're just starting out using authorizations in SAP HANA, let's get into this good habit right from the start. It really will make our lives easier later on.

Creating a role

Role creation is done, like all other SAP HANA development, in the Studio. If your Studio is currently closed, please open it, and then select the Modeller perspective. In order to create roles, privileges, and users, you will yourself need privileges. Your SAP HANA user will need the ROLE ADMIN, USER ADMIN, and CREATE STRUCTURED PRIVILEGE system privileges in order to do the development work in this article. You will see in the Navigator panel we have a Security folder, as we can see in Figure 12-2.

Figure 12-2   Security Folder

Please find the Security folder and then expand this folder. You will see a subfolder called Roles. Right-click on the Roles folder and select New Role to start creating a role as illustrated below in Figure 12-3.

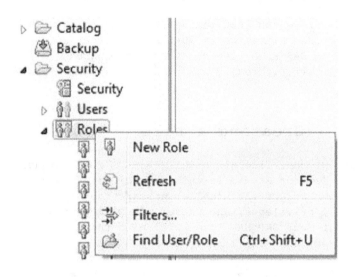

Figure 12-3 Roles

On the screen which will open, you will see a number of tabs representing the different authorization objects we can create as illustrated below in Figure 12-4:

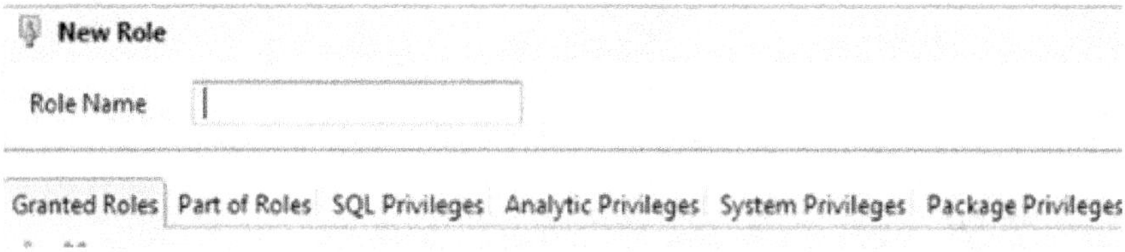

Figure 12-4 Create New Role

We'll be looking at each of these in turn, in the following sections, so for the moment just give your role
Name (BOOKUSER might be appropriate, if not very original).

Granted roles
Like many other object types in SAP HANA, once you have created a role, you can then use it inside another role. This makes authorizations a lot easier to manage. For

example. Let us assume company with two teams with different key functions:

- Sales
- Purchasing

And two countries, say:
- France
- Germany

We could create a role by giving access to sales analytic views, one giving purchasing analytic views, one giving access to data for France, and one giving access to data for Germany. We could then create new roles, say Sales-France, which don't actually contain any authorization objects themselves, but contain only the Sales and the France roles. The role definition is much simpler to understand and to maintain than if we had directly created the Sales-France role and a Sales-Germany role with all the underlying objects. Once again, as with other development objects, creating small self-contained roles and reusing them when possible will make your (maintenance) life easier. In the Granted Roles tab we can see the list of sub roles this main role contains. Note that this list is only a pointer, you cannot modify the actual authorizations and the other roles given here, you would need to open the individual role and make changes there.

Part of roles

The Part of Roles tab in the role definition screen is exactly the opposite of the Granted Roles tab. This tab lists all other roles of which this role is a sub role. It is very useful to track authorizations, especially when you find yourself in a situation where a user seems to have too many authorizations and can see data they shouldn't be able to see. You cannot manipulate this list as such, it exists for information only. If you want to make changes, you need to modify the main role of which this role is a sub role.

An SQL privilege is the lowest level at which we can define restrictions for using database objects. SQL privileges apply to the simplest objects in the database such as schemas, tables and so on. No attribute, analytical, or calculation view can be seen by SQL privileges. This is not strictly true, though you can consider it so. What we have seen as an analytical view, for example, the graphical definition, the drag and drop, the checkboxes, has been transformed into a real database object in the _SYS_BIC schema upon activation. We could therefore define SQL privileges on this database object if we wanted, but this is not recommended and indeed limits the control we can have over the view. We'll see a little later that SAP HANA has much finer-grained authorizations for views than this.

An important thing to note about SQL privileges is that they apply to the object on which they are defined. They restrict access to a given object itself, but do not at any point have any impact on the object's contents. For example, we can decide that one of our users can have access to the CUSTOMER table, but we couldn't restrict their access to only CUSTOMER values from the COUNTRY USA.

SQL privileges can control access to any object under the Catalogue node in the Navigator panel. Let's add some authorizations to our BOOK schema and its contents. At the top of the SQL Privileges tab is a green plus sign button. Now click on this button to get the Select Catalogue Object dialog as illustrated below in Figure 12-5 :

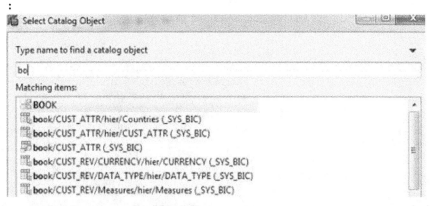

Figure 12-5 Select Catalog Object

As you can see in the screenshot, we have entered the two letters into the filter box at the top of the dialog. As soon as you enter at least two letters into this box, the Studio will attempt to find and then list all database objects whose name contains the two letters you typed. If you continue to type, the search will be refined further as illustrated below in Figure 12-6.

Granted Roles	Part of Roles	⚠ SQL Privileges	Analytic Privileges

✚ ✖ ▽ ↕ ▼	**Privileges for 'BOOK'**
SQL Object	
🔑 BOOK	Grantable to others
	☐ CREATE ANY ⚪ Yes ⚪ No
	☐ ALTER ⚪ Yes ⚪ No
	☐ DROP ⚪ Yes ⚪ No
	☐ EXECUTE ⚪ Yes ⚪ No
	☐ SELECT ⚪ Yes ⚪ No
	☐ INSERT ⚪ Yes ⚪ No
	☐ UPDATE ⚪ Yes ⚪ No
	☐ DELETE ⚪ Yes ⚪ No
	☐ INDEX ⚪ Yes ⚪ No

Figure 12-6 SQL Privileges

The first thing to notice is the warning icon on the SQL Privileges tab itself:
[SQL Privileges] - This means that your role definition is incomplete, and the role cannot be activated and used as yet. On the right of the screen, a list of checkbox options has appeared. These are the individual authorizations appropriate to the SQL object you have selected. In order to grant rights to a user via a role, you need to decide which of these options to include in the role. The individual authorization names are self-explicit. For

example, the CREATE ANY authorization allows creation of new objects inside a schema.

The INSERT or SELECT authorization might at first seem unusual for a schema, as it's not an object which can support such instructions. However, the usage is actually quite elegant. If a user has INSERT rights on the schema BOOK, then they have INSERT rights on all objects inside the schema BOOK. Granting rights on the schema itself avoids having to specify the names of all objects inside the schema. It also future-proofs your authorization concept, since new objects created in the schema will automatically inherit from the existing authorizations you have defined. On the far right of the screen, alongside each authorization is a radio button which gives an additional privilege, the possibility for a given user to, in turn, gives the rights to a second user.

This is an option which should not be given to all users, and so should not be present in all roles you create; the right to attribute privileges to users should be limited to your administrators. If you give just any user the right to pass on their authorizations further, you will soon find that you are no longer able to determine who can do what in your database. For the moment we are creating a simple role to show the working of the authorization concept in SAP HANA, so we will check all the checkboxes, and leave the radio buttons at No as illustrated below in Figure 12-7:

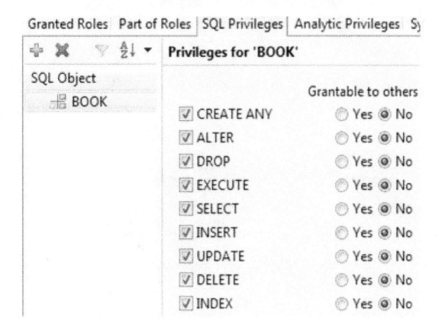

Figure 12-7 SQL Object

There are some SQL privileges which are necessary for any
user to be able to do work in SAP HANA. These are listed
below. They give access to the system objects describing
the development models we create in SAP HANA, and if a user
does not have these privileges, nothing will work at all;
the user will not be authorized to do anything. The SQL
privileges you will need to add to the role in order to
give access to basic SAP HANA system objects are:

- The SELECT privilege on the _SYS_BI schema
- The SELECT privilege on the _SYS_REPO schema
- The EXECUTE privilege on the REPOSITORY_REST procedure

As you can see with the configuration we have just done,
SQL privileges allow a user to access a given object and
allow specific actions on the object. They do not however
allow us to specify particular authorizations to the
contents of the object. In order to use such fine-grained

rights, we need to create an analytic privilege, and then add it to our role, so let's do that now.

Analytic Privileges

An analytic privilege is an artefact unique to SAP HANA; it is not part of the standard SQL authorization concept. Analytic privileges allow us to restrict access to certain values of a given attribute, analytic, or calculation view. This means that we can create one view, which by default shows all available data, and then restrict what is actually visible to different users. We could restrict visible data by company code, by country, or by region. For example, our users in Europe would be allowed to see and work with data from our customers in Europe, but not those in the USA. An analytic privilege is created through the Quick Launch panel of Modeller, so please open that view now (or switch to the Quick Launch tab if it's already open). You don't need to close the role definition tab that's already open; we can leave it for now, create our analytic privilege, and then come back to the role definition later. From the Quick Launch panel, select Analytic Privilege, and then Create.

As usual with SAP HANA, we are asked to give Name, Description, and select a package for our object. We'll call it AP_EU (for analytic privilege, Europe), use the name as the description, and put it into our book package alongside our other developments. As is common in SAP HANA, we have the option of creating an analytic privilege from scratch (Create New) or copying an existing privilege (Copy From). We don't currently have any other analytic privileges in our development, so leave Create New selected, and then click on Next to go to the second screen of the wizard as illustrated below in Figure 12-8:

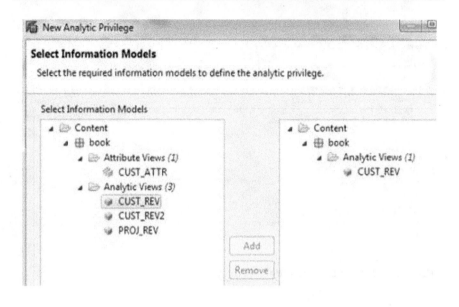

Figure 12-8 Analytic Privilege

On this page of the dialog, we are prompted to add development models to the analytic privilege. This will then allow us to restrict access to given values of these models. In the previous screenshot, we have added the CUST_REV analytic view to the analytic privilege. This will allow us to restrict access to any value we specify of any of the fields visible in the view. To add a view to the analytic privilege, just find it in the left panel, click on its name and then click on the Add button. Once you have added the views you require for your authorizations, click on the Finish button at the bottom of the window to go to the next step. You will be presented with the analytic privilege development panel, reproduced here as illustrated below in Figure 12-9:

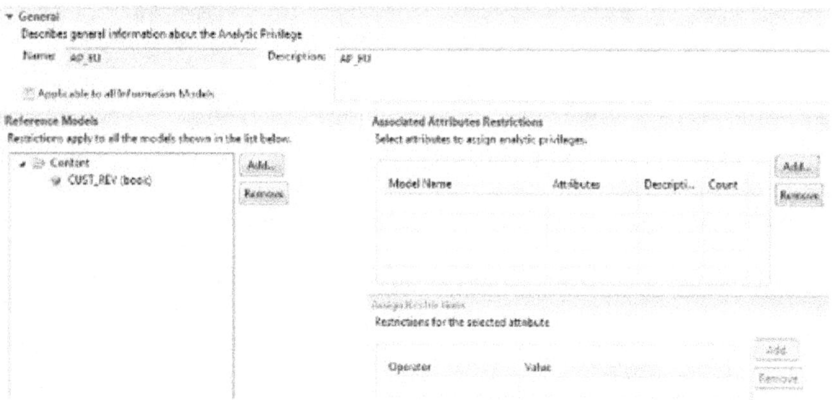

Figure 12-9 Attribute Restriction

This page allows us to define our analytic privilege completely. On the left we have the list of database views we have included in the analytic privilege. We can add more, or remove one, using the Add and Remove buttons. To the right, we can see the Associated Attributes Restrictions and Assign Restrictions boxes. These are where we define the restrictions to individual values, or sets of values. In the top box, Associated Attributes Restrictions, we define on which attributes we want to restrict access (country code or region, maybe). In the bottom box, Assign Restrictions, we define the individual values on which to restrict (for example, for company code, we could restrict to value 0001, or US22; for region, we could limit access to EU or USA). Let's add a restriction to the REGION field of our CUST_REV view now. Click on the Add button next to the Associated Attributes Restrictions box, to see the Select Object dialog as illustrated below in Figure 12-10:

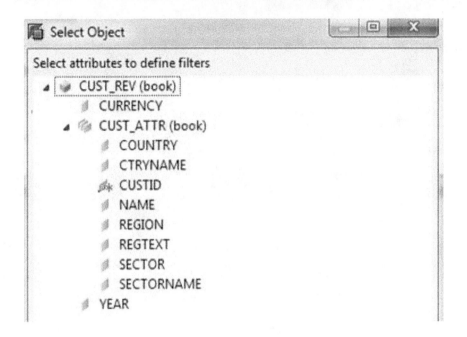

Figure 12-10 Select Attributes

As can be expected, this dialog lists all the attributes in
our analytic view. We just need to select the appropriate
attribute and then click on OK to add it to the analytic
privilege. Measures in the view are not listed in the
dialog. We cannot restrict access to a view according to
numeric values. We cannot therefore, make restrictions to
customers with a revenue over 1 million Euros, for example.
Please add the REGION field to the analytic privilege now.
Once the appropriate fields have been added, we can define
the restrictions to be applied to them. Click on
the REGION field in the Associated Attributes
Restrictions box, then on the Add button next to the Assign
Restrictions box, to define the restrictions we want to
apply as illustrated below in Figure 12-11.

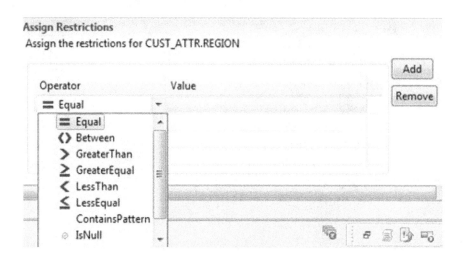

Figure 12-11 Assign Restriction

As we can see, restrictions can be defined according to the usual list of comparison operators. These are the same operators we used earlier to define a restricted column in our analytic views. In our example, we'll be restricting access to those lines with a REGION column equal to EU, so we'll selectEqual.In the Value column, we can either type the appropriate value directly, or use the value help button, and the familiar Value Help Dialog which will appear, to select the value from those available in the view. Please add the EU value, either by typing it or by having SAP HANA find it for us, now. There is one more field which needs to be added to our analytic privilege, and the reason behind might seem at first a little strange. This point is valid for SAP HANA SP5, up to and including (at least) release 50 of the software. If this point turns out to be a bug, then it might not be necessary in later versions of the software. The field on which we want to restrict user actions (REGION) is not actually part of the analytic view itself. REGION, if you recall, is a field which is present in CUST_REV, thanks to the included attribute viewCUST_ATTR.

In its current state, the analytic privilege will not work, because no fields from the analytic view are actually present in the analytic privilege. We therefore need to add at least one of the native fields of the analytic view to the analytic privilege. We don't need to do any restriction on the field; however it needs to be in the privilege for everything to work as expected.

Refer SAP Note # 1809199, SAP HANA DB: debugging user authorization errors.

Only if a view is included in one of the cube restrictions and at least one of its attribute is employed by one of the dimension restrictions, access to the view is granted by this analytical privilege. Not an explicit description of the workings of the authorization concept, but close. Our analytic view CUST_REV contains two native fields, CURRENCY and YEAR. You can add either of these to the analytic privilege. You do not need to assign any restrictions to the field; it just needs to be in the privilege.

Here is the state of the analytic privilege when development work on it is finished as illustrated below in Figure 12-12:

Figure 12-12 Attributes Restrictions

The Count column lists the number of restrictions in effect for the associated field. For the CURRENCY field, no restrictions are defined. We just need (as always) to activate our analytic privilege in order to be able to use it. The activation button is the same one as we have used up until now to activate the modelling views, the round green button with the right-facing white arrow at the top-right of the panel, which you can see on the preceding screenshot.

Please activate the analytic privilege now. Once that has been done, we can add it to our role. Return to the Role tab (if you left it open) or reopen the role now. If you closed the role definition tab earlier, you can get back to our role by opening the Security node in the Navigator panel, then opening Roles, and double-clicking on the BOOKUSER role. In the Analytic Privileges tab of the role definition screen, click on the green plus sign at the top, to add an analytic privilege to our role. The analytic privilege we have just created is called AP_EU, so type ap_euinto the search box at the top of the dialog window which will open. As soon as you have typed at least two characters, SAP HANA will start searching for matching analytic privileges, and your AP_EU privilege will be listed, as we can see here as illustrated below in Figure 12-13:

Figure 12-13 Select Analytic Privilege

Click on OK to add the privilege to the role. We will see in a minute the effect our analytic privilege has on the rights of a particular user, but for the moment we can take a look at the second-to-last tab in the role definition screen, System Privileges.

System Privileges

Eventually, these projects fail to yield expected ROI. Hence, as a Project Manager As its name suggests, system privileges gives to a particular user the right to perform specific actions on the SAP HANA system itself, not just on a given table or view. These are particular rights which should not be given to just any user, but should be reserved to those users who need to perform a particular task. We'll not be adding any of these privileges to our role, however we'll take a look at the available options and what they are used for.

Click on the green plus-sign button at the top of the System Privileges tab to see a list of the available privileges. By default the dialog will do a search on all available values; there are only fifteen or so, but you can as usual filter them down if you require using the filter box at the top of the dialog as illustrated below in Figure 12-14:

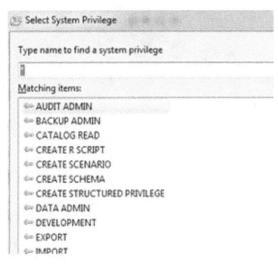

Figure 12-14 Select System Privilege

For a full list of the system privileges available and their uses, please refer to the SAP HANA SQL Reference, available on the help.sap.com website at http://help.sap.com/hana/html/sql_grant.html.

Package Privileges

SAP HANA delivers "better, faster, cheaper" alternative. The latest release is service pack SPS 10 for the SAP HANA platform, helping customers successfully extending core functionalities to deliver growing business requirements. For example, SAP delivered, Internet of Things (IoT) at enterprise scale, manage Big Data more effectively, further extend high availability of data across the enterprise and develop new applications. The SAP HANA provides a robust platform for SAP and non-SAP applications for transactional and analytical processing. Further, it extends to synchronizing data to any remote systems, high availability and disaster recovery of enterprise data to support advanced analytics. The last tab in the role definition screen concerns Package Privileges. These allow a given user to access those objects in a package. In our example, the package is called book, so if we add the book package to our role in the Package Privileges tab, we will see the following result as illustrated below in Figure 12-15:

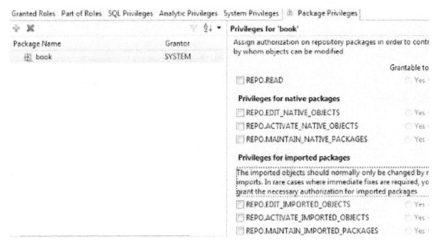

Figure 12-15 Package Privileges

Assigning package privileges is similar to assigning SQL privileges we saw earlier. We first add the required object (here our book package), then we need to indicate exactly which rights we give to the role. As we can see in the preceding screenshot, we have a series of checkboxes on the right-hand side of the window. At least one of these checkboxes must be checked in order to save the role. The individual rights have names which are fairly self-explanatory. REPO.READ gives access to read the package, whereas REPO.EDIT_NATIVE_OBJECTS allows modification of objects, for example. The role we are creating is destined for an end user who will need to see the data in a role, but should not need to modify the data models in any way (and in fact we really don't want them to modify our data models, do we?). We'll just add the REPO.READ privilege, on our book package, to our role. Again we can decide whether the end user can in turn assign this privilege to others. And again, we don't need this feature in our role.

At this point, our role is finished. We have given access to the SQL objects in the BOOK schema, created an analytic privilege which limits access to the Europe region in our CUST_REV model, and given read-only access to book package. After activation (always) we'll be able to assign our role to a test user, and then see the effect our authorizations have on what the user can do and see. Please activate the role now.

Users

There are various options provided by SAP. One of the fundamental questions is to go for pure cloud or hybrid on premise solution. Well, I wouldn't advocate entirely cloud or on premise and/or hybrid as it entirely depends on the customer situation. Perhaps, we can discuss it in detail about a viable option in "Chapter 15 - Transform your enterprise to SAP S/4 Cloud"

For example, an enterprise with subsidiaries can go for the SAP Cloud finance edition for shared service centres, the cloud-enterprise edition for group subsidiaries. The on premise edition for core processes such as ERP. The enterprises can choose from the best suited operating models. Now, let's see HANA on cloud illustrated in Figure 1-9 for reference. Let's explore each of the cloud editions in the next section.

Users are probably the most important part of the authorization concept. They are where all our problems begin, and their attempts to do and see things they shouldn't are the main reason we have to spend valuable time defining authorizations in the first place. In technical terms, a user is just another database object. They are created, modified, and deleted in the same way a modelling view is. They have properties (their name and password, for example), and it is by modifying these properties that we influence the actions that the person who connects using the user can perform. Up until now we have been using the SYSTEM user (or the user that your database administrator assigned to you). This user is defined by SAP, and has basically the authorizations to do anything with the database. Use of this user is discouraged by SAP, and the author really would like to insist that you don't use it for your developments. Accidents happen, and one of the great things about authorizations is that they help to prevent accidents. If you try to delete an important object with the SYSTEM user, you will delete it, and getting it back might involve a database restore. If however you use a development user with less authorization, then you wouldn't have been allowed to do the deletion, saving a lot of tears. Of course, the question then arises, why you have been using the SYSTEM user for the last couple of hundred pages of development. Let create a new user now, and assign the role we have just created. From the Navigator panel, open the Security node, right-click on User, and select New User from the menu to obtain the user creation screen as illustrated below in Figure 12-16:

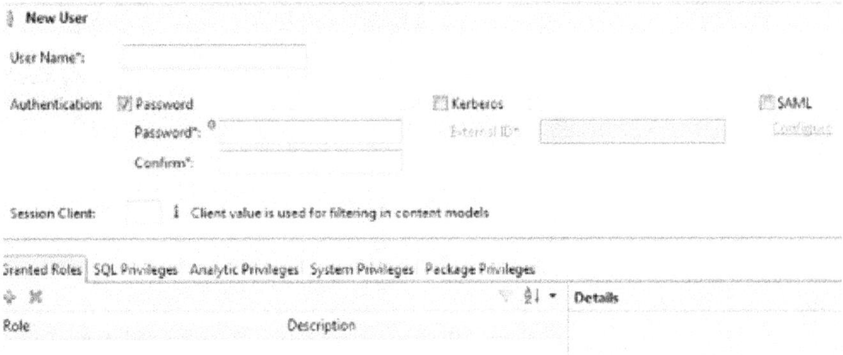

Figure 12-16 Grant Roles

Defining a user requires remarkably little information:

User Name: The login that the user will use. Your company might have a naming convention for users. Users might even already have a standard login they use to connect to other systems in your enterprise. In our example, we'll create a user with the (once again rather unimaginative) name overbook.

Authentication: How will SAP HANA know that the user connecting with the name of ANNE really is Anne? There are three (currently) ways of authenticating a user with SAP HANA.

Password: This is the most common authentication system, SAP HANA will ask Anne for her password when she connects to the system. Since Anne is the only person who knows her password, we can be sure that Anne really is ANNE, and let her connect and do anything the user ANNE is allowed to do. Passwords in SAP HANA have to respect a certain format. By default this format is one capital, one lowercase, one number, and at least eight characters.

You can see and change the password policy in the system configuration. Double-click on the system name in the Navigator panel, click on the Configuration tab, type the word pass into the filter box at the top of the tab, and scroll down to indexserver.ini and then password policy. The password format in force on your system is listed as password layout. By default this is A1a, meaning capitals, numbers, and lowercase letters are allowed. The value can also contain the # character, meaning that special characters must also be contained in the password. The only special characters allowed by SAP HANA are currently the underscore, dollar sign, and the hash character. Other password policy defaults are also listed on this screen, such as maximum_password_lifetime (the time after which SAP HANA will force you to change your password).

Kerberos and SAML: These authentication systems need to be set up by your network administrator and allow single sign-on in your enterprise. This means that SAP HANA will be able to see the Windows username that is connecting to the system. The database will assume that the authentication part (deciding whether Anne really is ANNE) has already been done by Windows, and let the user connect.

Session Client: As we saw when we created attribute and analytic views back at the start of the book, SAP HANA understands the notion of client, referring to a partition system of the SAP ERP database. In the SAP ERP, different users can work in different Clients. In our development, we filtered on Client 100. A much better way of handling filtering is to define the default client for a user when we define their account. The Session Client field can be filled with the ERP Client in which the user works. In this way we do not need to filter on the analytic models, we can leave their client value at Dynamic in the view, and the actual value to use will be taken from the user record. Once again this means maintenance of our developments is a lot simpler.

If you like, you can take a few minutes at the end of this article to create a user with a session client value of 100, then go back and reset our attribute and analytic views' default client value to Dynamic, reactivate everything, and then do a data preview with your test user. The result should be identical to that obtained when the view was filtered on client 100. However, if you then create a second user with a session client of 200, this second user will see different data. We'll create a user with a password login, so type a password for your user now. Remember to adhere to the password policy in force on your system. Also note that the user will be required to change their password on first login.

At the bottom of the user definition screen, as we can see from the preceding screenshot, we have a series of tabs corresponding to the different authorizations we can assign to our user. These are the same tabs we saw earlier when defining a role. As explained at the beginning of this article, it is considered best practice to assign authorizations to a role and then the role to a user, rather than assign authorizations directly to a user; this makes maintenance easier. For this reason we will not be looking at the different tabs for assigning authorizations to our user, other than the first one, Granted Roles. The Granted Roles tab lists, and allows adding and removing roles from the list assigned to the user. By default when we create a user, they have no roles assigned, and hence have no authorizations at all in the system. They will be able to log in to SAP HANA but will be able to do no development work, and will see no data from the system. Please click on the green plus sign button in the Granted Roles tab of the user definition screen, to add a role to the user account. You will be provided with the Select Role dialog, shown in part here as illustrated below in Figure 12-17:

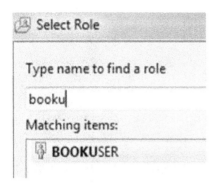

Figure 12-17 Select Role

This dialog has the familiar search box at the top, so typing the first few letters of a role name will bring up a list of matching roles. Here our role was called BOOKUSER, so please do a search for it, then select it in the list and click on OK to add it to the user account. Once that is done, we can test our user to verify that we can perform the necessary actions with the role and user we have just created. We just need, as with all objects in SAP HANA, to activate the user object first. As usual, this is done with the round green button with the right-facing white arrow at the top-right of the screen. Please do this now.

CASE STUDY

Testing user and role

The only real way to check if the authorizations we have defined are appropriate to the business requirements is to create a user and then try out the role to see what the user can and cannot see and do in the system. The first thing to do is to add our new user to the Studio so we can connect to SAP HANA using this new user. To do this, in the Navigator panel, right click on the SAP HANA system name, and select Add Additional User from the menu which appears.

This will give you the Add additional user dialog, shown in the following screenshot as illustrated below in Figure 12-18:

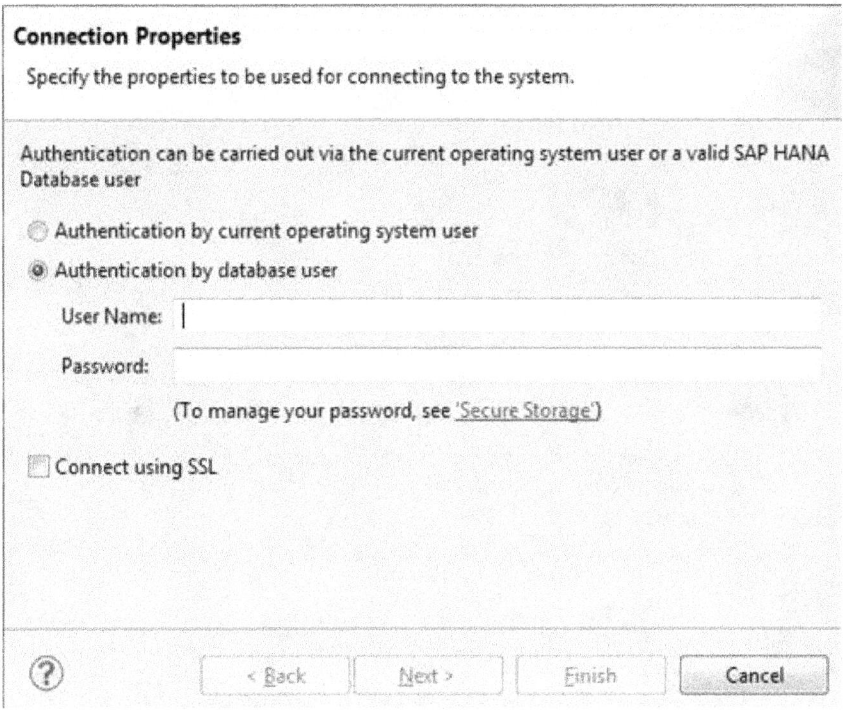

Connection Properties

Specify the properties to be used for connecting to the system.

Authentication can be carried out via the current operating system user or a valid SAP HANA Database user

○ Authentication by current operating system user

◉ Authentication by database user

User Name: |

Password:

(To manage your password, see 'Secure Storage')

☐ Connect using SSL

⑦   < Back   Next >   Finish   Cancel

Figure 12-18 User Authentication

Enter the name of the user you just created (BOOKU) and the password you assigned to the user. You will be required to change the password immediately as illustrated below in Figure 12-19:

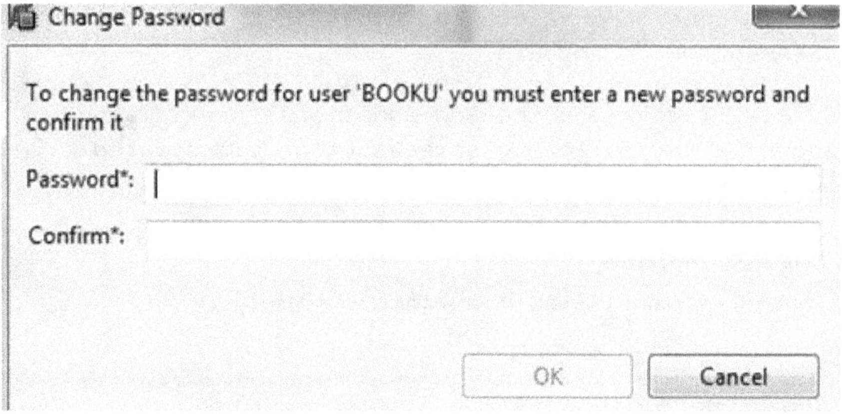

Change Password

To change the password for user 'BOOKU' you must enter a new password and confirm it

Password*: |

Confirm*:

OK   Cancel

Figure 12-19 Change Password

Click on Finish to add the user to the Studio. You will see immediately in the Navigator panel that we can now work with either our SYSTEM user, or our BOOKU user as illustrated below in Figure 12-20:

Navigator

- HN5 (BOOKU) Internal HANA Te:
  - Catalog
  - Security
  - Content
- HN5 (SYSTEM) Internal HANA Te
  - Catalog
  - Backup
  - Security
  - Content

Figure 12-20 Navigator

We can also see straight away that BOOKU is missing
the privileges to perform or manage data backups;
the Backup node is missing from the list for
the BOOKU user. Let's try to do something with
our BOOKU user and see how the system reacts. The
way the Studio lets you handle multiple users is
very elegant, since the tree structure of database
objects is duplicated, one per user, you can see
immediately how the different authorization
profiles affect the different users. Additionally,
if you request a data preview from
the CUST_REV analytic view in the book package
under the BOOKU user's node in the Navigator panel,
you will see the data according to the BOOKU user's
authorizations. Requesting the same data preview
from the SYSTEM user's node will see the data
according to SYSTEM's authorizations. Let's do a
data preview on the CUST_REV view with
the SYSTEM user, for reference as illustrated below
in Figure 12-21:

	test	SECTOR	NAME	SECTORNAME	REGTEXT	CTRYNAME	REGION	COU
2		ENT	Jacques	Enterprise Customer	Europe	France	EU	FR
4		SMB	Jones	Small and Medium ...	North America	United States of A...	NAR	US
1		SMB	Smith	Small and Medium ...	Europe	Great Britain	EU	GB
3		IND	Martin	Individual Owner	Europe	Great Britain	EU	GB
4		SMB	Jones	Small and Medium ...	North America	United States of A...	NAR	US
4		SMB	Jones	Small and Medium ...	North America	United States of A...	NAR	US
3		IND	Martin	Individual Owner	Europe	Great Britain	EU	GB
3		IND	Martin	Individual Owner	Europe	Great Britain	EU	GB
1		SMB	Smith	Small and Medium ...	Europe	Great Britain	EU	GB
2		ENT	Jacques	Enterprise Customer	Europe	France	EU	FR
1		SMB	Smith	Small and Medium ...	Europe	Great Britain	EU	GB
2		ENT	Jacques	Enterprise Customer	Europe	France	EU	FR

Figure 12-21 System Users

As we can see, there are 12 rows of data retrieved,
and we have data from the EU and NAR regions. If we

ask for the same data preview using our BOOKU user, we can see much less data:

test	SECTOR	NAME	SECTORNAME	REGTEXT	CTRYNAME	REGION	CO
2	ENT	Jacques	Enterpose Customer	Europe	France	EU	FR
3	IND	Martin	Individual Owner	Europe	Great Britain	EU	GB
1	SMB	Smith	Small and Medium ...	Europe	Great Britain	EU	GB
2	ENT	Jacques	Enterprise Customer	Europe	France	EU	FR
1	SMB	Smith	Small and Medium ...	Europe	Great Britain	EU	GB
3	IND	Martin	Individual Owner	Europe	Great Britain	EU	GB
3	IND	Martin	Individual Owner	Europe	Great Britain	EU	GB
1	SMB	Smith	Small and Medium ...	Europe	Great Britain	EU	GB
2	ENT	Jacques	Enterprise Customer	Europe	France	EU	FR

Figure 12-22 Rows retrieved

BOOKU can only see nine of the 12 data rows in our view, as no data from the NAR region are visible to the BOOKU user. This is exactly the result we aimed to achieve using our analytic privilege, in our role, assigned to our user.

The adoption trend for software-as-a-service (SaaS) is significant for SAP's business with over $1 billion in subscription.

Refer: http://help.sap.com/hana_platform/

Summary

In this chapter, you have looked at various aspects of the authorization concepts in SAP HANA. We examined the different authorization levels available in the system, from SQL privileges, analytic privileges, system privileges, and package privileges. We saw how to add these different

366

authorization concepts to a role, a reusable group of authorizations. You've created a new user in our SAP HANA system, examining the different types of authentications available, and the assignment of roles to users. Finally, we logged into the Studio with our new user account, and found out the first-hand effect of authorizations had on what the user could see and do.

■   ■   ■

3

A

B

C

D

E

F